WINSTER
People and Places in Postcards

Michael Greatorex

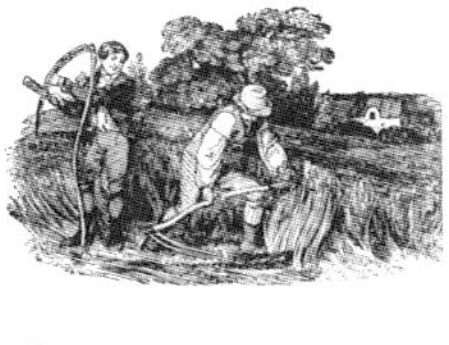

Country Books

Published by Country Books/Ashridge Press
Courtyard Cottage, Little Longstone, Bakewell, Derbyshire DE45 1NN
Tel: 01629 640670
e-mail: dickrichardson@country-books.co.uk

ISBN 978-1-906789-43-5

British Library Cataloguing in Publication Data.
A catalogue record for this book is available from the British Library.

Printed and bound by HSW Print

CONTENTS

FOREWORD

This book is about Winster's Picture Postcards up to the 1960s: of people, places and publishers. It discusses the work of Winster's Edwardian publishers (Marshall and Heathcote) and suggests clues to try and identify the work of the former. It includes sections about the work of some Edwardian itinerant photographers who visited the village and the images are supported with notes about the Winster people who either sent or received or are pictured or mentioned in the cards.

The original postcards illustrated throughout the book measured 5½" x 3" approx ("Golden Age" size). It was sadly impracticable to reproduce them at full size.

I am indebted to many people interested in Winster's local history who have contributed towards my understanding of Winster's postcards – there are too many of these people to personally acknowledge here (and I would probably miss someone out) but I am grateful to them all. My wife, Moira, has supported me throughout the time spent preparing this book and I thank her for her generous encouragement and patience. I am also grateful to my publisher, Dick Richardson, who listened patiently to my initial ideas for the book and then encouraged me to complete it. He was particularly understanding when one or two "deadlines" which we had agreed for the project had to be revised as more pressing aspects of my life interrupted the work.

Michael Greatorex
2010

INTRODUCTION

I will admit it straightaway: this book is about a love affair. There – I feel better already. A love affair both with the village of Winster, Derbyshire, (my birthplace) and with its picture postcards. Winster lies between the towns of Matlock and Bakewell and grew out of the lead mining industry during the 18th century. At that time it was a place of some importance but declined when lead mining too declined. Today it strives with some success to retain the charm and character of a bygone era – a time before the advent of the Town and Country Planning Acts – and is still able to remind us how such settlements developed piece-meal. We are also reminded that the village (as many villages else-where) was built for an age which did not have to accommodate the motor-vehicle.

What follows does not claim to be a definitive review of Winster's post-cards: it is a selection of both topographical cards and other cards from the Edwardian period to the 1960s. Many of the cards included are from my own collection. Many too are from the Eric Brassington collection of which I am fortunate to be the present custodian. I have tried to use sparingly non-postcard images as the theme of this book is "Postcards" but in places the temptation to include non-postcard images has been too great and a few have crept in. I hope they add to the text and your enjoyment of the true postcard images. There are innumerable photo-graphs of Winster Morris Dancers published elsewhere but you will not find many (if any) here. That is not because I am not a Winster Morris fan – I am – but the topic deserves a separate book.

Topographical cards are easy for us all to understand. They show a local view of a place or a piece of countryside. Many of us collect them; the places where we have lived or have visited. We have certainly sent them to family and friends from places where we have spent holidays. Winster has its share of these topographical cards.

Other cards – of people, events, all printed with a traditional postcard back but often with no description of the picture nor identifying the photographer, are probably nearly as well known but not often collected. This book tries to deal with these Winster cards too. They are not often collected unless they can be identified by place, photographer, subject or person. These too form part of Winster's postcard legacy and some are included here along with the more common topographical examples. These unidentified cards have often either been lost or unrecognised by later generations; unless someone has left a note, or word of mouth has passed down the generations whereby we have been fortunate to recognise a place, a scene or the person the subject of the card. Such cards are commonplace throughout England but difficult to identify arising from the lack of information printed on them. With the passage of time there is a danger that these cards will be lost. How often have you been associated with clearing out the effects of an aged family member recently deceased? Perhaps the last member of an earlier generation and have been confronted with a shoebox of memorabilia some of it about people long since dead and unknown to you or other living relatives. This is when such items are in danger of being "lost." And then later something may arise to remind you that you were hasty in throwing the items away. You might discover that the items have some monetary value (rarely) but suddenly reveal their importance as items of sentimental or historical value to a local area. So there is a dearth of these items which manage to survive. The ones that do tell a story of a bygone age most noticeable by the different clothes of the people captured in the photographs. In some cases such cards can be identified with a little research, local knowledge, and a lot of luck. Often the quality of the photographs is high – with distinct sharp images – they are attractive and collectable for that reason and doubly so if you are able to identify the people or the places and the age in which they were all captured by the camera.

This book is an attempt to try and group together some of these "Winster People Postcards" and to bring them to the attention of readers who may be interested in the people depicted and their place in Winster's photo-history.

It was during the latter part of the Victorian and the start of the Edwardian periods that photography and printing techniques developed apace. With that rapid growth came a growth in the popularity of the picture postcard. From the start of the 20th century to the end of the Great War in 1918 the postcard was the favoured reliable means of mass written communication. There are many examples today of old postcards which were posted late one day and addressed to someone in another locality announcing the writer's arrival the following day and suggesting to the recipient that it would be a splendid idea for him/her to meet and to renew their acquaintance. An age when the postal system was reliable and well used before the advent of the telephone and computer and the modern systems of communication that we now take for granted. This period became "The Golden Age of Postcards." Not only were they sent in their millions but they were also avidly collected too. A postcard collecting craze developed encouraged by the early commercial photographers who recognised and encouraged the business opportunities thus presented; many became itinerants moving from locality to locality and from village to village taking photographs which they published as post-cards and then returned to sell to local shopkeepers. In turn these shop-keepers sold them to the local public and visitors. Winster had its visiting itinerant photographers too (more of them later) but was fortunate in that it had its own resident photographer, Albert Marshall (1860-1918), whose postcard work fills many of these pages. Marshall was also a printer who printed for many Winster organisations and those of neighbouring villages too. Many of these documents have survived.

Marshall, as a resident Winster Edwardian photographer, must have taken photographs of individuals, couples, small family groups and the like including Winster events – these too he would have furnished to his private customers printed with a postcard back but lacking a printed description of the event or person depicted and, crucially, also unidentified with his name as the photographer. This book offers some ideas as to identifying "Marshall People Postcards."

"But how did your love affair with postcards begin?" you may be wondering. Most likely with the first card I decided to keep. (See p.9.)

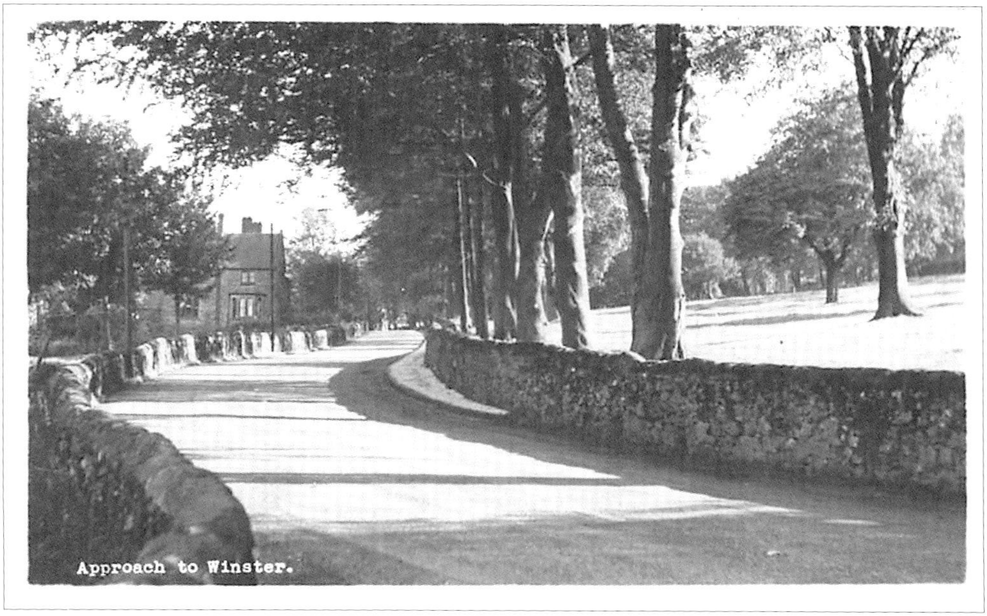

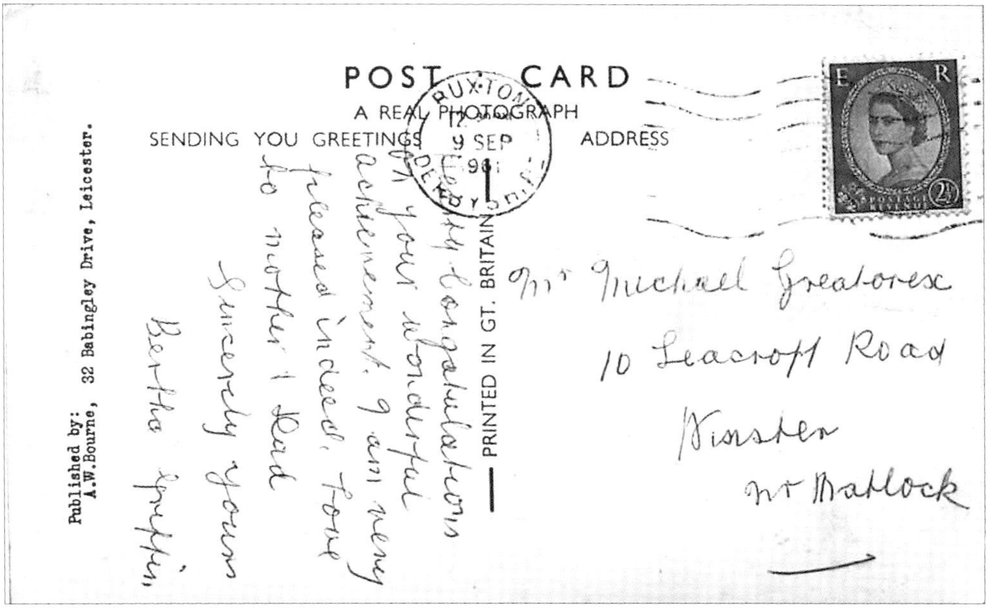

Posted from Buxton on 9th September 1961 to the author at 10 Leacroft Road.

This card was sent to me by a relative, Bertha Griffin. In 1961 I was a 16 year old boy living with my parents and family at 10 Leacroft Road.

"Happy congratulations on your wonderful achievement. I am very pleased indeed. Love to mother & dad."

The "wonderful achievement", I recall, was passing some exams. This card exemplifies everything I like about a picture postcard:

The View – Vicarage Hill, the approach to Winster from the west, is unchanged since 1961. The house at left is the Vicarage and to the right is Oddo Park.

The Postmark – the postage stamp remains and the cancellation strike is legible and it is often (with much older cards) the only reference which we have as to the approximate time when the photograph was taken viz it is obvious that this one was taken not later than 9 September 1961. The photograph itself may have been taken well before the date of the cancellation strike.

The Name and Address of the Recipient – Again, with older cards these are invaluable aids to identifying people and places. The recipient's name can often be found in Census Returns and information about them from other sources too. A "good address" as here is often unavailable on older cards. Winster developed before addresses did. Sometimes Winster people called their homes by names such as "Rose Cottage, East Bank". A later occupant might not like the name "Rose Cottage" and change it to "Clough View, East Bank." The problems that this creates for the local historian are obvious. Oh, just in case you are wondering – these two examples of names are fictitious and invented by me just to illustrate my point.

The Message – Often this is inconsequential and commonplace. Sometimes the message is humorous or may even help in identifying other family members of the sender or the recipient.

The Publisher/Photographer – In the case of this card, we have his name and address, A.W. Bourne, 38 Babingly Drive, Leicester. That opens up further opportunities for research into other cards published by the publisher and about the publisher too. Back in 1961 I was unaware and not at all remotely interested in the identity of this publisher. It was many, many years later when I came across some of his other Winster cards and also became aware of his wider work too, that I started to take note of him and his postcard work. More about A.W. Bourne later, let me continue with the work of that Winster man, Albert Marshall.

CHAPTER 1

ALBERT MARSHALL (1860 -1918)

Albert Marshall had a business in the late 19th and early 20th centuries as a printer and stationer in Winster. He was a photographer too and published many postcards of Winster and the surrounding villages. Some examples of his topographical cards of neighbouring villages are included later for the sake of completeness.

Albert was born into a family of lead miners on 14 September 1860. His Father, Daniel, was born in Elton in 1822 and died suddenly on 29 May 1867. "Suddenly" does not remotely do justice to the circumstances of his death. The Vicar at the time (the Rev. Herbert Milnes (1832 – 1909) thought the circumstances to be of interest enough to make a note in the burial register thus: "Accidentally shot dead May 29 in Tragues leaving a widow and eight children – a handsome subscription has been raised for him." Tragues was either a farm on the border between Wensley and Winster or was in France. I guess it was the farm.

Albert's Mother, Sarah Jackson, was born in Winster in 1819 and died in 1890. The Rev. Milnes was still Vicar in 1890 and again helpfully notes in the register that she "died from dropsy." I suppose there might be interest enough in recording notes made in Winster registers by clergy but that might take me too far from the ambit of this book. However, I'll content myself with just one more because it is remotely connected to Albert. In 1891 Albert's niece, Elsie Marshall, died, aged 11, – here the Rev. Milnes left us with this gem: "Died from some kind of brain attack. Her parents thought that she had worked too hard at her lessons as in her delirium she spoke about her school. Buried 3 October 1891."

Albert had eleven siblings all born in Winster. In 1881 at the age of 20 he was still living at home on East Bank by which time his mother was a farmer and Albert was a lead miner.

In 1891 Albert had become a farmer/lead miner and was the head of a household still at East Bank. His younger sister, Adeline, was housekeeper and his younger brother, William, was a domestic gardener. Emily Burton, aged 13, Albert's niece also lived with him. During this year Albert married Eliza Nunn who was born in Gravesend, Kent.

In 1888 there is a mention in *Winster Parish Magazine* of a "Mr. A. Marshall" (it might have been Albert) in connection with a collection for the Organ Fund. In February 1893 Albert's work as a printer is also mentioned in the Magazine where he is recorded as receiving a salary in connection with printing for Winster Parish Council.

At the start of the 20th century Albert was living in the Angel Yard, Main Street, near the Market House. He had made the transition from farmer/lead miner to become a printer and stationer on his own account. He had a son, Albert Nunn Marshall, aged 8. Albert's brother, Herbert, lived nearby as the publican of the Angel Inn and Herbert also ran a business as a cab proprietor on his own account.

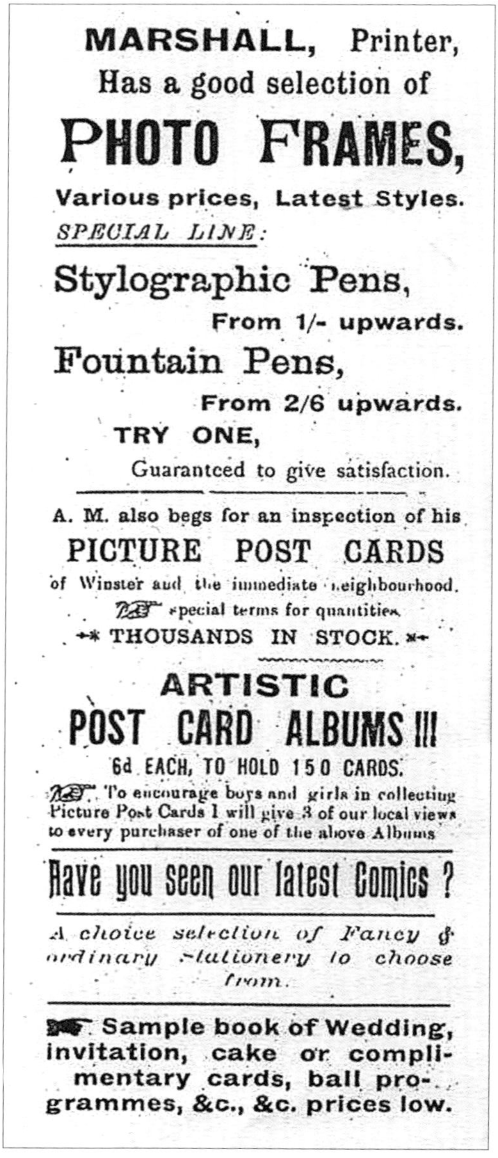

Albert Marshall advertisement – possibly from Parish Magazine.

There are a number of references to Albert in the *Parish Magazine* during the period 1900 to 1915 in connection with printing; the Horticultural Society Show; the Primitive Methodists; as the supplier of a new Church Hymn Book and in connection with a "song" by him at Bank House, West Bank, and as a donor to a jumble sale (with his wife).

In her 1985 publication *A Winster Scrapbook No. 4 Winster Parish Records. Researched by Margery Rodger, August 1985*, Mrs Rodger reproduces two advertisements by Albert. Unfortunately, she makes no mention as to where she found these adverts but I suspect they were from the Parish Magazine in the early 20th century. In the example here Albert refers to his "Picture Postcards of Winster and the immediate neighbourhood – special terms for quantities." He goes on to refer to having "thousands in stock" (probably an advertising puff). He also not surprisingly reveals his interest in promoting the sale of his cards by stating that he has "*Artistic Post Card Albums 6d each to hold 150 cards to encourage boys and girls in collecting Picture Post Cards I will give three of our local views to every purchaser of one of the above albums*." In the second advertisement (not illustrated) Albert repeats the publicity for the albums and his offer to the boys and girls and goes on to say that he has "Photographic views (cabinet size) of the Church, P.M. (Primitive Methodist) Chapel, New Road, Robin Hood, The Street and Market House etc at a reasonable price."

By 2nd April 1911, the date of the Census of that year, Albert was still living in Winster (the exact address is not given) with his wife and son, Albert Nunn Marshall. Albert Senior was described as a Printer & Stationer and was employed at home on his own account. Albert Junior, aged 18, was employed as a worker in his father's office.

The business founded by Marshall was carried on by his family until the mid 1930s. It is first listed in *Kelly's Directory* in 1895 with Albert as a printer; in 1899 as a printer and stationer and then in 1906-07 as a printer, stationer, newsagent and fancy goods dealer, Market Place. In 1916 Albert's son, Albert Nunn Marshall, is playing an active part in the business and is mentioned in *Kelly's Directory* for the first time – "Albert & Son". In 1928 Mrs. A.E. Marshall & Son are listed and the last listing is in 1936.

Albert died suddenly in Winster on 23 May 1918 from pneumonia after a few days' illness. He was buried in Winster churchyard on 27 May 1918.

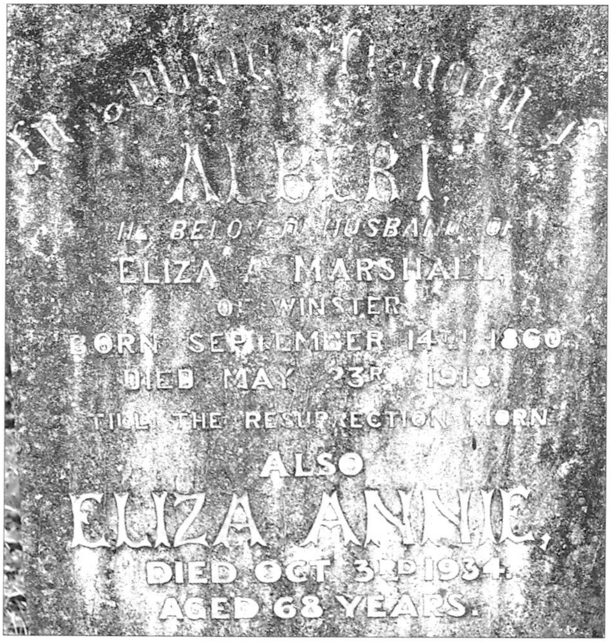

Albert & Eliza Marshall gravestone in Churchyard.

There is a short account of his funeral and those attending in The *High Peak News*, 1st June 1918. There is also an obituary in the June 1918 issue of *Winster Parish Magazine*. The *Derbyshire Times* dated Saturday June 1st, 1918 also gave publicity to the following unfortunate incident:

"Dragged Up By Bell
Winster Sexton's Extraordinary Mishap

An extraordinary accident occurred at the Winster Church on Friday. Mr. A. Roberts, an elderly resident of the village and for several years the Church Sexton, was ringing the passing bell for the late Mr. A. Marshall when by some unaccountable means, the bell turned right over. Its tremendous weight dragged the unfortunate sexton up to the belfry, and his left hand, which was tightly wrapped in the upper part of the rope, had all the four fingers ripped off as the rope passed through the rope in the ceiling. Mr. Roberts fell to the floor, but the room is by no means lofty, and he sustained no further injury. A taxi was procured and Mr. Roberts was taken to the Whitworth Hospital, Darley Dale, where his injuries received attention."

Consolation indeed that after having "all four fingers ripped off" the *Derbyshire Times* notes for posterity that, in falling to the floor, "he sustained no further injury." What a relief!

The extent of the involvement of Albert's son (Albert Nunn Marshall (1892 – 1931)) and indeed Albert Senior's wife (Eliza Annie Nunn (1866 – 1934)) in the postcard side of the business is unknown.

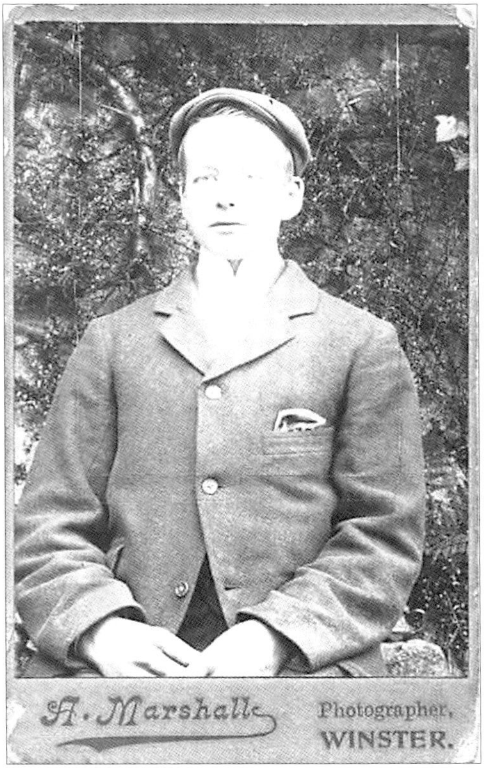

This might be a photograph of Albert Nunn Marshall (1892 – 1931) taken by his father, Albert Marshall Sen (1860 – 1918). The back of the image is printed but without reference to Marshall. At bottom right of the back is printed "Copyright 31379." Albert Sen probably bought in a supply of these cards with the pre-printed back which he then sold to customers with their images stuck on the front.

I suspect that Albert Senior was the major player right up to his sudden death in 1918, aged 58. I noted earlier that Albert Junior was living with his parents as recorded by the 1911 Census. The year before that on 19th November 1910, aged 18, he was proposed for membership of The Odd Fellows (The Loyal Triumphant Hope Lodge No. 1646) by Ernest and Fred Mosley. Albert Junior was then described as a printer resident in Winster. The following year on 14th November he was married at the Wesleyan Methodist Chapel, Matlock Street, Bakewell, to Ellen Osborne who was living at Rowsley but who was born in Hertfordshire. Both Albert Junior and Albert Senior's occupations were given as Printer on the Wedding Certificate.

By 1912, Albert Junior would be 26.

The short report of Albert Senior's funeral mentions that he left "a widow and one son, who is missing, we hope a prisoner in Germany." Albert Junior, like many Winster men, was serving in the Great War (1914 – 1918). He was Private No. 91585 in the Notts & Derby Regiment of the Sherwood Foresters. Wherever he was "missing" he fortunately found his way back home and died in 1931 three years before his mother. Albert Junior was a morris dancer and also ran or was a member of Marshall's Dance Band. His wife, Ellen, may also have been a member – she "*was a very good violinist… and used to teach*" as recalled by her daughter, Phyllis Taylor and reported at p133 of "*Winster A Peak District Village Remembers*."

Eliza Marshall, Albert Senior's wife, probably played a significant part in running the business, and certainly did so after her husband's sudden death in 1918. *Kelly's Directory* notes in 1895 that "Mrs Eliza Marshall" had a private school in Winster. Her first mention in Kelly's in relation to her late husband's business was in 1928 along with Albert Junior. Albert's sister, Adeline Marshall (1864 – 1932) died on 9 February 1932. An undated extract from an unidentifed newspaper article in the collection of Winster Local History Group gives a brief account of her funeral. Herbert (b.1856) and James Marshall (1859 – 1953), Adeline and Albert Senior's brothers are mentioned as "at the printers, Winster," so it seems that there might have been a considerable involvement in the business by other family members after Albert Senior's death.

CHAPTER 2

MARSHALL'S PLACES POSTCARDS

The bulk of Marshall's cards were printed. He also produced real photographic cards. Real photographic means what it describes – a postcard with an obvious glossy real photographic image. This multi-view greetings card is a good example.

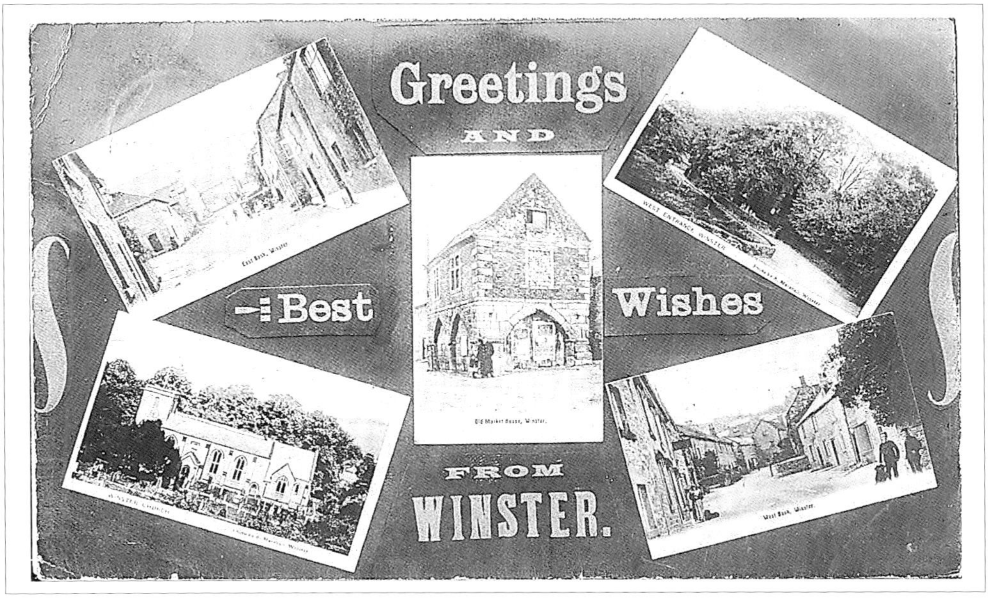

The places depicted are the Church, East Bank, Market House, West Entrance and West Bank. This card has been made by placing five other

Winster cards (illustrated elsewhere) and laying them around what appears to be a "*homemade*" Greetings text and then photographing the ensemble. This card was postally used from Winster. Marshall also published what he called his "*Real Photo Series*." Unfortunately, these were not numbered. Here we have two examples from this Series both postally used:

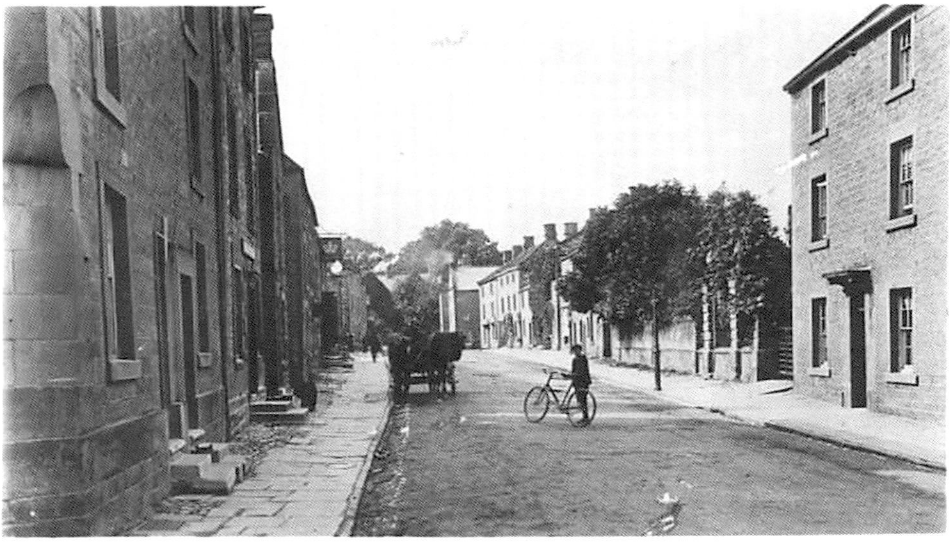

MAIN STREET, WINSTER

Posted from Winster on 18 August 1909.

The second example has a back which reveals plenty of information. It was posted from Manchester on 10 May 1910 to a Mrs Alice Angel at Golf Club House, Offerton Road, Stockport. In the 1911 Census Alice was still at the Golf Club – she was then aged 47 and gave Darley Dale as her birthplace. She was living with her husband who was the green-keeper. The couple had no children and had been married for 17 years. The sender of the card, Adeline, sent it from 23 Portman Street, Moss Side. The message reads:

"Dear Alice
What day next week will be best for me to come & see you. I think I can arrange for any day except Tuesday & that may be our Big Washday. Monday would be best if right for you. But I am afraid it wont, but let me know & I will try & arrange for one of the others. All news when I see you.
Love from Adeline."

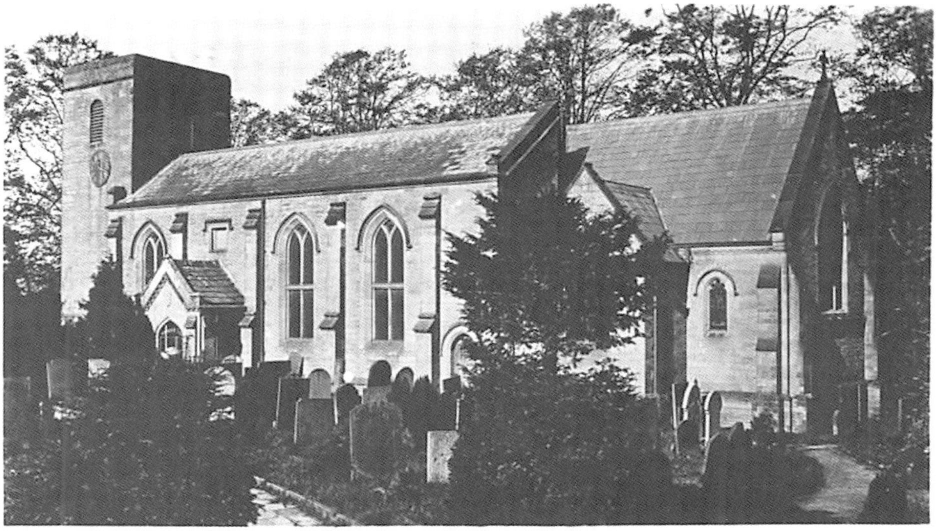

WINSTER CHURCH

It is tempting to imagine that Adeline was Adeline Marshall (1865 – 1932), Albert's sister. If Adeline Marshall did post the card she would have been about 45 roughly in the same age-bracket as Alice. Adeline Marshall was described as of Manchester at Albert's funeral in 1918 and she died at Manchester on 9th February 1932.

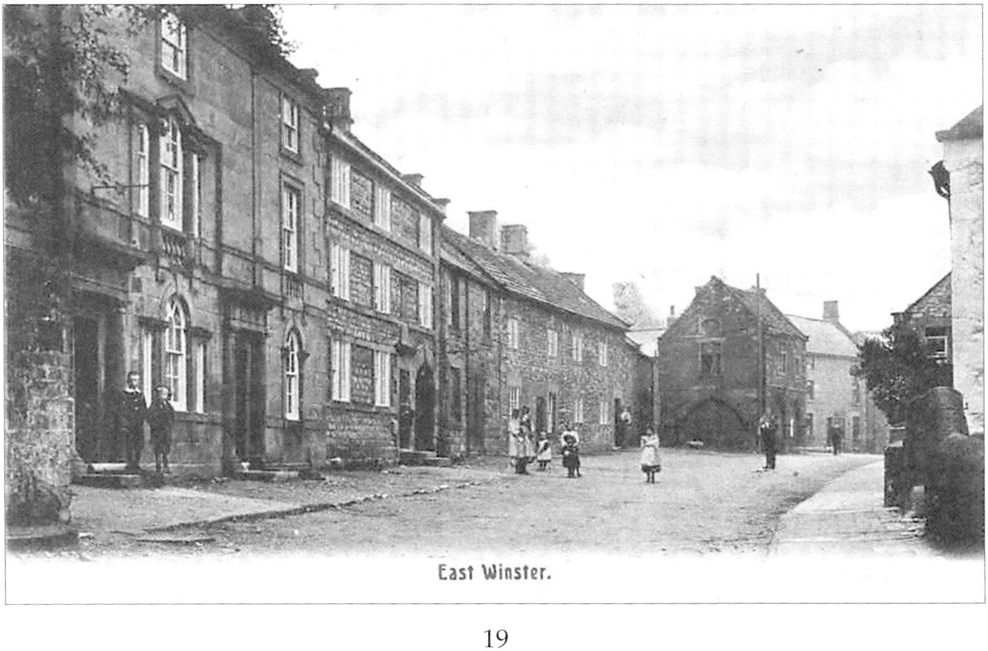

East Winster.

Marshall had a business arrangement with The Artistic Publishing Co., 9 Bury Court, St. Mary Axe, London, which printed the card of East Winster on the previous page and the next two cards of West Bank and the Old Market House.

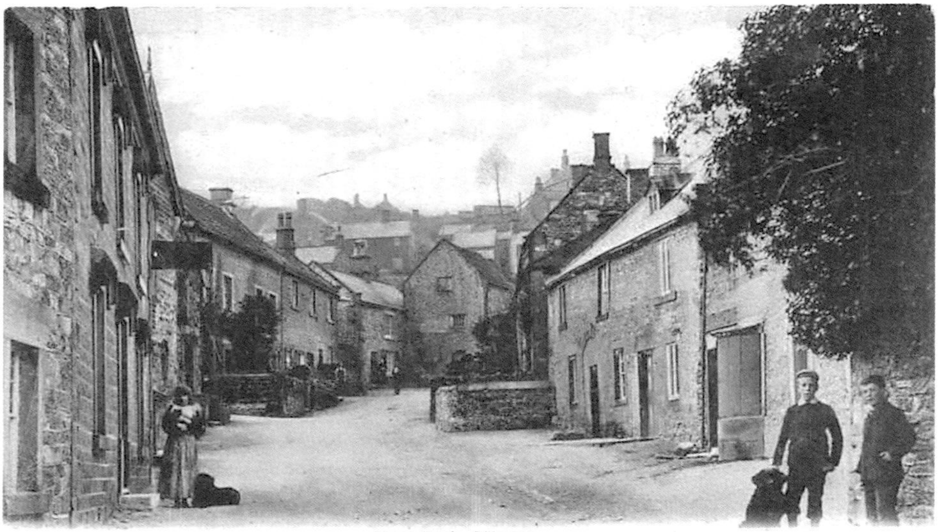
West Bank, Winster.

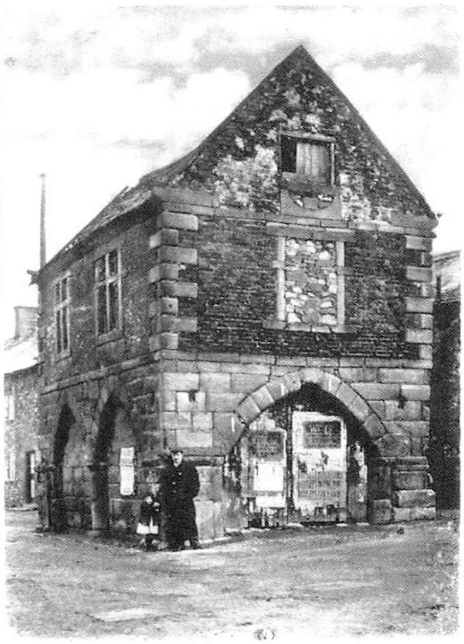
Old Market House, Winster.

These last three cards have identical fonts in red for the descriptions of the views and identical backs save for the Series Numbers. The West Bank card is Series No. 507, the East Winster is Series No. 499 and the Market House is Series No. 506. The Series No. was probably used by The Artistic Publishing Co. and not by Marshall – it may simply be the identification number for the view. The backs state that the cards were phototyped in Bavaria. Germany was a popular country for postcard publishers to get their cards printed in the Edwardian period. As the Series numbers are relatively close to each other, it suggests that Series Nos. 499 to 506 might be at least a total of seven Winster views. You will find The Crucifix, Cratcliffe (Series No. 500) illustrated later (see p29). So there may be at least five other Series numbers not yet discovered by me namely, Series Nos. 501, 2, 3, 4 and 5. The West Bank, Winster, card was postally used on 30 December 1905 and the Old Market House card was postally used on 10 February 1905. This latter card was sent by H.A. Fearn to Miss Remmer, Knedlington, Howden, Yorkshire. The text reads:

"Main St Winster
Matlock Bath
Feb 10th 1905

Dear Miss Remmer
I expect you know I came home on Wednesday. I travelled as well as could be expected. I keep much about the same any pain does not go away yet. But I think it will in time. The Dr ordered one home for a month's rest. I should have like to have seen you before I came away intended writing to tell you. I am taking my food a little better remember me to all friends. Best love your loving friend H.A. Fearn."

There are other cards in this book sent by H.A. Fearn (see p.168). Harriet Ann Fearn was born in Winster in 1877. The 1901 Census found her, aged 23, living with her parents, a brother and two sisters on Main Street. Her occupation then was not stated – her father was an Insurance Agent. The 1905 card states that Harriet had returned home for a month on "*doctor's orders*" to recover from her illness. Harriet may have been working in the Howden area where Miss Remmer was one of her Yorkshire friends.

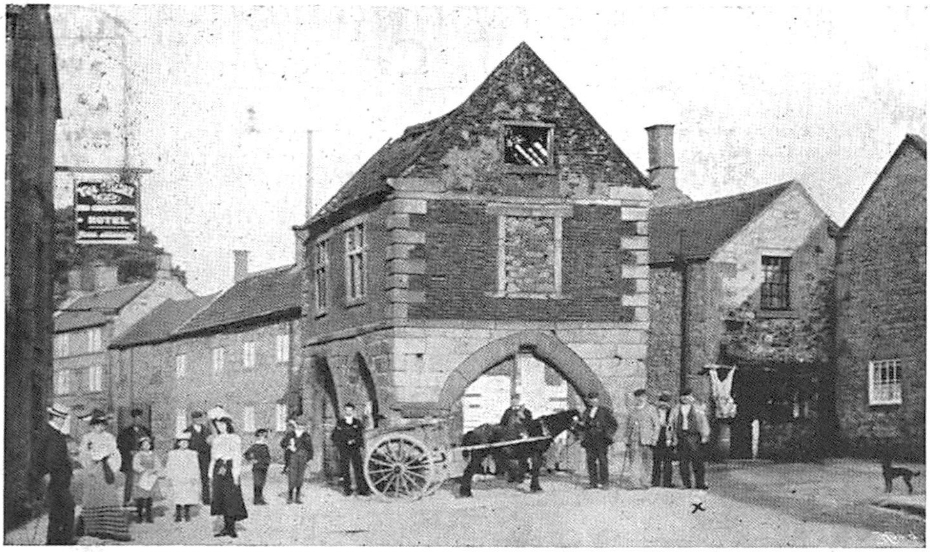

MARKET PLACE, WINSTER. Photo by A Marshall, Winster

An earlier generation of Winster local historians left us some information about the identity of the people on this card which was postally used on 26 April 1907. But first, the message is of interest – it reads:

"The gentleman on the extreme right of this picture is the stout gentleman we had at our table. The one who wanted double quantity of ham and eggs. This is how he appears during working hours. He is an engine driver."

The image was reproduced in the *Winster Festival of Britain Celebrations Programme* 1951 with this comment:

"We are fortunate in being able to reproduce two pictures of Winster's old Market House and we feel that the one prior to restoration, somewhere about 1890, has a special significance this Festival year since we are able to name at least four of the people on the picture who have sons or daughters living in Winster today.

On the right of the picture is the late Mr. George Greatorex, father of Mr John Isaac Greatorex, Newholme, Main Street; third from right is the late Josiah Smith, father of Mrs. Ernest Mosley (Winster's R.D.C.

representative); fourth right is the late Mr. Samuel Heathcote whose son Samuel, and daughter Miss Louisa, still reside in East Bank; the late Mr. John Heathcote (standing behind the horse) is father of Mrs. Harold Wild, Sunny Bank, Winster."

I doubt whether the photograph was taken around 1890. It is, I suggest, unlikely that Marshall would have used this image for a postcard that we know was posted 17 years later in 1907. If it was taken in 1890 then the "stout gentleman" at right, if it was George Greatorex (1855 – 1908), would have only been 35 at the time of the photograph. The image suggests a much older man. My guess is that the photograph was taken early in the 20th century. The Market House was restored in 1905. In 1900 George Greatorex would have been 45 and if it was taken, say in 1905, then he would have been 50 which seems more likely.

You will note the butcher's shop at right. Of the people identified in the photograph in 1951 these notes about their identities and life spans may be of interest:
George Greatorex (1855 – 1908)
John Isaac Greatorex (1881 – 1960)
Josiah (or Joshua) Smith born about 1841
Mrs. Ernest Mosley née Grace Smith (1882 – 1960)
Samuel Heathcote (1849 – 1905)
Samuel Heathcote (1877 – 1959)
Louisa Heathcote (1879 – 1956)
John Heathcote (1852 – 1925)
Mrs. Harold Wild née Minnie Heathcote (1888 – 1993)

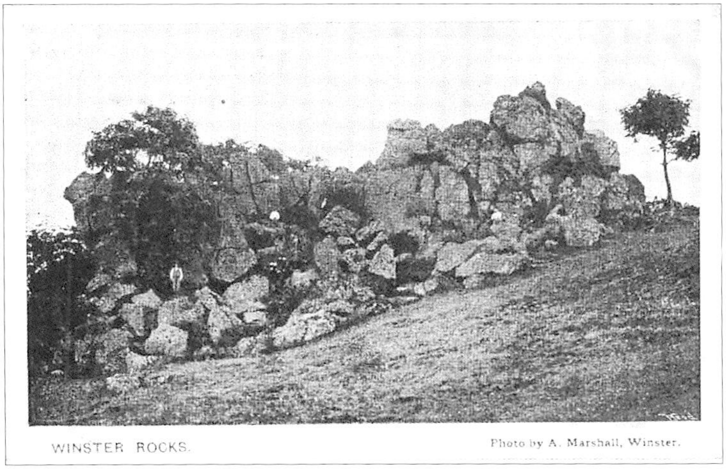

Postally used 14 April 1906

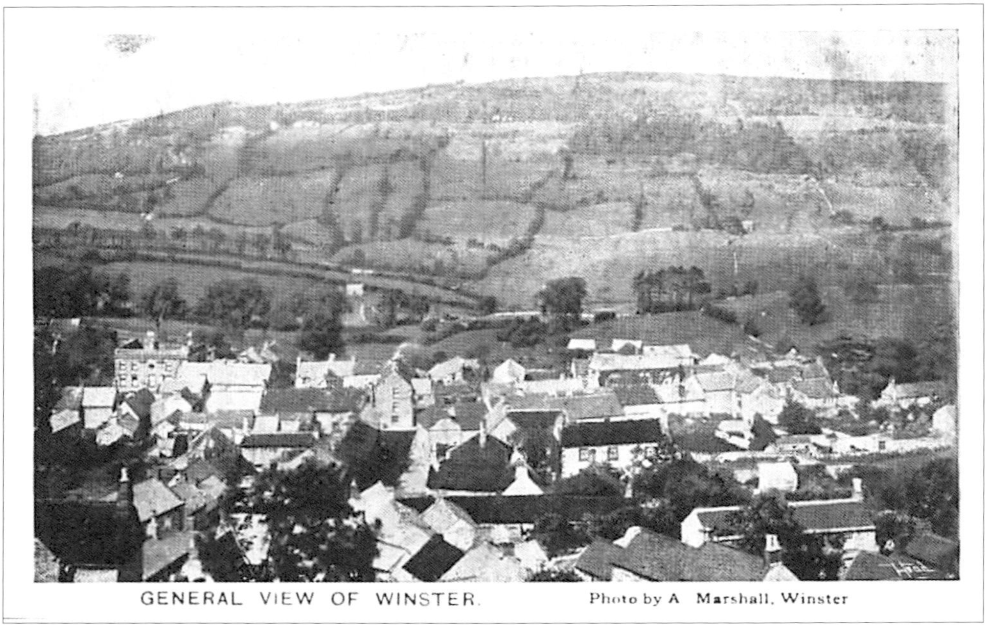

Postally used 13 July 1907

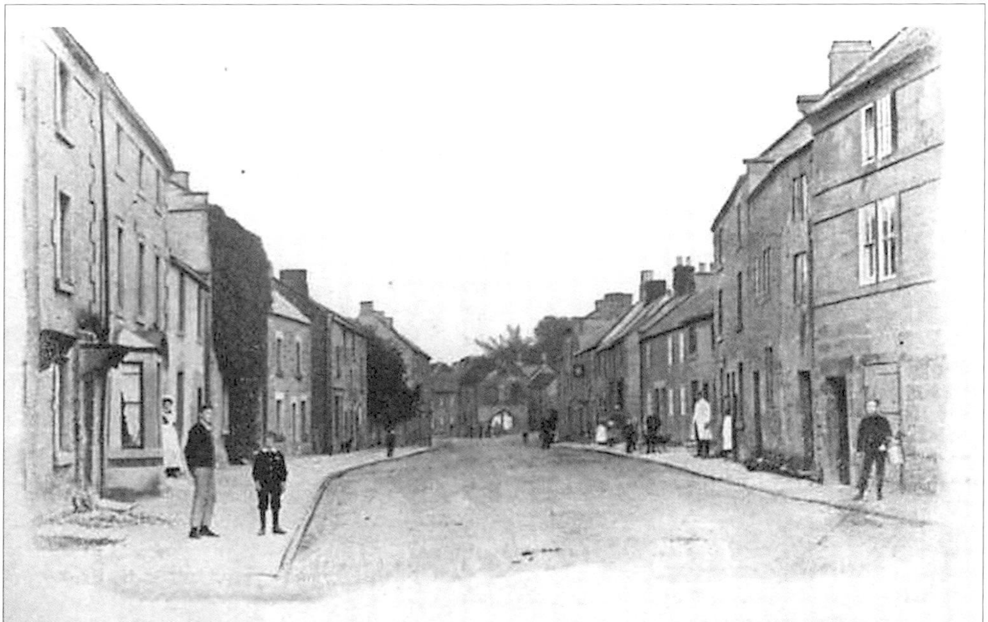

Unused – this card has the same back as the previous card
Photo produced by courtesy of M. Saxton

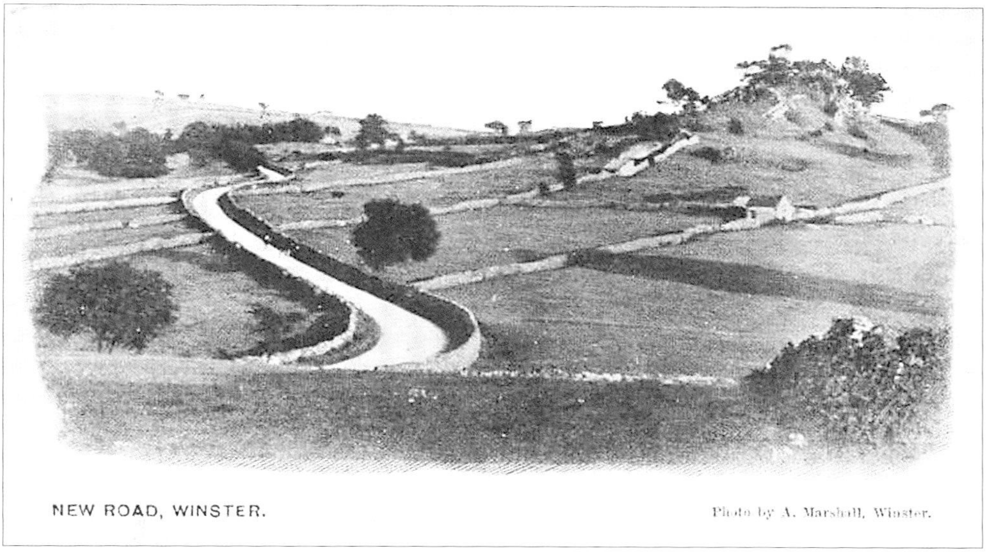

The above card (unused) suggests a semi-vignette style which was popular in the period when no message was allowed on the back. Senders often included messages on the picture side and so postcard

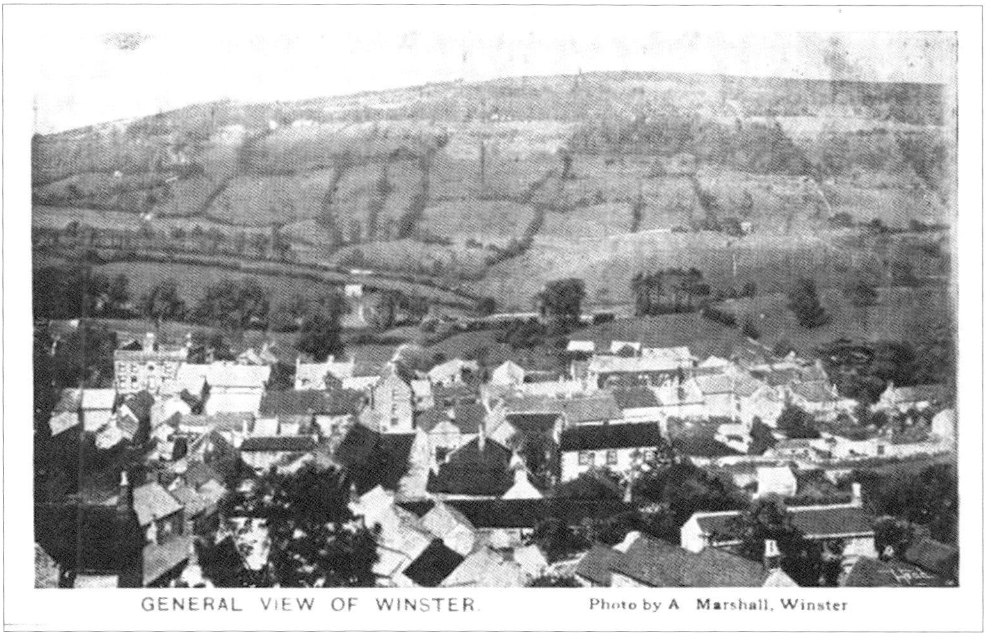

Posted from Birchover on 22 August but the year is illegible to Mr. E.A. Gill, 86 Exeter Road, Sherwood Ris(e), Nottm. The message is simply "From Annie G." Derbyshire Artistic Series No. 3007 and 7726

publishers printed cards in this form which readily allowed the sender to include some text. The Post Office Regulations were changed in 1902 to allow the back of the card to be divided into the now traditional form – address on the right and message on the left. The back of this card is printed with the easily recognisable divided back and is also printed in the same colour with this message at the top of the message space:

"This space, as well as the back may now be used for communication – Inland Postage Only. Post Office Regulation."

Of course, the text is confusing – it refers to *"this space, as well as the back..."* and is printed on the back itself! Should it have been printed – *"this space, as well as the front..."* That would have made more sense. The conclusion I draw here is that this card was probably printed after 1902.

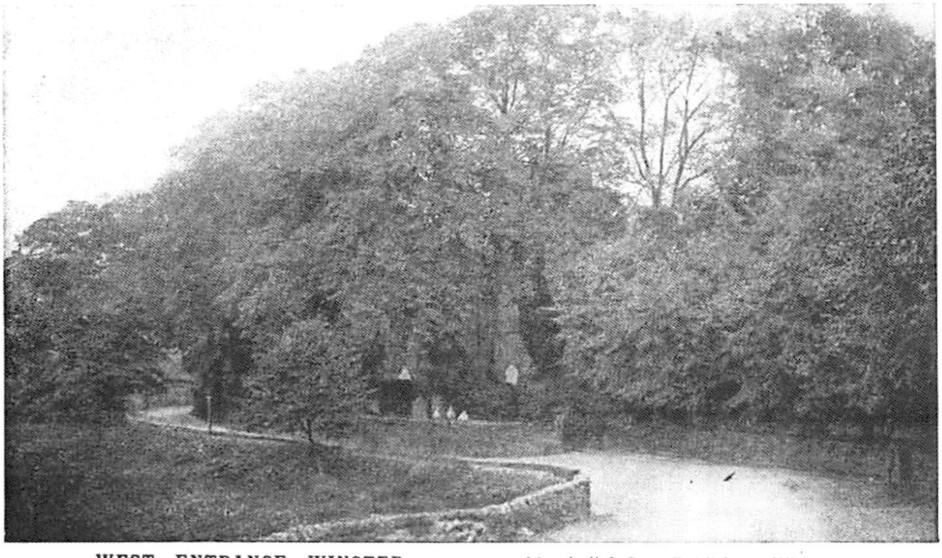

WEST ENTRANCE WINSTER. Marshall & Son, Publishers, Winster.

The above card (unused) would win no prizes for interest. It is completely dominated by trees. Only those who know Winster will realise that behind the trees is Winster Church. If you peer closely, you will just be able to see three people posing for the camera behind the churchyard wall.

Marshall Cards Of Neighbouring Villages

Marshall published postcards of neighbouring villages – they are included here for the sake of completeness.

Robin Hood's Stride – This beauty spot lies about 2 miles to the north-west of Winster, alongside Cratcliff Rocks.

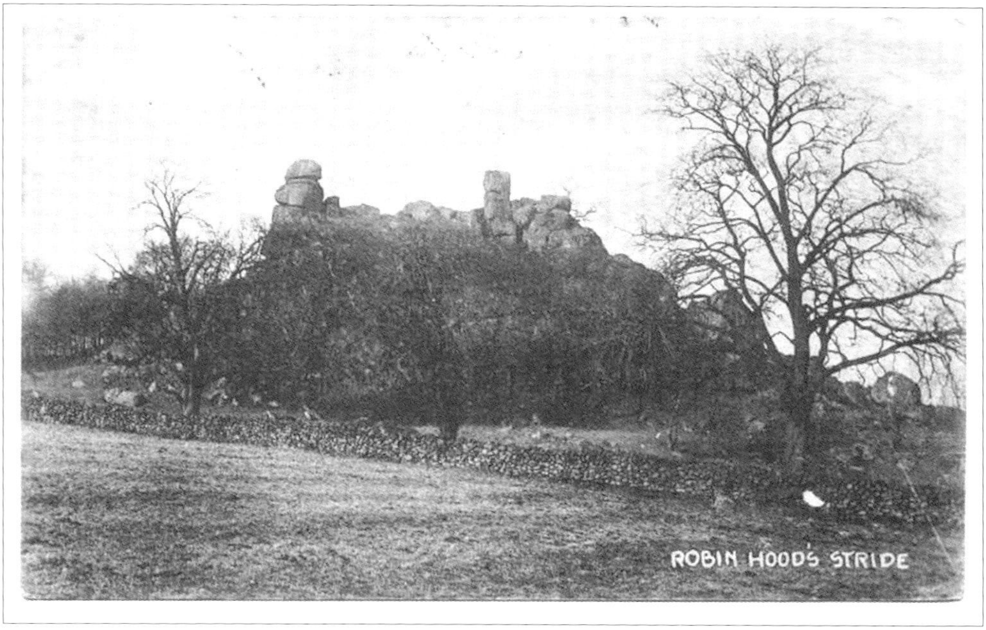

I have two different cards where the same photograph has been used for both. The one above is sepia coloured and was used (unfortunately not postally). It was sent to a Mrs. Sidebotham, 3 Hardman Street, Longsight, Manchester (witten in pencil in an adult hand). The message (also written in pencil but clearly in a child's hand) seems to be addressed *"Dear Brother"* and is illegible but it refers to Winster: the Rock Field, East Bank, and Shothouse. The signature looks like *"Arthur."* The other version (not illustrated) is unused. It has a caption on the front at top and a different printed back. Both are printed on the back *"Published by A. Marshall, Winster."*

Cratcliff House and Rocks – Cratcliff or Cratcliffe lies next to Robin Hood's Stride between Elton and Birchover. It is a local beauty-spot and the rocks are a magnet for climbers wanting to hone their skills.

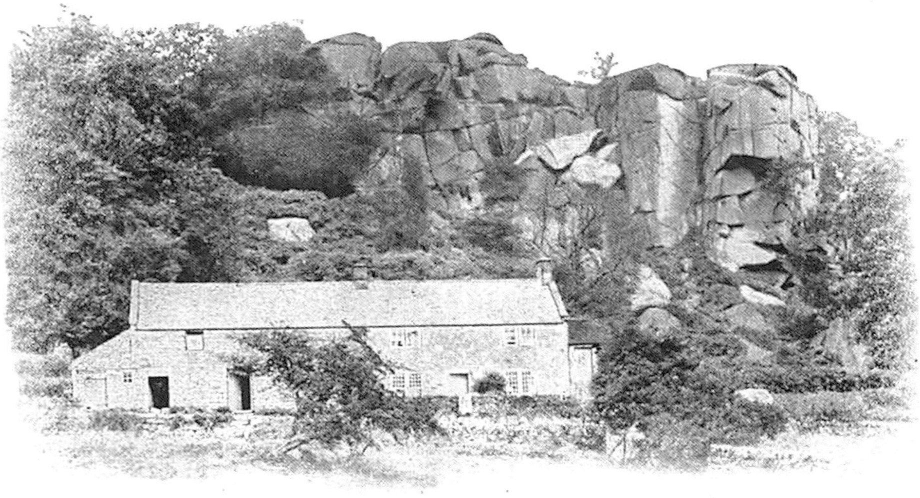

CRATCLIFFE ROCKS. Photo by A. Marshall, Winster.

Unused

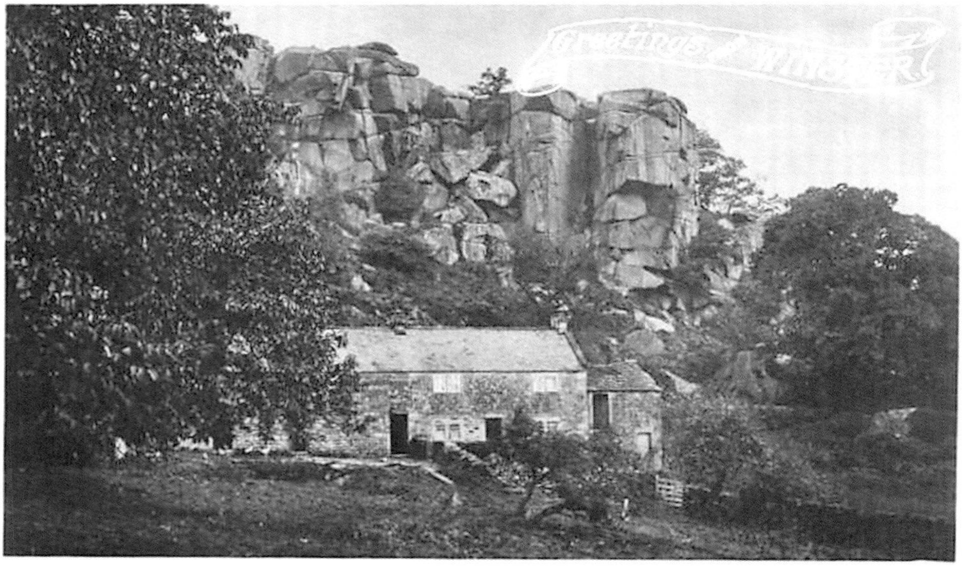

CRATCLIFFE ROCKS NEAR WINSTER.

Unused

Cratcliff Crucifix – Behind Cratcliff House and nestled at the bottom of the Rocks is a cave or rather a space of about up to 10 feet further back from the overhang of the Rocks. Locals refer to it as *"the Hermit's Cave."* On the far wall from the entrance is the Crucifix cut into the wall and protected by metal railings.

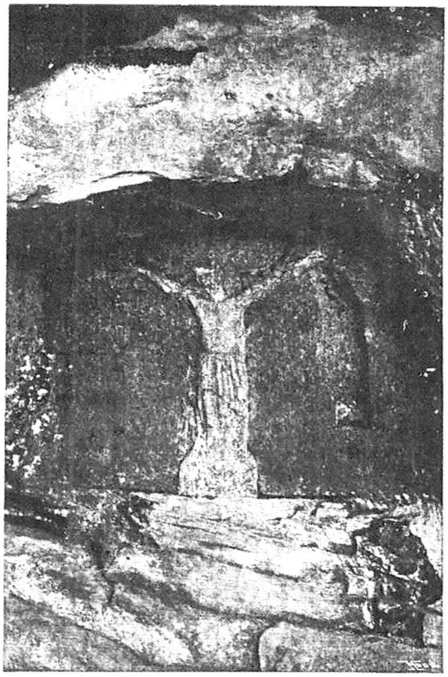

CRUCIFIX, CRATCLIFF. Marshall & Son, Publishers, Winster.

This card is Series No. 500 published by Marshall with The Artistic Publishing Co – it is unused

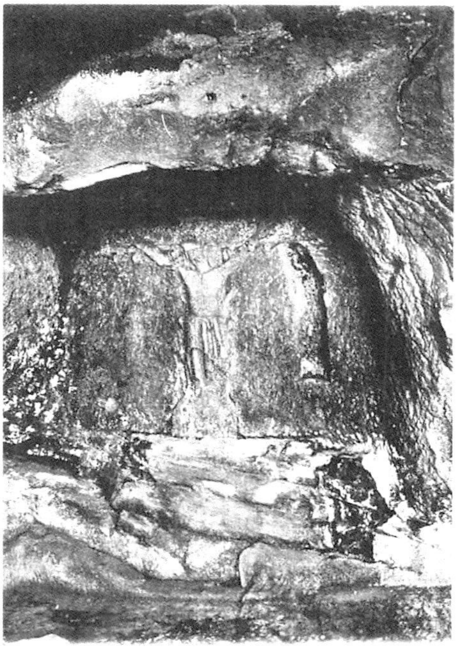

The Crucifix, Cratcliffe.

Unused

Birchover – is north of Winster connected by Birchover Lane which is now unsuitable for the passage of modern motor-vehicles. The longer but safer route for the motorist is west out of Winster, turning right on to the B5056 towards Bakewell – then passing Robin Hood's Stride and Cratcliff Rocks at the bottom of the hill which are away in the left distance before taking the right hand turn about half a mile along the valley bottom onto an unclassified road up into Birchover. As the motorist ascends The Mires to the top of the climb and into Main Street and the village proper, Birchover Rocks (also known as Rowtor Rocks) are to the right behind the public house. As a child in the 1950s I recall that the Rocks were a local attraction open to the public, I think, on payment of a fee. The attraction of Rocks for children to clamber upon is self-evident.

There are five Marshall postcards in this small collection only one of which was postally used.

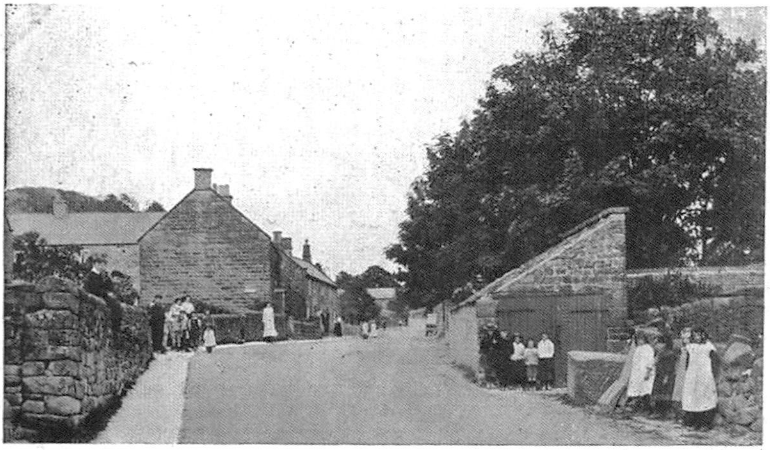

BIRCHOVER STREET Photo by A. Marshall, Winster.

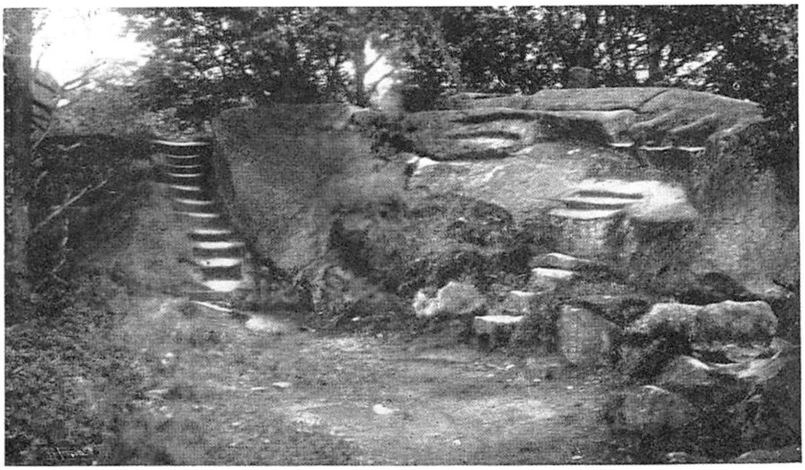

ARM CHAIRS, BIRCHOVER ROCKS Photo by A. Marshall, Winster.

Postally used on 4 December 1904

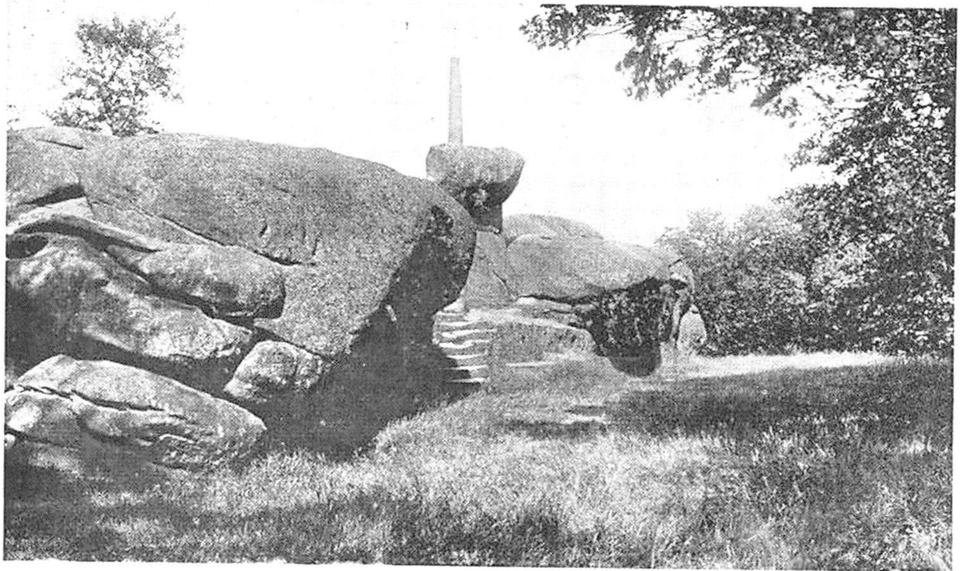

THE NEEDLE, ROWTOR ROCKS Photo by A. Marshall, Winster

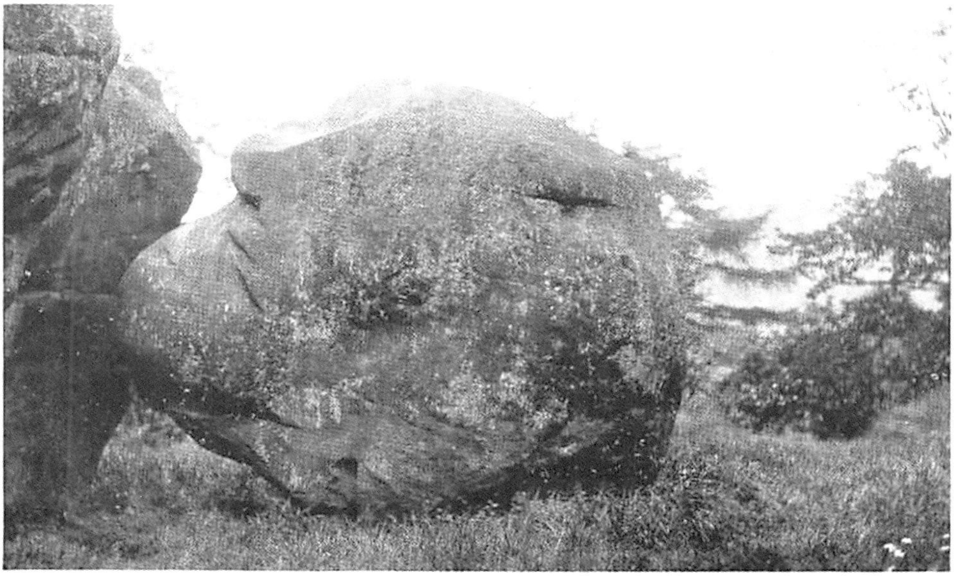

ROCKING STONE, BIRCHOVER ROCKS. Photo by A. Marshall, Winster

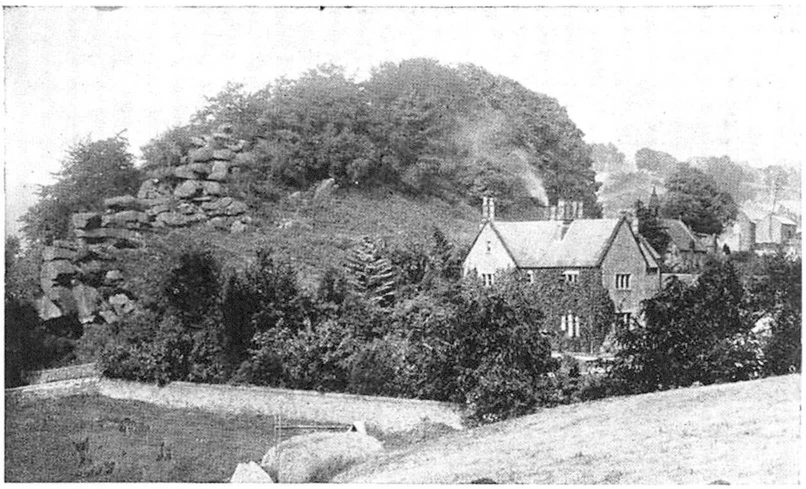

BIRCHOVER ROCKS AND VICARAGE   Photo by A Marshall, Winster

Elton – Elton is west of Winster – the two are within a short walking distance. If Winster is considered by some to be remote then Elton is remoter. West of Elton village is a gated road (unsuitable for modern motor vehicles) linking Elton with the much larger village of Youlgreave.

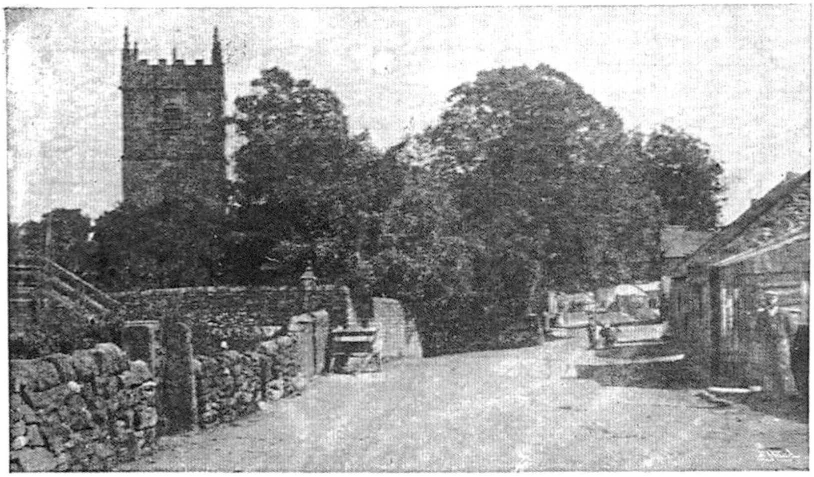

ELTON STREET.   Marshall & Son, Publishers, Winster.

This card was posted from Winster but, unfortunately, the cancellation strike is poor and the all-important date is missing

Stanton-in-the-Peak – This village is north of Winster and beyond Birchover. Both the following cards were used – the one of the Church was posted from Stanton-in-the-Peak on 26 January 1910 to an address in Devon. The other card, of the Hall, was not postally used but was addressed to an address in Heeley (Sheffield) and is crammed with a message on almost every available spot of the back including *"I wrote this PC late last night & it is no use to write a letter now. The recipe came this morning & I can get them here."* This message too lacks a date.
The same image of the Hall was posted on 10 June 1908 to Miss Greatorex, Bilton House, Harrogate, without a message.

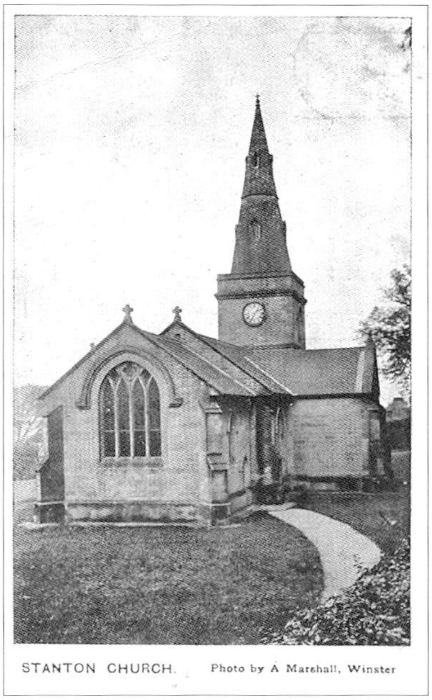

Postally used on 26 January 1910

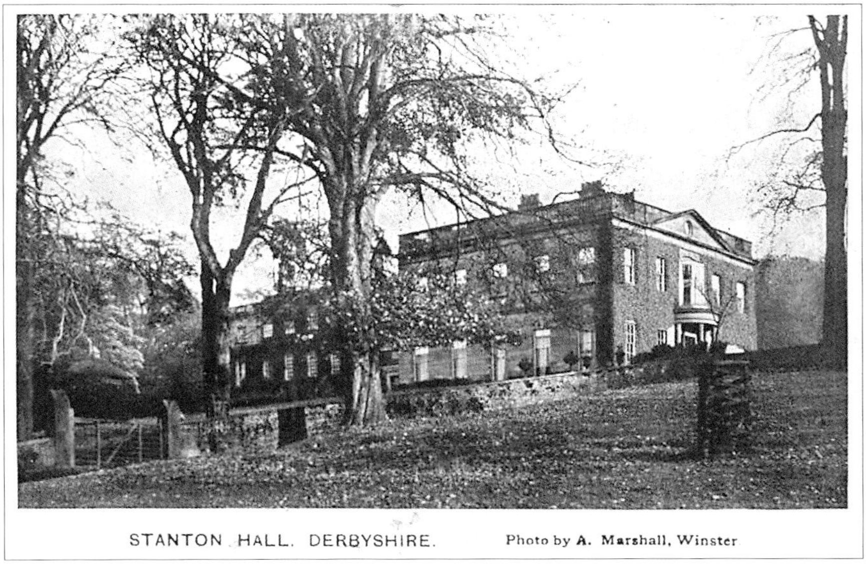

The most recent Marshall topographical card in my collection (not illustrated) is a printed colour-tinted view of Main Street looking east and printed on the back *"Published by E.A. Marshall & Son, Winster, Matlock"* – Rextone Series.

CHAPTER 3

MARSHALL'S PEOPLE POSTCARDS

Late in my many years' collecting Marshall's postcards I had still not discovered a card by Marshall taken in his studio (I assumed he had one) – and then along came this lovely card of Sarah Winifred (Winnie) Brassington (1909 – 2000) which is identified on the back by an inked stamp: *"Marshall & Son, Photo, Winster Matlock."*

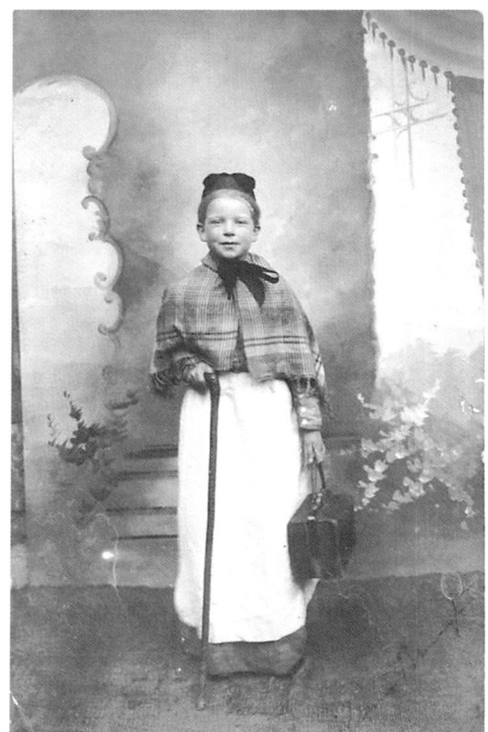

Sarah Winifred Brassington (1909 – 2000). There is an ink stamp on the back *"Marshall & Son, Photo, Winster, Matlock."*

The image has Sarah's name (she was known throughout her life as "*Winnie*") written in fading ink at bottom right of the picture. The date of the image is about 1919.

This card of Winnie was from the collection of Eric Brassington, Winnie's nephew. I will deal shortly with how this card led me to other possible Marshall cards but, first, some details and postcards illustrating Winnie's life.

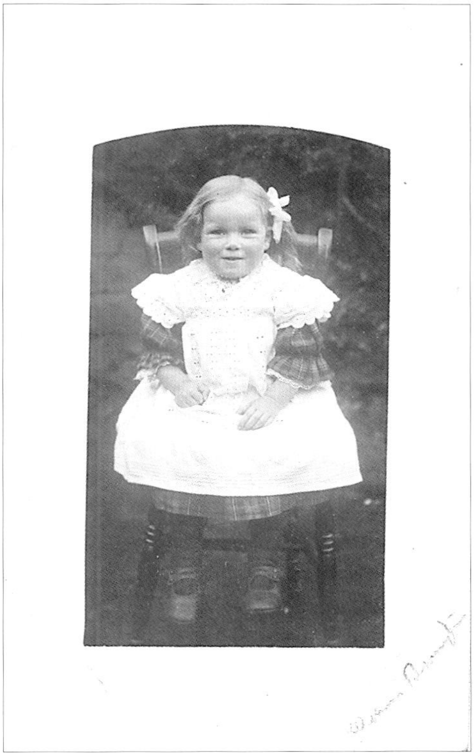

Winnie Brassington as a child c1913

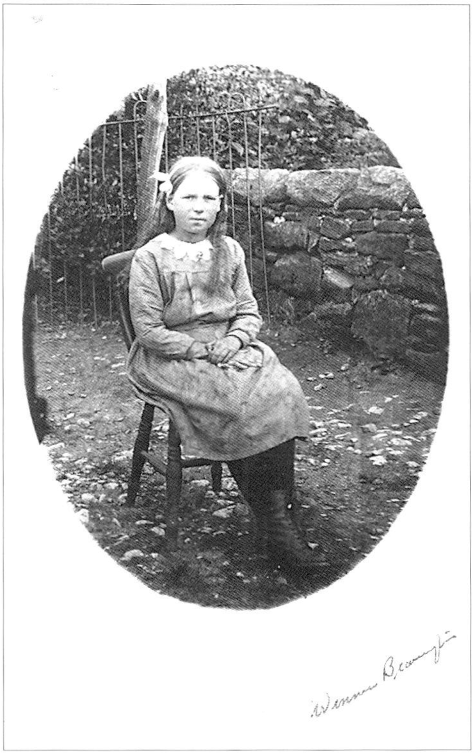

Winnie Brassington, aged about 12, c1921, at Winster School

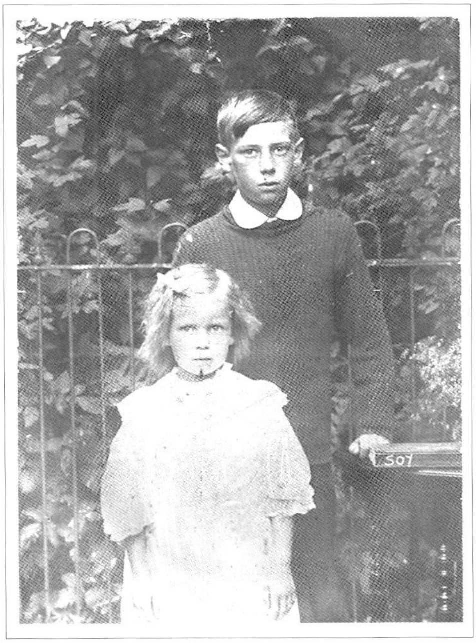

Winnie Brassington & her brother, Ben. This is not a postcard. The original print is about 6″ X 4″ with a plain back. Note the railings which might be the same railings at Winster School in front of which Winnie posed in the preceding image

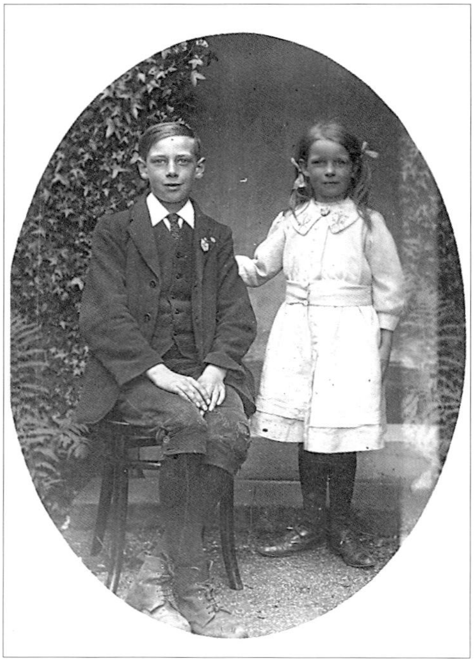

Winnie Brassington with her brother, Ben

These two postcards of Winnie Brassington were taken at While U Wait Studios, Blackpool, early in the 1930s.
They were taken at different times – note Winnie's different clothing. In one image she is with her Winster friend, Gladys Hardy (1905 – 2005)

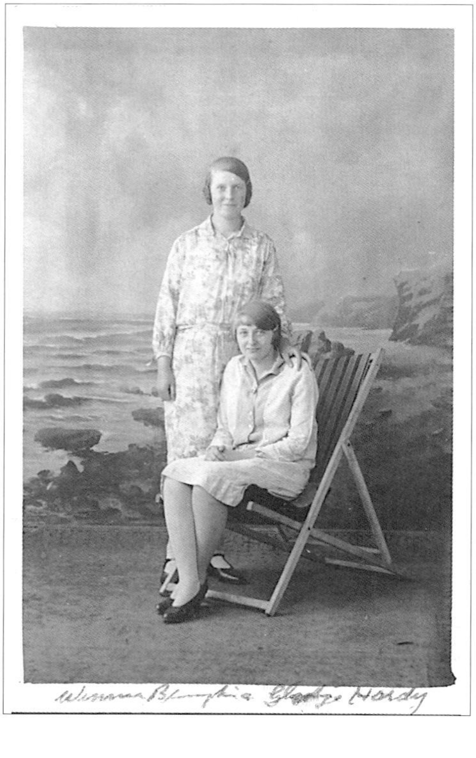

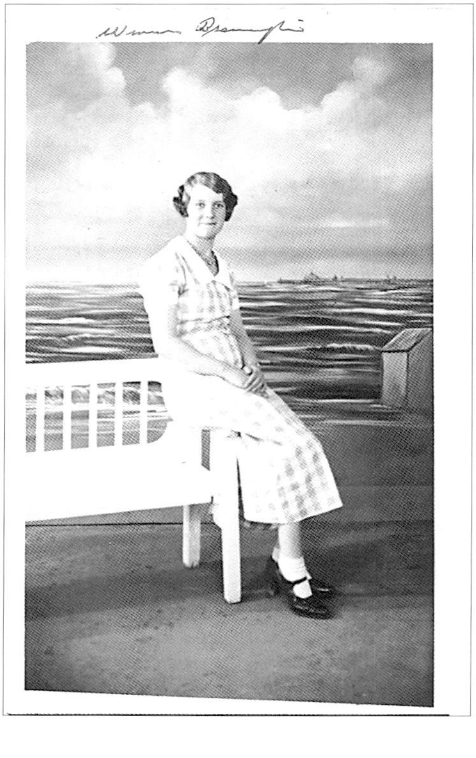

Winnie was born in 1909 and died in 2000. In the 1911 Census she is living with her parents and two brothers on East Bank, Winster. She was educated at Winster School. After School, unlike many Winster girls who went to work in local Mills, Winnie went into service with Dr. Meecham, Dale Road, Matlock. She continued this job during the time she was an auxiliary nurse at the RAF rehabilitation unit in Matlock caring for recovering aircrew. At Dr. Meecham's she was to learn the skills of housekeeping and cooking. She worked every day of the week and only had Wednesday afternoons off.

In the 1930s it became a weekly treat for Winnie's nephew and niece (who both lived in Winster) to have tea with their grandparents in Winster when *"Aunt Winnie"* came *"home"* to visit on Wednesday afternoons. She always brought cakes and treats for the children. The only other time the children saw Winnie was when they were taken to Matlock and called at the Doctor's house where Winnie would provide a drink and a home made biscuit.

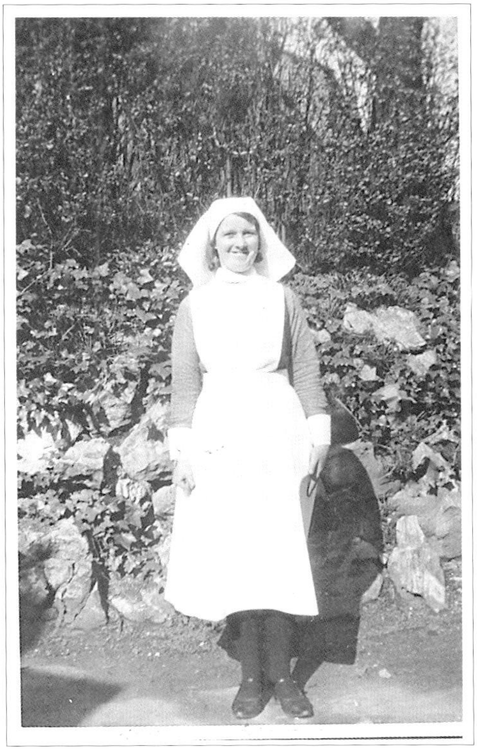

Winnie Brassington as a Nurse during World War 2

In 1947 Winnie married Roy Ollerenshaw and then lived in a cottage at the top of Willersley Lane, Starkholmes. Roy was a widower with 2 children.

Winnie was an enthusiastic supporter of local cricket and football teams. In later life she was a member of Derbyshire County Cricket Club and enjoyed attending matches at Derby and Chesterfield. She was a keen supporter and worker for Matlock Town Football Club organising events to pay for the match ball or towards the cost of new kit. One aspect of her fund raising involved making knitted dolls which she produced in large numbers. Much later when one of Winnie's nephews visited her with his own children the children always left with a knitted doll.

Winnie resisted attempts by relatives to get her a television and preferred to listen to Radio Derby and was a regular respondent by telephone to comment on items and to answer questions about local issues, sport and religion.

Following the death of her husband Winnie continued to live at Starkholmes until she became too infirm and then moved to Darley Dale where she died on 4 May 2000. Her funeral service was at Winster Methodist Chapel (her father had been a local preacher and she maintained strong Methodist connections throughout her life) followed by cremation at Chesterfield.

And now, back to the significance of the first postcard of Winnie illustrated on p.34. You will note that Winnie appears to be dressed as a "character" and that the photograph was taken in a studio in front of a backcloth. The original card has her name written across the bottom right-hand corner. Winnie's nephew (Eric Brassington) confirmed that the image was indeed that of his Aunt. From Winnie's known age, the photograph may date from c1918 which fits in with when Albert Marshall Junior would be actively involved in the business. You will recall that Albert Senior died in 1918 when the younger Albert would be about 26. The backcloth is typically that which a photographer would use as background for some of his studio portraits. He may have had other backcloths and would give customers a choice of which backcloth to use. In Eric Brassington's collection were other cards and one in particular caught my eye – it had the identical backcloth to that used

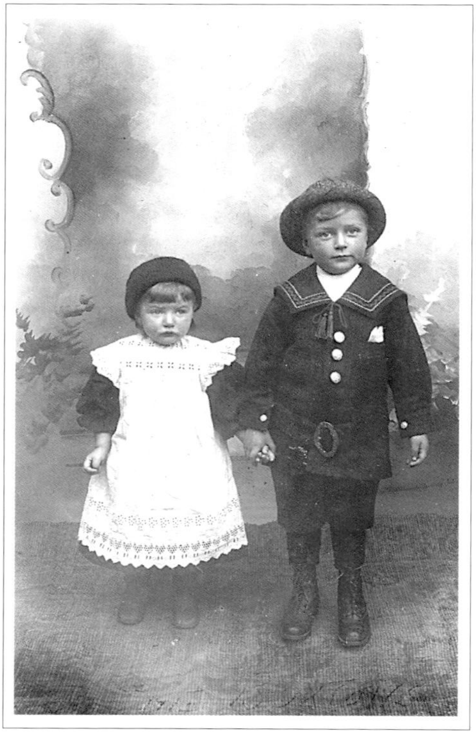

Note the backcloth is identical to that used in the Sarah W. Brassington card

for Winnie Brassington – it was of Billy Buxton and his sister. (See p.38.)

Although this image is not endorsed as being by Marshall it is likely that it is his work because of the backcloth. Eric was unsure as to the identity of Billy Buxton and his sister and their connection with his or the other Winster families included in his collection. This is one of four unused postcards of Billy and his sister – there is nothing to identify the children other than the name *"Billy Buxton"* or *"the Buxtons"* or *"Billy Buxton & Sister"* written on either the front or back of some of the cards. In two of the cards Billy is dressed in identical clothing suggesting that the photographs were taken during the same session. In these images too the background suggests that they were taken in an outdoor location. This location has ferns and paving stones which is the same background for other cards of the same period in which the subjects were Winster people. If these cards were the work of Marshall then I speculate that they were taken by him in the yard of the Angel Inn/Hotel on the north side of Main Street opposite the Market House. But back to the puzzle – who was Billy and his sister? Were they Winster people? Here are the three other cards.

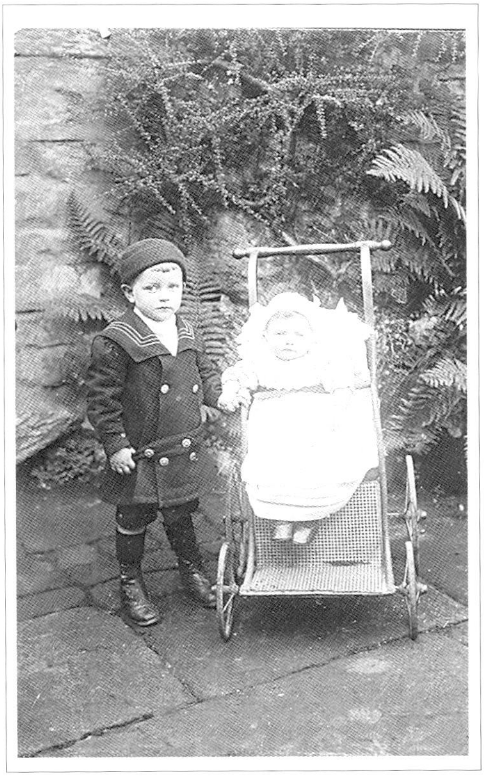

Billy Buxton & His Sister – Note the ferns and the paving slabs which are the background for other similar postcards

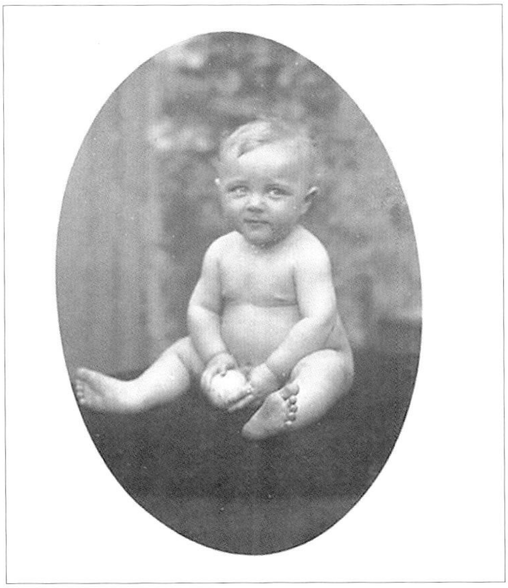

Billy Buxton as a baby

The 1911 Census records William Buxton, aged 32, living with his wife, Jane, aged 31, at East Bank. They had a son, William A. Buxton, aged 4 months, living with them. William and Jane were married and William was described as a Banksman at a lead mine.

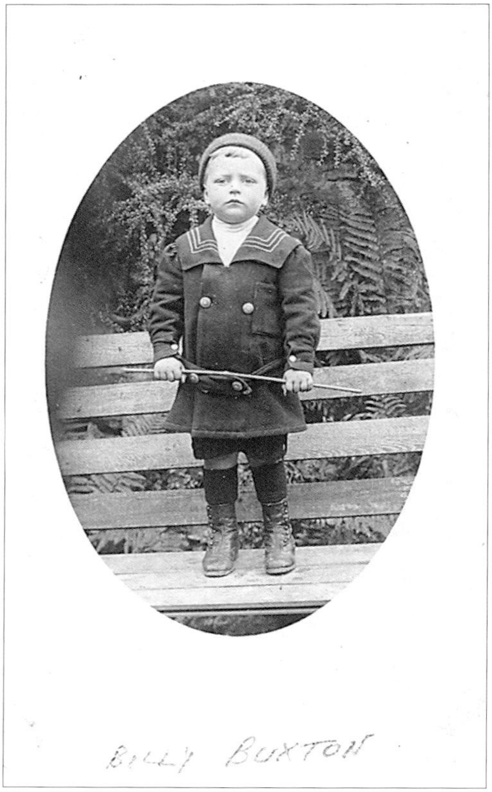

Billy Buxton – again note the back-ground of ferns. Note also that Billy is dressed in the same clothes as in the previous postcard

In Winster's *Parish Magazine* for September 1912, there is a note that William Anthony, the son of William and Jane Buxton, was baptised on 18 August. Confusingly, there was a William A. Buxton's birth registered in the October Quarter in Bakewell District in 1916. In the *Parish Magazine* for April 1918 it was noted that Alice, the daughter of William and Jane Elizabeth Buxton was baptised on 31 March 1918.

When a child was baptised is not a reliable date even to infer when a child might have been born. Oft times, especially in the late 19th century, children were not baptised soon after birth but much later – sometimes siblings might be baptised together or at some significant time during family life. So, for the moment the enigma of Billy Buxton and his sister remains – possibly to be solved by a reader of this book!

Other possible Marshall portraits with the similar ferns and paving slabs are the following:

At the bottom of the next image someone has written "*Mrs. H. Hardy & Mary.*" By a roundabout process I wondered if Mrs. H. Hardy was, in fact, Maud Hardy. In the 1911 Census she was living on East Bank, aged 24, the wife of Charles Herbert Hardy. Charles, aged 27, was a stationary engineman at a Lead Ore Mine (Mill Close Mine) and was born in

Winster. Maud was born in Starkholmes. Later, John Marsden, a former Winster resident, saw the image and recognised the woman as his grandmother and the child as his mother, Rose Mary Hardy.

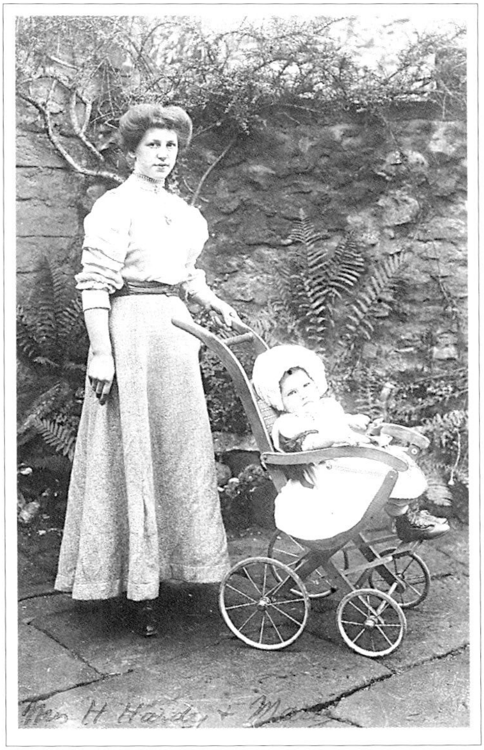

Mrs. H. Hardy & Mary c1911

In the 1911 Census Charles and Maud lived with their daughter, Rose Mary Hardy, aged 3, who had also been born in Winster. Maud was born Maud Blackham at Starkholmes, Matlock. In the 1901 Census she was living at West Bank, aged 15, working as a nurse/ domestic, at the home of her uncle, John Rouse (b.1864). John was married living with his wife, three sons and two daughters. Frank Blackham, aged 19, John's nephew and probably Maud's brother, was also living in the household and working as a lead miner. Maud married Charles in 1907. Rose Mary (1908 – 1970) was married in 1929 to William (Bill) Marsden and she lived in Winster for most of her life.

The Newton Family

This group of cards feature a Winster Newton family and particularly a trio of Newton girls. Ernest Newton (1877 – 1920) and Hannah Newton (nee Stone b.1888) the parents of the Newton Girls Trio were both born in Winster and married about 1902. Ernest's ancestors had lived in Winster since 1775 and Hannah's since 1795. The 1911 Census notes that they were living on West Bank. Ernest was a lead miner (Hewer) at a lead ore mine. They had their three girls living with them: Ada, Doris May and Gladys Lena. They also had a son, Ernest Henry Newton, but he was not at home on Census night and therefore went unrecorded with the remainder of the family. Winster's *Parish Magazine* also records in 1901 that another son, Herbert, was baptised in Winster Parish Church on 3 August 1901.

Ada Newton (1901 – 1988) married William Henry Gregory (1899 – 1956) in 1926. They had no children. She was the Winster May Queen in 1907.

Doris (*"Dolly"*) May Newton (1905 – 1999) married Ben Brassington (1903 – 1971) in 1929. Ben Brassington is someone we will meet later in this book. Dolly was a prize winner in the girls' 13-18 race at Winster's Peace Celebrations held on 19 July 1919.

Gladys Lena (known as Lena) Newton (1908 – 1995) married John (Jack) Walker (1905 – 1950) in Winster in 1937. They had two children and lived on West Bank. Lena too was a prize winner at the 1919 Peace Celebrations in the girls' race 9-11. For many years she was Winster's postwoman and as such must have been an authority on every Winster nook and cranny and who lived there.

Ernest Henry Newton (1908 – 1991) married Doris L. Travis in 1940. During World War 2 Ernest saw service in Burma and later returned to his job at Patons and Baldwins, Matlock, where he continued to work until his retirement.

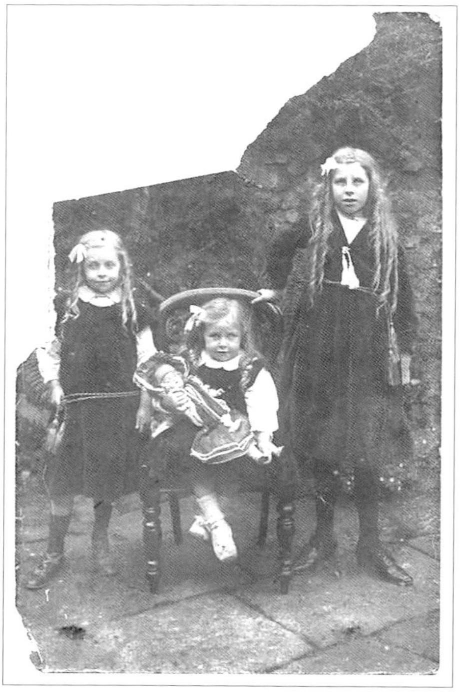

Newton Trio c1913

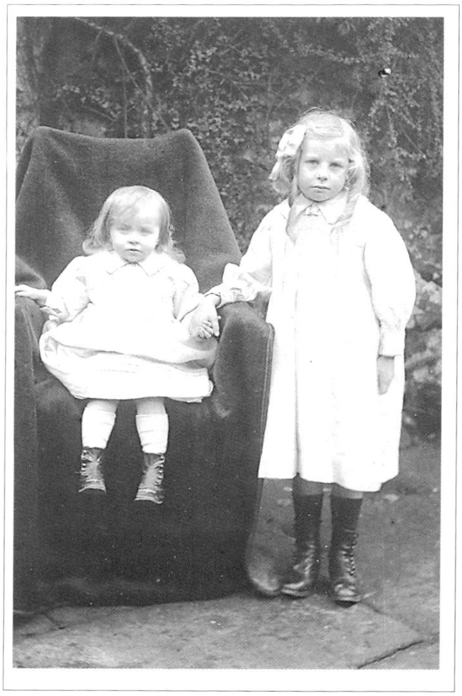

Ada & Dolly Newton c1910

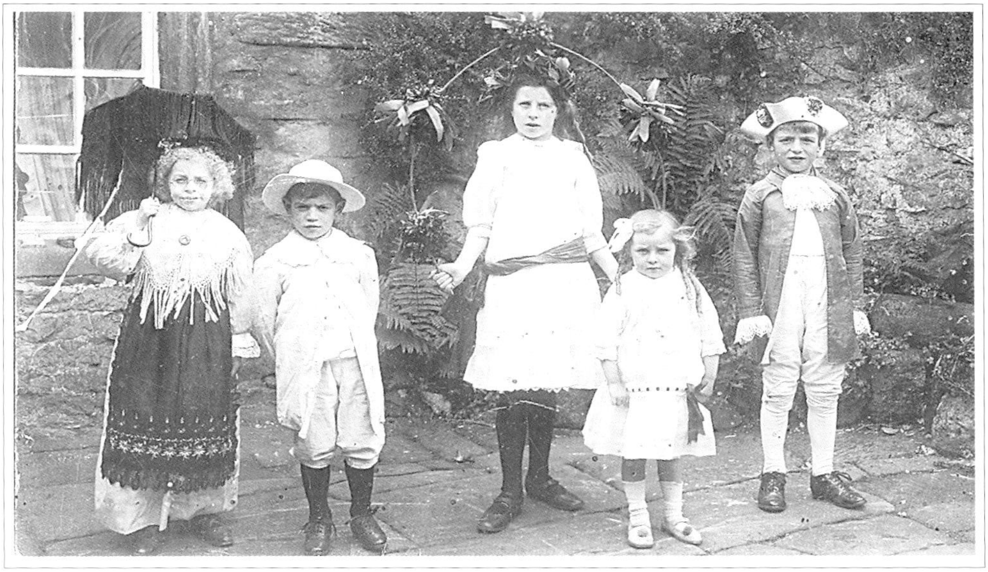

From left to right – Dolly, Ernest Henry, Ada and Lena.
The boy at far right may be Eric Henry Stone (possibly 1904 – 1923). c1910

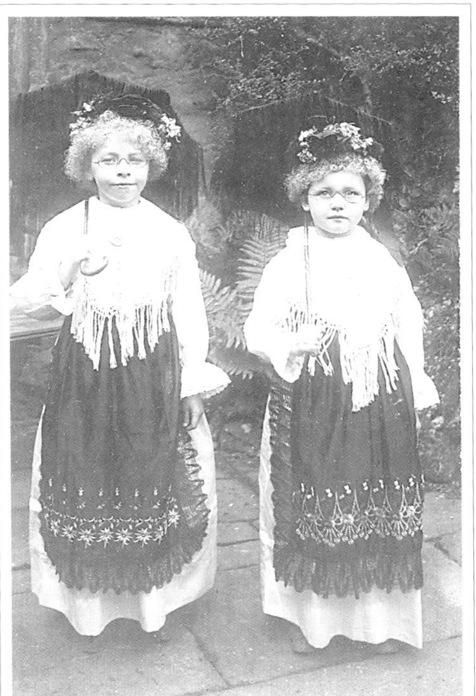

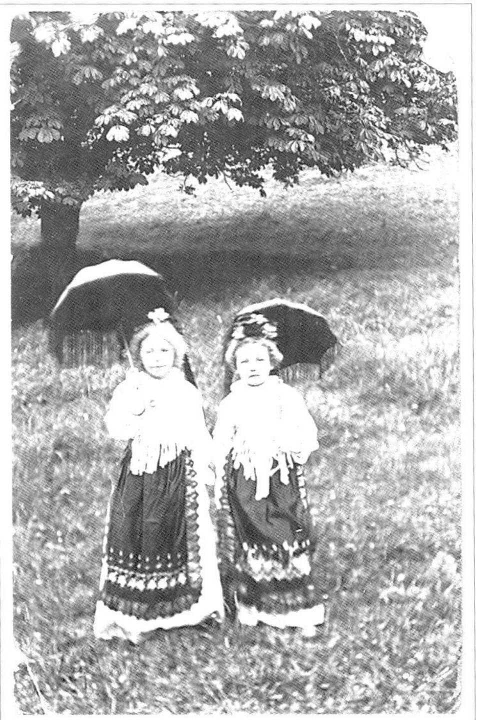

Dolly Newton & Florrie c1910

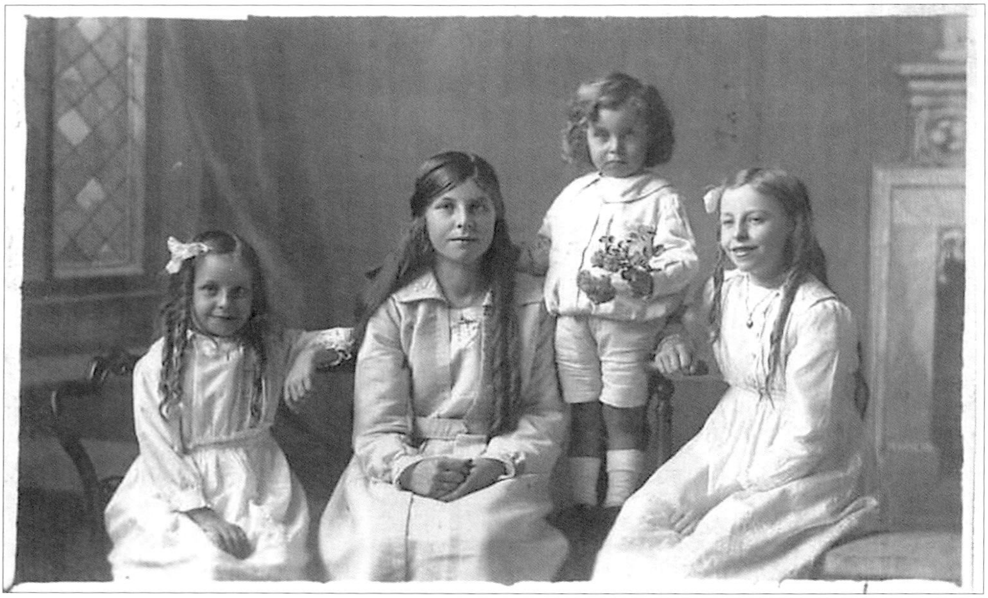

From left to right – Lena, Ada, Ernest & Dolly Newton c1915

The condition of the damaged card of the Newton Trio (see p.42) is testament enough that it is lucky to have survived. What a magnificent doll Lena is holding.

The ferns and the paving slabs are apparent in four of these cards and suggest that they are by Marshall. The card of Dolly and Florrie in the field was probably taken on the same day as the others where they are wearing identical costumes and I guess that it too is a Marshall card. The occasion of these costumed cards may have been a Winster May Day Celebration and I date them around 1910. Ada was May Queen in 1907 and no doubt the May Day Celebrations were held in other years too when the Newton children may have been photographed. I have been unable to establish the identity of the child, Florrie.

We can see something of the lives of the family in adulthood too through postcards.

Ada Newton

You may recall that Ada was married in 1926: on 19 August to be precise – in Winster Parish Church. Her groom was William Henry (known as Henry) Gregory. We will meet Henry again later. A cutting survives (not illustrated) of a report of the wedding which appeared in a local unidentified newspaper. This report informs us that the couple were married by the former Vicar, the Rev. W. H. Nixon, M.A., and that Ada's home was at Bank House, Main Street (immediately to the east of Woolley's Yard and then next door to the Post Office). The groom's father is given as George Gregory, the bride was given away by her uncle (Herbert Stone) and the report identifies the bride's sisters as two of the three bridesmaids. The best man was Tommy Gregory, brother of the groom. We are informed too that "*amongst the many presents was a pair of blankets from friends at Derwent Mills, Matlock*." This was probably the workplace of Ada or her groom or both.

Such an item is, of course, a wonderful aid to descendants of the couple or the other people mentioned in the report and assists too in identifying people captured by postcards/photographs whom later family tree enthusiasts might want to trace. You will be aware, though, of the old adage that "you should never believe what you read in the 'papers." That is true, I suspect, of all documentary sources except official records and it was certainly true in the case of this cutting. The cutting got the name of one of the bride's sisters wrong and also mixed up the identity of the best man (the best man is correctly identified above). "Living memory" put matters right as the cards and the cutting passed into my possession. It is a salutary lesson to be recalled whenever one deals with such sources.

A group of Ada's wedding photographs survive and are illustrated too for the sake of completeness although I can only be certain that one of them is an unused postcard. One of the photographs was taken outside the gates of Bank House and all the others were taken towards the bottom of Woolley's Yard. When enjoying the former photograph note that at the time of this wedding (and for many years later well into the 1950s at least) the ground floor of Bank House doubled up as a Bank. The sign in the window at right states that the Bank was "*Open*." The wedding was by tradition on a Saturday and it is probably safe to presume that the Bank was, in fact, closed at the time the photographs were taken!

Note too that there are two group photographs – one depicts the happy couple with their bridesmaids and other identified people. The face just visible over the bride's right shoulder is unidentified. We know that the bride's father, Ernest, died in 1920, and that she was given away by her uncle. Could this unidentified face be that of Ada's mother? In the other group photograph, apart from the bride and groom, we are only able to suggest that the girl at left might be Sarah Ann (Nancy) Staton (1910 – 1989). In this image, perhaps Herbert Stone is another who this time also peeps over the bride's right shoulder. The older behatted couple on either side of Ada and William may be William's parents. Note too the couple's more stilted pose – William wears his hat and stands apart with his hands at his side in contrast to the traditional stance in the other group photograph.

The last image of Ada and William shows them on their honeymoon at Blackpool a popular venue for many honeymooners from Winster. This image is helpfully marked with the date – 28th August 1926 – on the back. It is clearly a professional studio portrait.

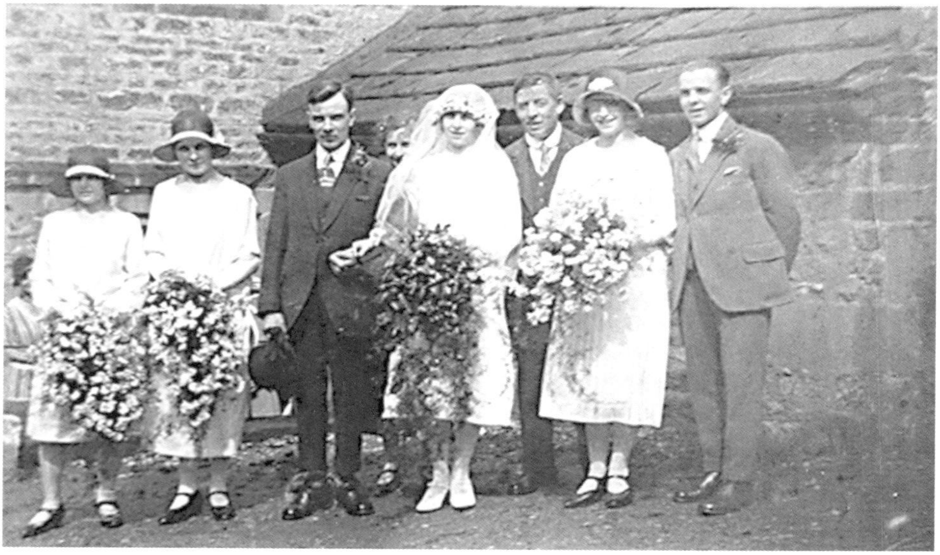

From left to right – Lena Newton, Lilian Gregory (sister of the groom), Groom, unidentified possibly Bride's mother, Bride, Herbert Stone (bride's uncle), Dolly Newton and Tommy Gregory (best man and groom's brother)

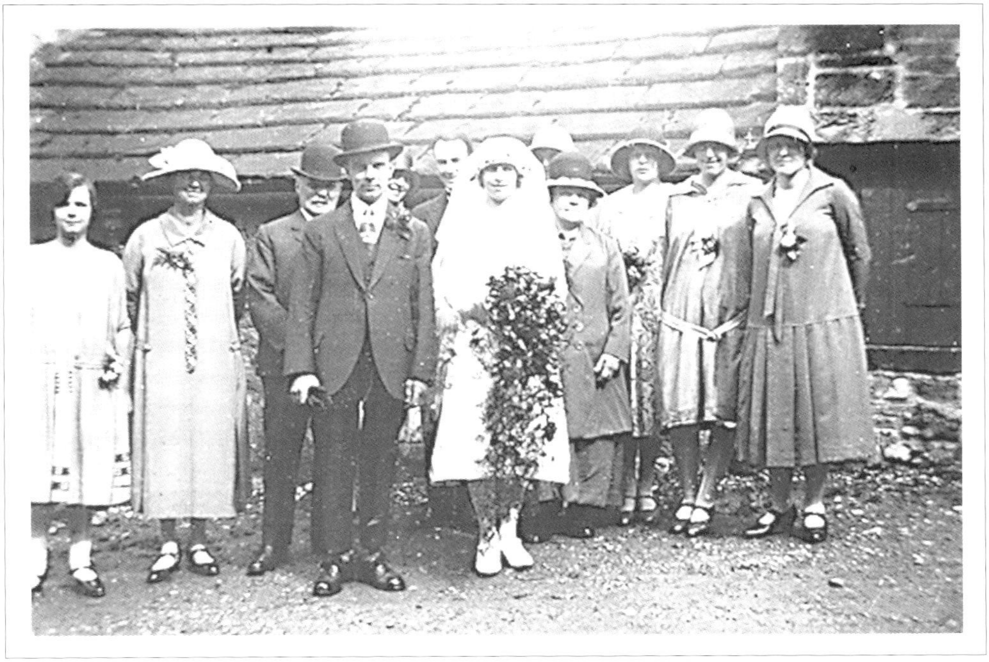

At left possibly Sarah Ann Staton (1910 - 1989). The older couple immediately behind the Bride and Groom may be the Groom's parents

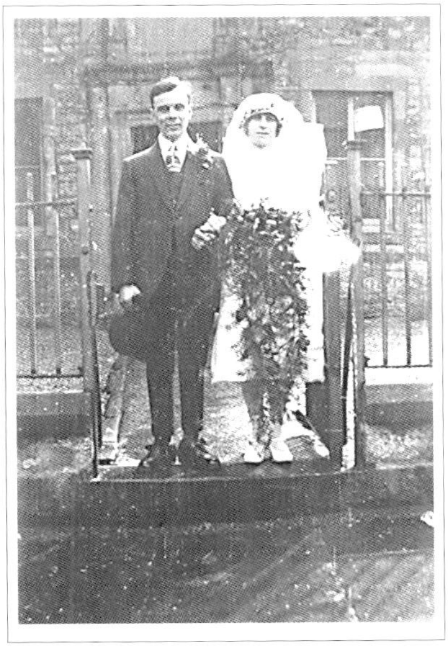

Ada & William Outside Bank House, Main Street

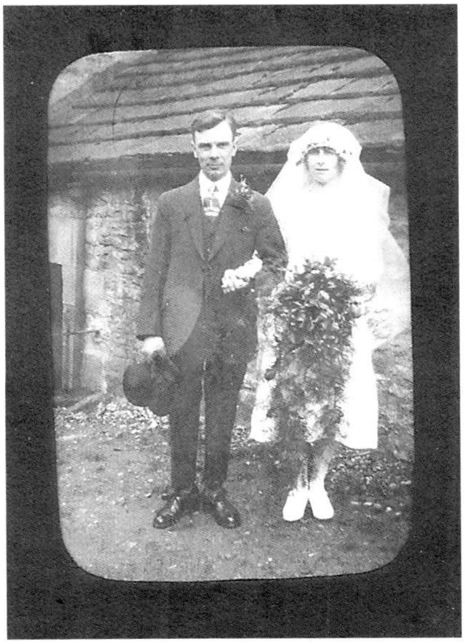

Ada & William in Woolley's Yard

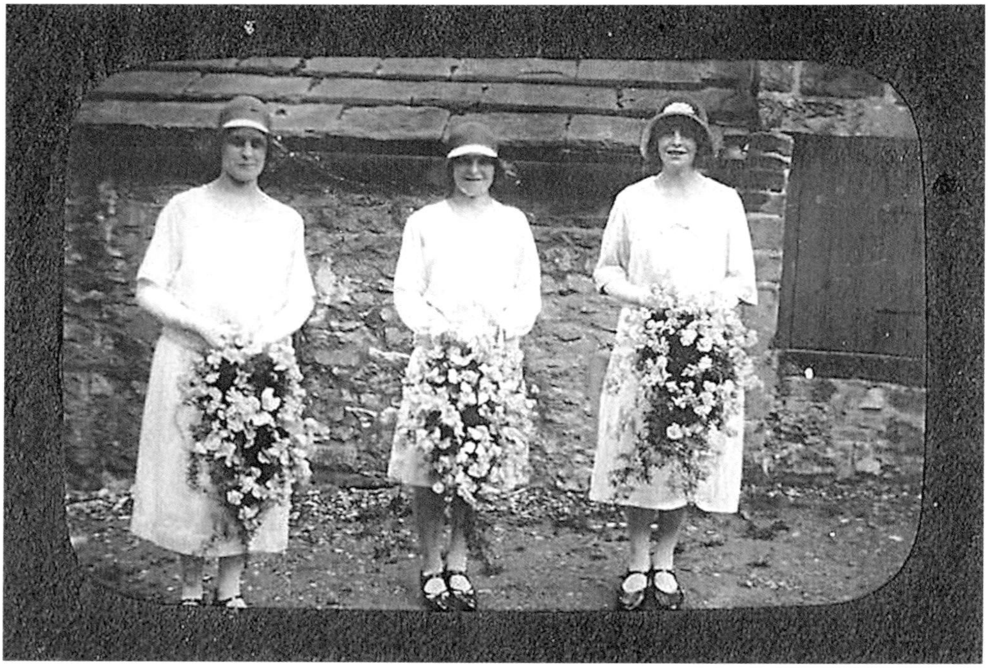

From left to right –
Lilian Gregory, Lena & Dolly Newton
in Woolley's Yard

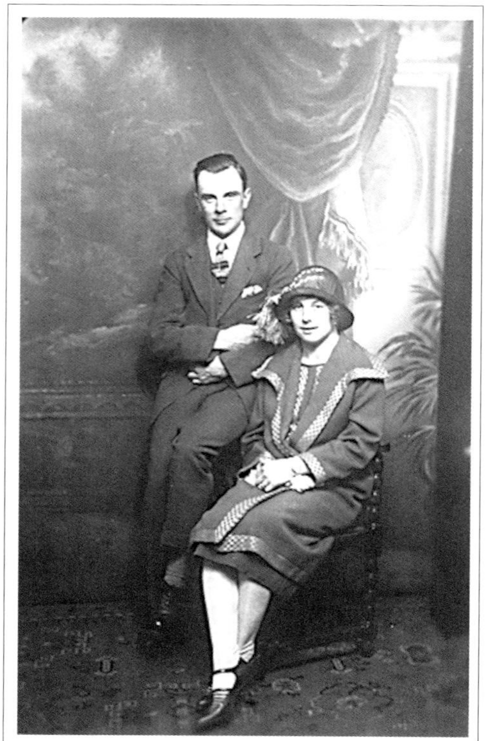

Ada & William on Honeymoon,
Blackpool, 28th August 1926.
Reproduced by courtesy of
Eileen Crowder

Dolly Newton

Next are three images of Dolly: the first is not a postcard but is worthy of inclusion as it is a charming studio portrait by W.N. Statham, Matlock Bridge, c1908, showing Dolly as a child of about 2/3 years; the second shows her as a young woman in c1921/22 when she would have been about 16/17 – this image has a card back and appears to be the work of an unidentified professional photographer; and the third on her Wedding Day, 17 August, 1929, to Ben. Brassington.

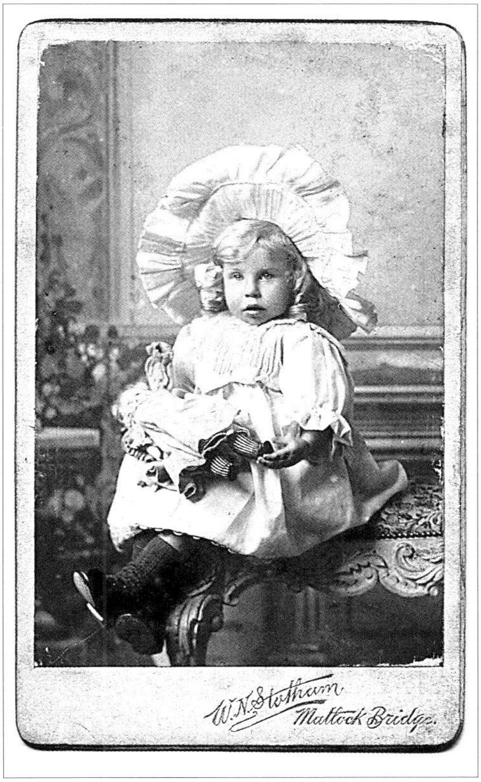

Dolly as a child by Statham

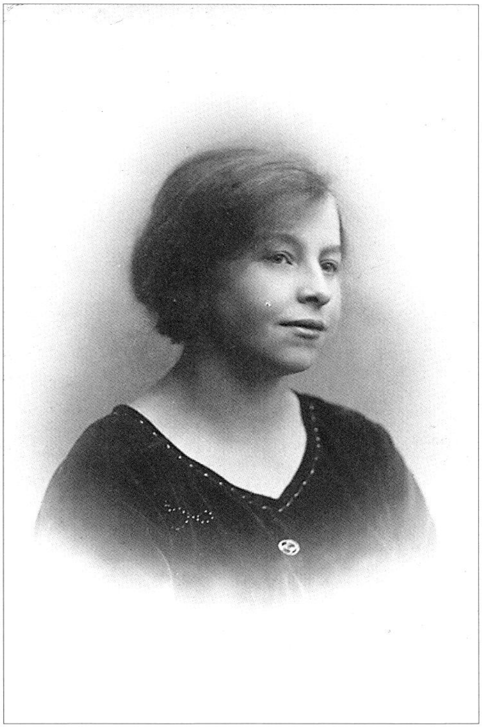

Dolly as young woman c1921/22)

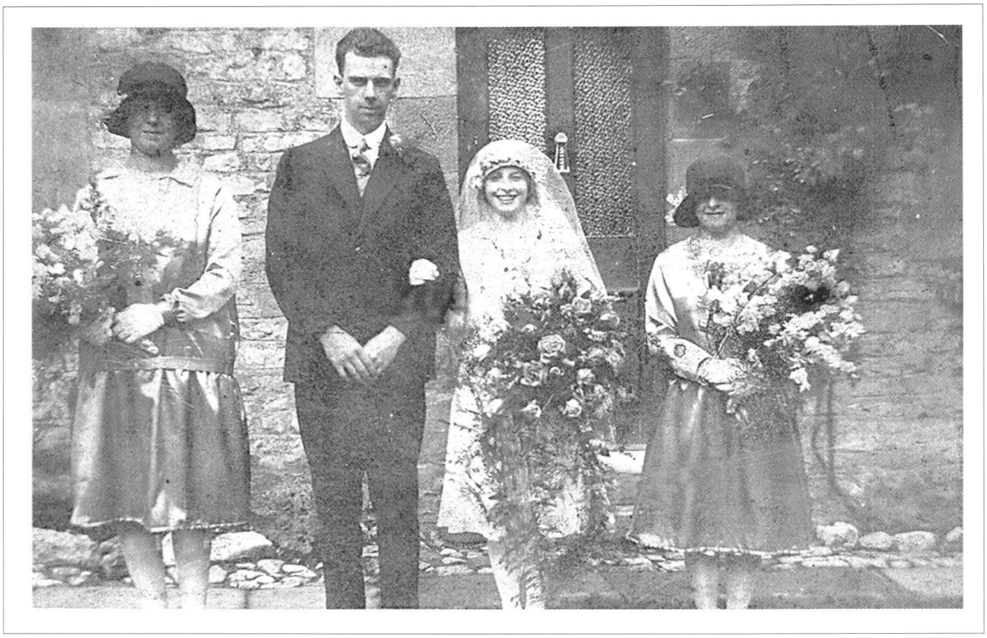

Ben Brassington and Dolly probably outside Dolly's home on East Bank

Lena Newton

As a child in the 1950s, I knew all the Newton sisters as individuals but did not know that they were sisters! I simply knew them as Mrs. Gregory (Ada), Mrs Brassington (Dolly) and Mrs. Walker (Lena). Many Winster families were inter-related during the latter part of the 19th Century and at least into the middle of the last century. This still came as a surprise to me as my interest in Winster local history developed in adulthood. Back during my 1950s childhood these inter-relationships were unknown to me.

I knew Lena more than the others as she was Winster's postwoman and therefore known to every villager, including children. I am including five photographs in this section although only the first mentioned is a card. It shows Lena as a young woman. Another is a Wedding Group to record her marriage to Jack Walker in 1937. In making this image available to me, Eric Brassington, (Lena's nephew) recalled in August 2009 that he was taken in a car (for the first time) down to Statham's in Matlock. He recalled too his father cutting his hair and not wanting to be dressed in red velvet! (Eric, that is.)

Then there are two photographs of Lena's children, Monica (1938 – 2005) and Malcolm (1941 – 2009) in childhood.

The image c1946 is helpfully marked on the back in ink – "*Best Wishes Christmas 1946 Monica 8 yrs 6 months Malcolm 5 yrs 8 months.*" I knew both of them. Monica was seven years my senior so I did not know her as well as Malcolm. I met her again towards the end of her life when attending meetings of Winster's Local History Group. Malcolm I knew well during my childhood. He was a few years older than me and was a life-long friend of my late brother, Kenneth Greatorex (1943 – 2003). The last photo on p.52 is of Malcolm, Ken and myself, all in regulation early 1950s style short-trousers, pictured on The Flat with three older Winster youths, Eric Brassington, Cedric Ellis and Malcolm White.

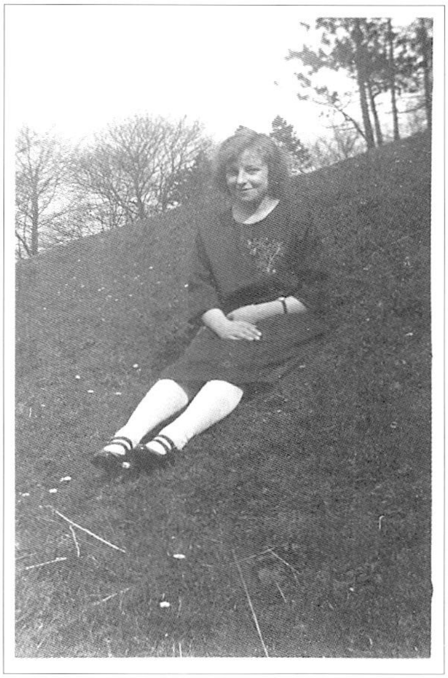

Lena Newton probably early 1920s

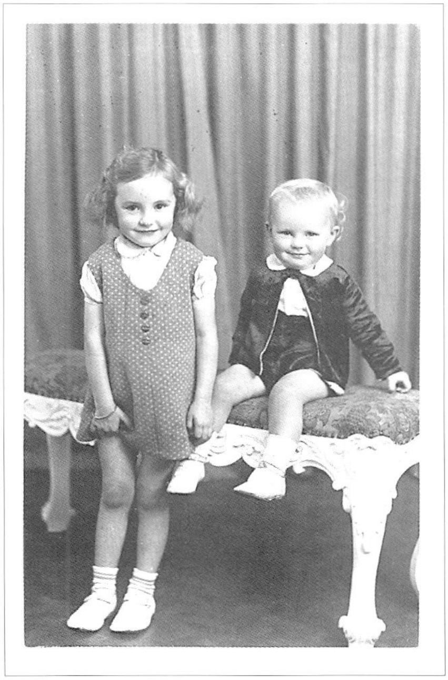

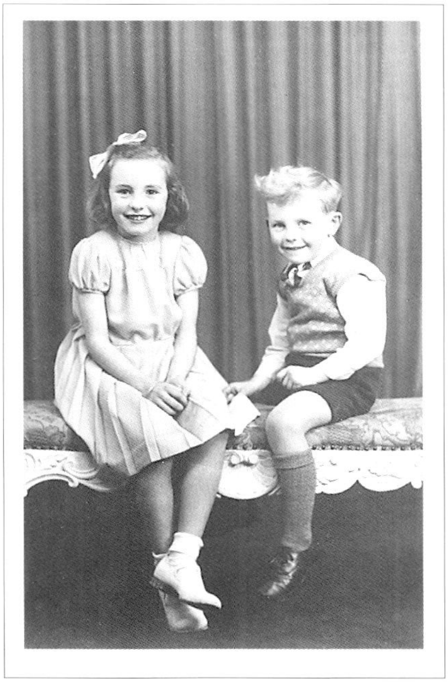

Monica & Malcolm Walker c1943 & c1946. Both photographs by Statham's, Matlock

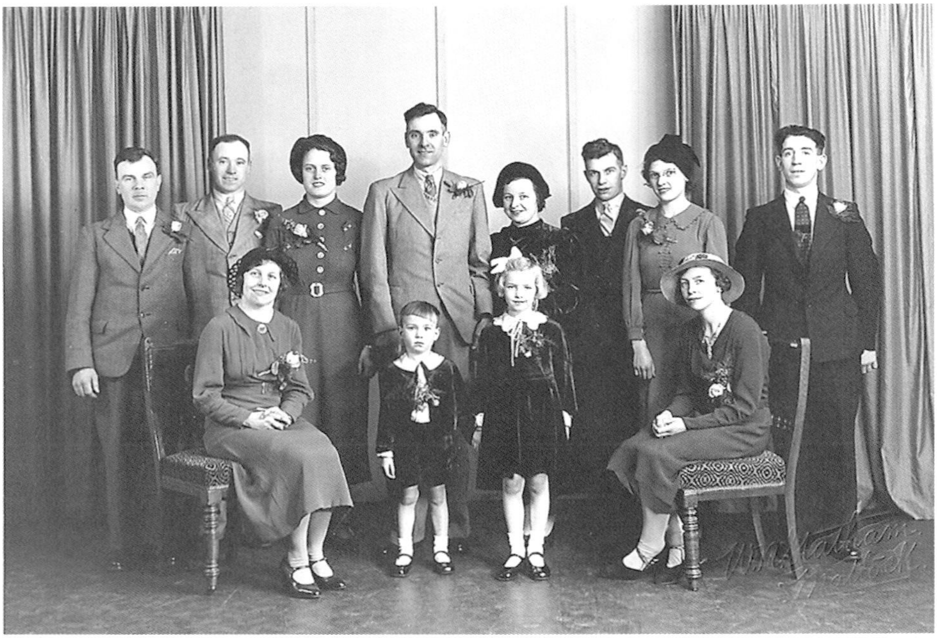

Lena Newton Wedding Group 1937. Left to right on back row
George Henry Gregory, Unidentified, Unidentified, John (Jack) Walker (Groom), Lena Newton (Bride), Ernest Newton (brother of the bride), Doris Travis (fiancé of Ernest Newton) and Bernard Stone.
Front Row – Ada Gregory (sister of the bride), Eric & Eileen Brassington (nephew & niece of the bride) and Dolly Brassington (sister of the bride).
Photograph by Statham's, Matlock

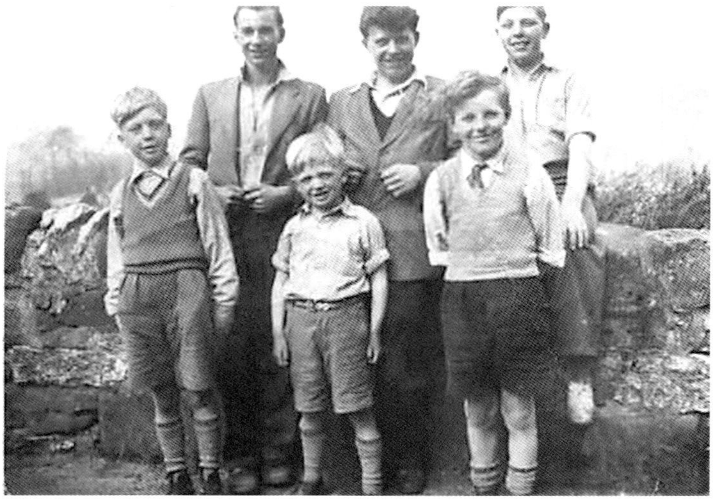

On The Flat Early 1950s – From left to right at back Eric Brassington, Malcolm White and Cedric Ellis. Front from left to right Ken Greatorex (1943 - 2003), The Author and Malcolm Walker (1941 - 2009)

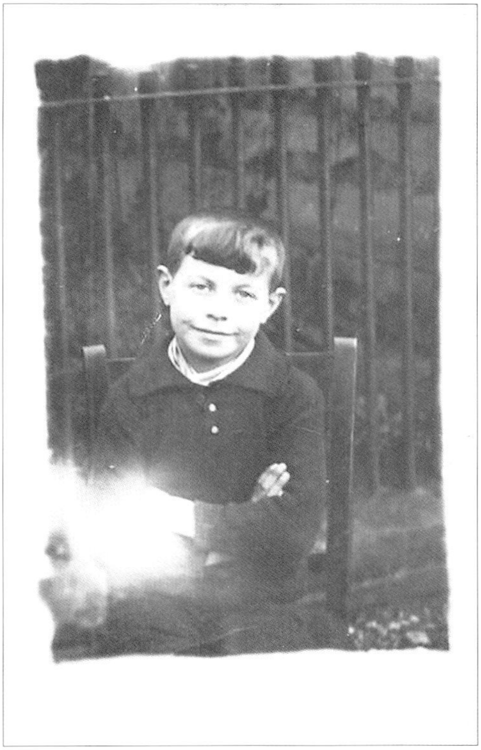

Ernest Newton c1916 probably at Winster School

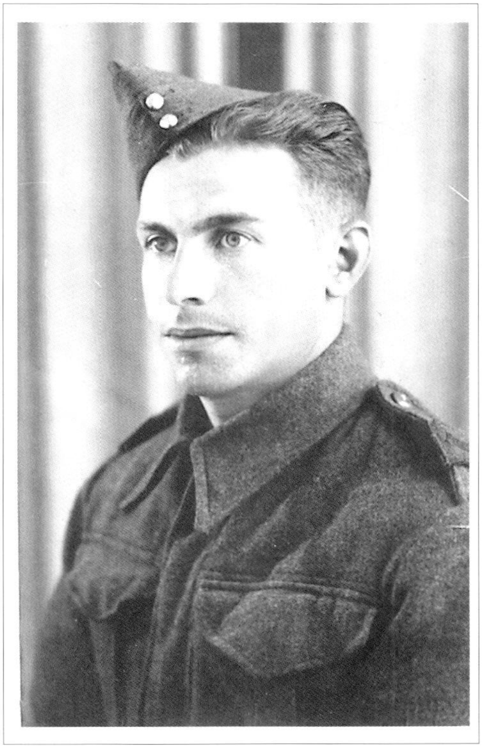

Ernest Newton – early 1940s.

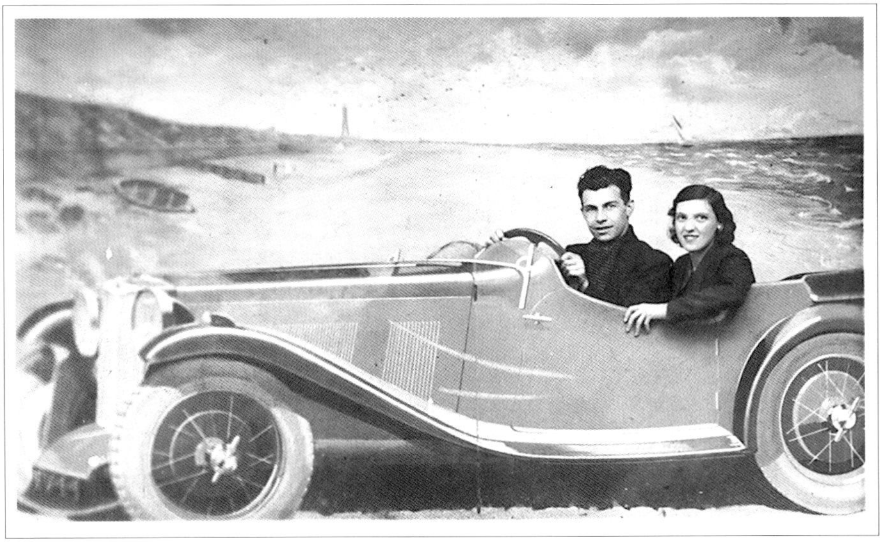

Ernest Newton & Doris L. Travis 1940 on honeymoon in Blackpool. Photograph by Will Cooper & Son

Ernest Henry Newton

The photograph of Ernest and Doris L. Travis in the studio "*car*" was probably taken during their honeymoon in Blackpool in early 1940. The plain back of the image is printed with this message:

"I thank you for your patronage and will always appreciate a return visit. Repeat copies can be had from this photograph. Return this picture. Will Cooper & Son, 125 Wellington Terrace, Blackpool. Phone Blackpool 1595 Residence – Marton 363."

The photograph of Ernest as a soldier was probably taken during the early 1940s. It has a plain back and is printed with the name "*Jerome*". It is also stamped 20 Jun but, unfortunately, there is no year.

A Newton Mystery

I mentioned earlier the problems presented when confronted by photographs of people in family memorabilia / albums passed down by earlier generations. With some photographs we are at a loss to identify the people pictured who are long since deceased. With others we might just have a name written on the back – a person we cannot readily "*place*" in the family story. This "*Newton Mystery*" involved one Thomas Newton. The temptation is to destroy these apparently unidentified items about people perhaps long-since deceased. But wait – consider the quality of these images and their potential as pieces of social history. Surely they are worth saving somehow, somewhere? The next three cards fall into this category. The best to be done for this trio is to preserve the originals and to set them into the context in which they came into my possession.

These three cards and the above Newton images were placed in my safe-keeping by Eric Brassington. Eric, like me, was born in Winster but no longer has any direct ties with the village. The cards and photographs were gathered together by Eric from old family albums and scrapbooks belonging to the Brassington, Newton, Gregory and Barnsley families of Winster. You will recall that I touched earlier on the inter-relationship of Winster families. That was the case with the content of Eric's collection – he had been unable to identify some of the people on some images. You, the reader, may be able to help identify them. That, and the quality of the images, is the best possible reason for reproducing them and preserving the collection.

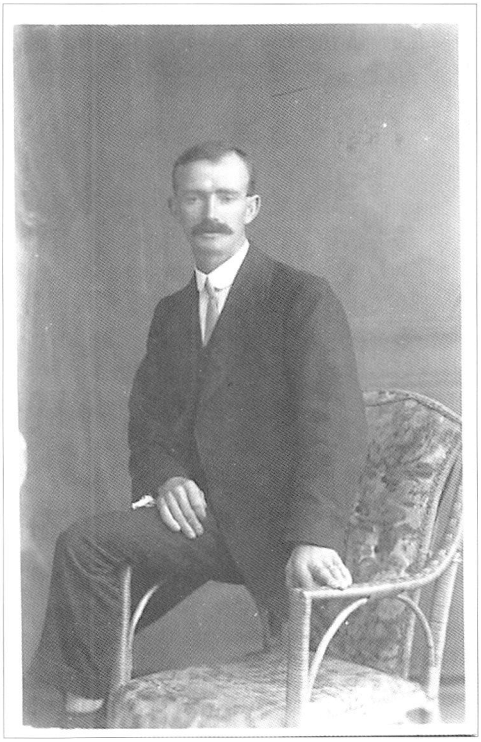

Thomas Newton

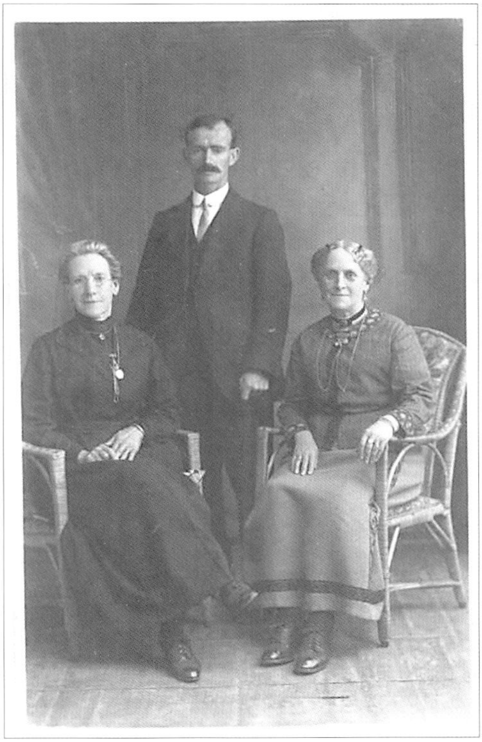

Thomas Newton with two unidentified women – Studio postcard by D.A. Maclean, Photographer, Promenade, Blackpool

The card with the man informally astride the chair has the name Thomas Newton written on the back. He is the same man in the card with the two women. He is wearing the same clothes and the same furniture is pictured in both cards. Even Dr. Watson might exclaim: *"Holmes, these photographs were taken at the same time!"* He might even go on: *"One of the cards has an inked stamp on the back with a photographer's name and address. Holmes, the evidence is conclusive – these images were definitely taken at the same time!"* The inked endorsement states that the photographer was D.A. Maclean, Promenade, Blackpool. Maclean was probably active c1910. But who was Thomas Newton? He, presumably, along with the two women, was a relative of the Winster Newtons.

Alas, the third card with the seated woman and girl has no clues to offer other than it was with the Newton papers. It is a glossy real photographic studio card illustrating the fashions of the day. There are many such cards available for purchase for a modest few pence by a collector at antique or collectors fairs. They are "*priceless*" if preserved in a family collection with the individuals identified and, hopefully, will increasingly populate local museum collections later in the 21st century.

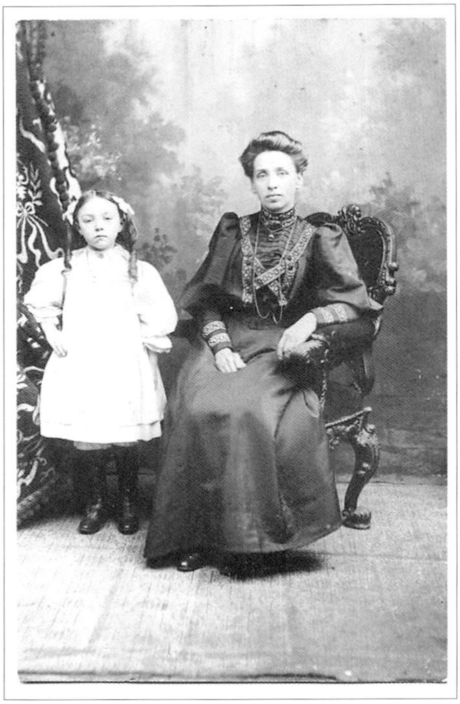

The Brassington Family

We met Winnie Brassington earlier. Now it's time to meet other members of her family and to learn a little about them as their images were captured in photographs/cards.

Joseph Albert Brassington

Winnie's parents were Joseph Albert Brassington (1877 – 1957) and Mary Emma nee Barnsley (1877 – 1954) who was born in Winster. Joseph was a Youlgrave man who lived there at least until the 1901 Census. On 21 August 1902, they were married at the Primitive Methodist Chapel on East Bank.

The first three images are not cards but are worthy of inclusion. They date from the end of the 19th Century.

Joseph had this cabinet portrait taken by E. T. & T.C. Evans' of Youlgrave. The image is pasted onto board which is printed with Evans name and address in gold – the back refers to "*Artistic Photography*" and is in standard form as probably supplied to countless photographers by the supplier who is unknown.

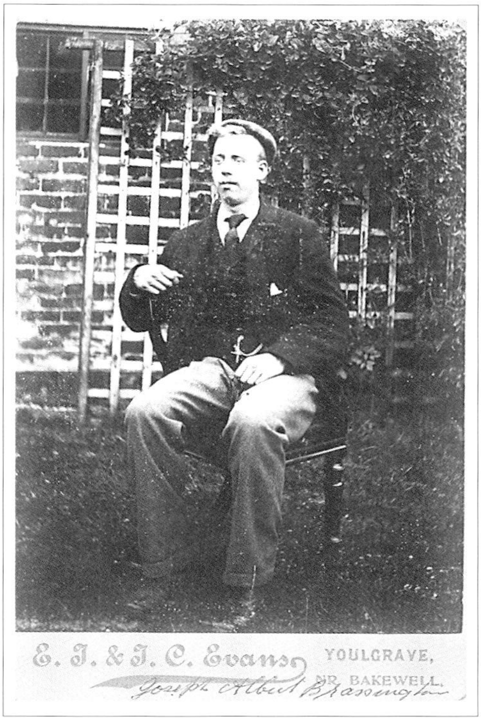

J.A. Brassington (1877 - 1957) by E.T. & T.C. Evans, Youlgrave – late 19th Century

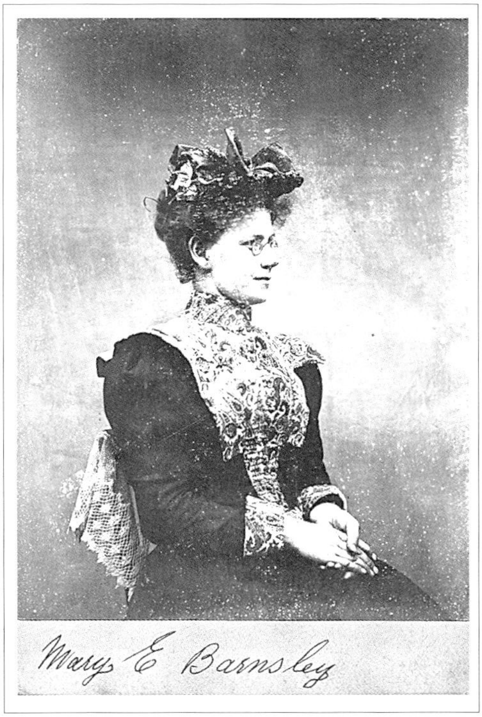

Mary E. Barnsley (1877 - 1954) – late 19th Century

Mary Emma Barnsley

The next two images are of Mary. The one with her name written across the bottom has a plain back. The other has a printed back referring to Allen Nield's "*Chief Office, printing & enlarging works at Rowland Road, Leeds.*" Two more addresses in Leeds are also referred to, namely at Queens Arcade and "*Lindenthorpe*" Villa also at Rowland Road. Then there are references to these other addresses – 105 Market Street, Manchester, 68 Wellington Road South, Stockport and Grosvenor Square, Stalybridge.

By the 1911 Census the couple had three children, Ben, George and Winnie. Joseph was then working as a gritstone quarry cutter. He worked at a Birchover quarry and walked to work both from Youlgrave and also from Winster after his marriage. Joseph was a Methodist lay preacher for fifty-nine years. As such he would travel around the Winster area to other villages on foot to fulfil preaching engagements. The card posted to him on 28th September 1922 was sent by another lay preacher and the message refers to the arrangements being made by the two men, probably for the forthcoming Sunday's service at Bonsall. It is the message side of this card which interests us but the picture side (not illustrated) would certainly interest Matlock postcard collectors. The picture is a printed image of a Matlock Cable car at the bottom of Bank Road, Matlock, and it is printed at left on the back: *"Denny's Innovation Series, Matlock."* The following *"Birthday Postcard"* sent to Mary has a Manchester cancellation strike of 31 March 1929 sent to her with greetings for her birthday the following day. So even in 1929 the sender had confidence that the postal service would deliver a message by postcard for the following day. The picture side of this card (not illustrated) is a view of The Painted Hall, Chatsworth, (just a short distance from Winster). The card is Nod. 1116 at bottom right of the picture and was published by Bamforth & Co., Holmfirth.

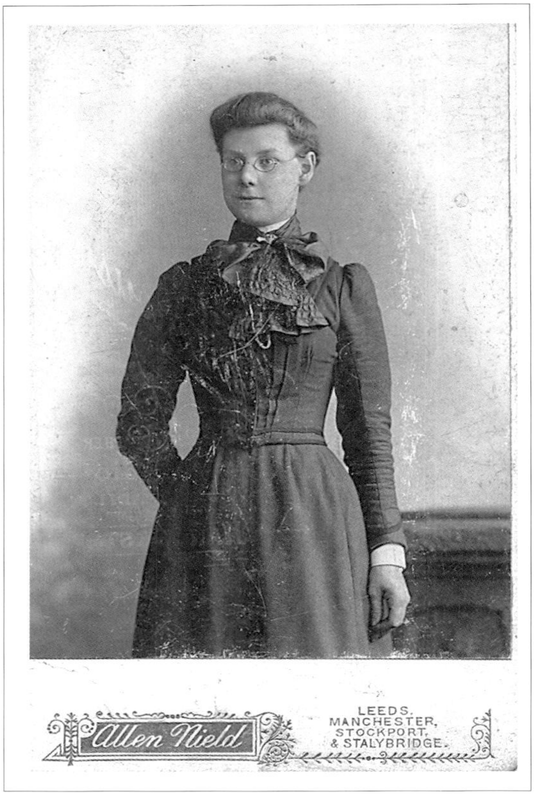

Mary E. Barnsley by Allen Nield – late 19th Century

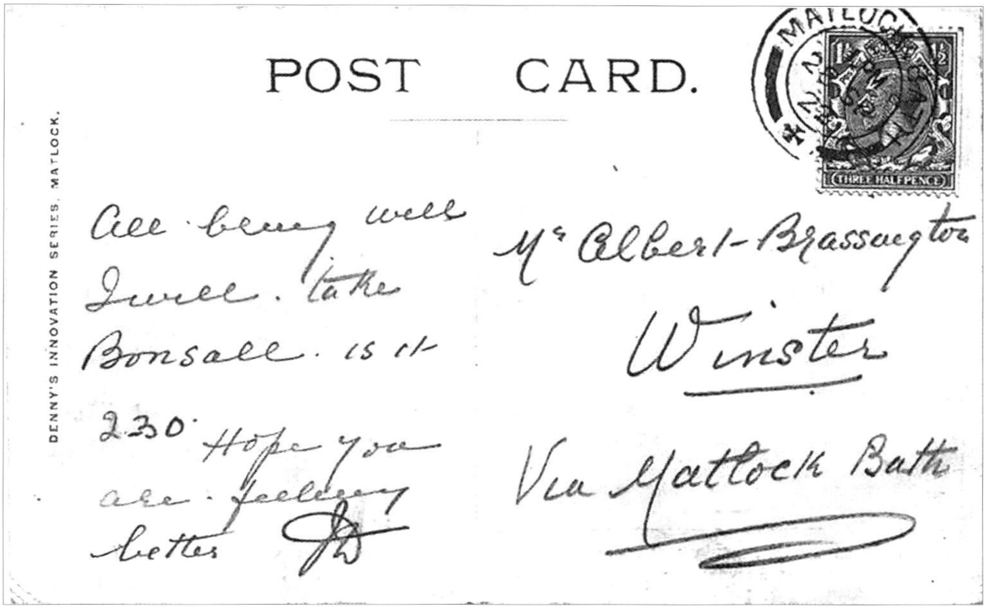

Postally used 28 September 1922

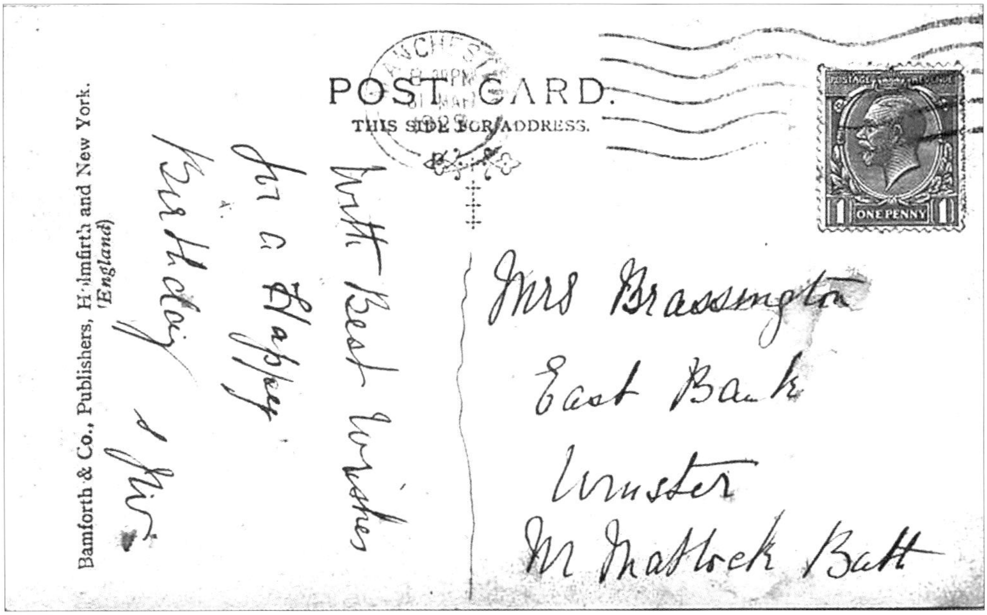

Postally used 31 March 1929

Finally, these last two images of Joseph and Mary in later life (on p61) are not cards but are included because they are lovely images and deserve to be published alongside the earlier ones.

Joseph's grandson, Eric Brassington, took the photograph in the 1950s of Joseph lighting his pipe outside his home on East Bank. The subject appears totally unselfconscious of the presence of the photographer who has captured that moment of bliss when the pipe-smoker carefully cradles his pipe as he is about to rekindle the bowl. The shadows cast by nearby foliage add to the charm. Joseph's clothes sum up what I recall my own grandfather wore in the 1950s; the obligatory flat cloth cap; the woollen short neckerchief possibly worn over a shirt with no collar; the waistcoat; and the cardigan. Note also the bushy eyebrows and the downward glance of the left-eye as single-minded concentration is directed to the important task in hand.

The second photograph of the couple was taken on a Methodist Church Sunday School trip to Skegness in the early 1950s. So far as senior male 1950s fashion is concerned, here Joseph sports a collar and tie and an albert chain as ornament to the pocket watch in the waistcoat. Also, he carries a mac over his left arm. In the background is a lovely art-deco style 1930s house. This image has a plain back and has been rubber-stamped:

"Fennells (?Chemist) Ltd
70 Castleton Boulevard
Skegness
For extra copies quote number hereon."

Just in case you would like to order a copy the number 27285 is also rubber-stamped on the back too but I have a feeling that the firm may no longer be in business.

Ben & George Brassington

The first card in this section is another one by Marshall. It is of two lads, Ben & George (their parents were Joseph and Mary) and here again we have the characteristic ferns and paving slabs of Marshall's outdoor "*studio*." This photograph was taken about 1908. On the face of the original someone has written the names of the two boys and that might be visible in the reproduction here.

The brothers lived at Woodland View, East Bank, near The Flat. At left is George who was born about 1906 and who died in 1912. The other lad, Ben, (1903 – 1971) is someone I knew as an adult during my Winster childhood in the 1950s. I did not know him well but I recall that he was a tall, big man.

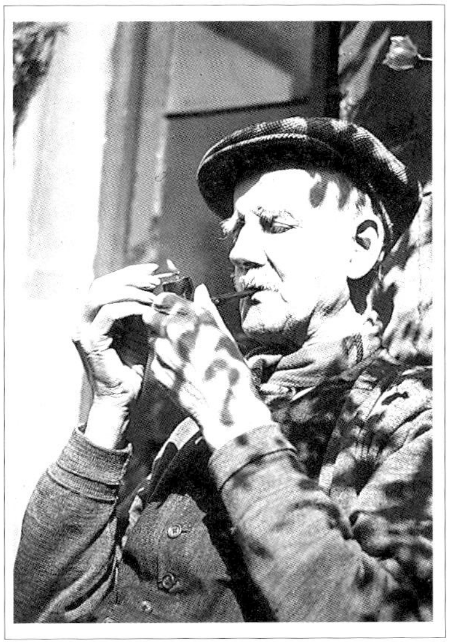

J.A. Brassington in 1950s – Photograph by Eric Brassington

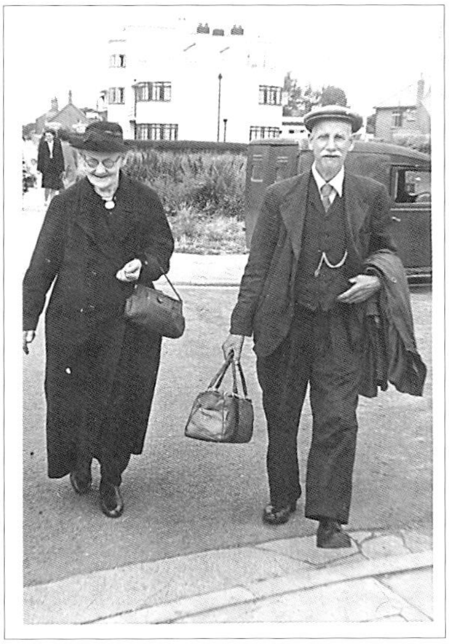

Mr. & Mrs. J.A. Brassington at Skegness in early 1950s

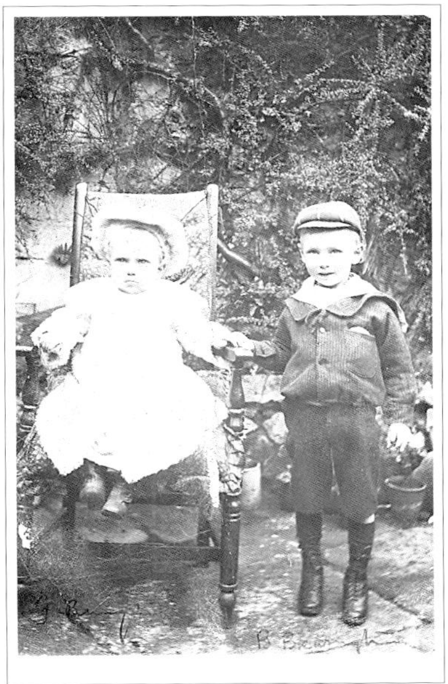

George & Ben Brassington c1908 by Marshall – Ben at right.

Ben worked at Mill Close Mine until it closed in 1939. During the World War (1939 – 1945) he worked at Rolls-Royce Ltd, Derby, and was an Air Raid Warden authorised by Bakewell District Council. After the War he worked for Firth Derihon Stampings Ltd, Darley Dale, until his retirement in 1968. He was born into a strong Methodist Family and was a Trustee of Winster Methodist Church, only a short walk from his home. During his youth he was a keen sportsman. He played for Winster teams at both football and cricket and was a member of Derbyshire County Cricket Club as was his sister, Winnie. With Winster St. John's, playing as a goalkeeper, he was a member of the teams which won the Cavendish Cup in 1924 and 1927. He was also a member of the team which were runners-up in 1926. In 1926, aged 23, he was probably in his prime as a footballer and his football was not limited to Winster. He was a professional with Matlock Town during the 1926/27 Season and during 1926 he also had a trial with Portsmouth. He was also a trialist with Stockport County.

On 17 August 1929 Ben married Doris (Dolly) Newton in Winster Parish Church. The couple had two children. Ben was a keen photographer who developed his own prints – an interest which he passed to his son, Eric. Ben was educated at Winster School, and is pictured there in 1908 (see p.175).

About 1910 Ben is captured in the unused card view of a crowd at the back of the Market House where he is the boy marked with an X and the name Ben and faces the camera with some confidence. In this image a maypole is in the middle distance and Edwardian fashion is to the fore complete with umbrellas/parasols warding off the Sun. The sign of the Angel Inn is prominent at centre-right. The expanse of Main Street

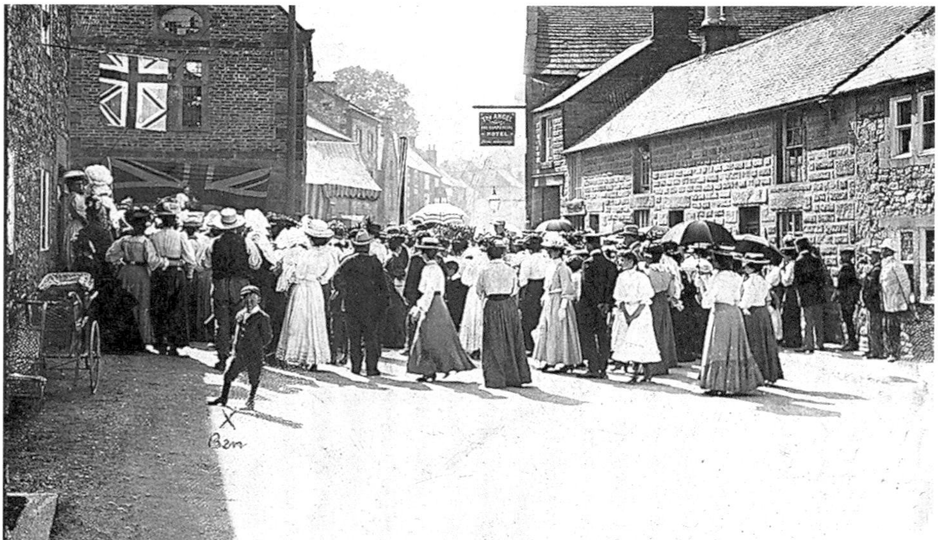

in the foreground is also prominent as the photographer has stepped back so that he could include the width of the substantial crowd.

The card message sent to Ben from Gibralter in 1911 is of interest to Winster Brassington and Barnsley genealogists and only the message side need concern us. It was rightly described to me in October 2008 by Ben's son, Eric, *"as a real gem."* I will let Eric take up the story:

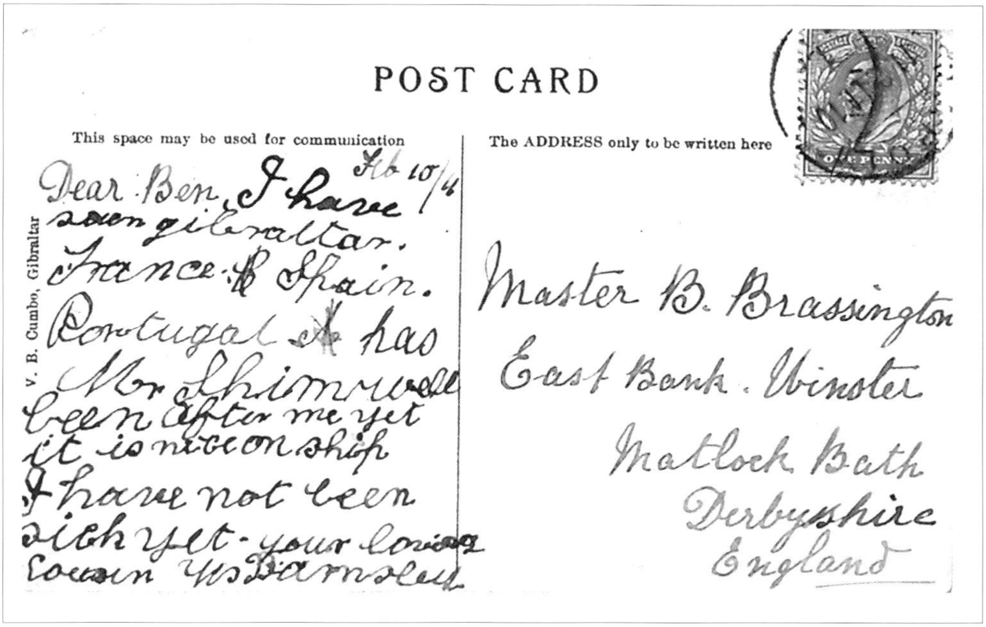
POST CARD

This space may be used for communication

The ADDRESS only to be written here

V. B. Cumbo, Gibraltar

Feb 10/11
Dear Ben I have
seen gibraltar.
France & Spain.
Portugal & has
Mr Shimwell
been after me yet
it is nice on ship
I have not been
sick yet. your loving
cousin W Barnsley

Master B. Brassington
East Bank. Winster
Matlock Bath
Derbyshire
England

Message on postcard sent to Ben Brassington in 1911 from Gibralter

"This had been ignored as just another postcard. But the message gives me the answer to a question that Frank Barnsley (Eric's cousin) and I had never found. We had details of the Barnsley immigrants to Canada on the SS Peruvian and of William Barnsley who immigrated to Canada later only to return, then set off again with his son, William, for Australia. We never knew when he had gone. On the back of the card is the answer, early in 1911, posted from Gibralter as they were on their way. They sailed on 3 February 1911 from London bound for Freemantle, Australia, on the SS Otway."

William Barnsley Senior was born in Winster in 1872 and died in Australia in about 1930.

The portrait card of Ben, aged about 25, is by Gale's Studios Ltd. The publisher's name is printed on the back and the card is helpfully stamped on the back with the date, 14 Jun 1928. The Morris Dancing Group pictured in front of the Market House is from the 1920s. Ben is the penultimate dancer on the back row at right. The image of Ben (possibly) at Aldwark Hen Races in the 1920s/30s is not a card. The identity of the young assistant is unknown. When I first saw this image I had never heard of Aldwark Hen Races or any other

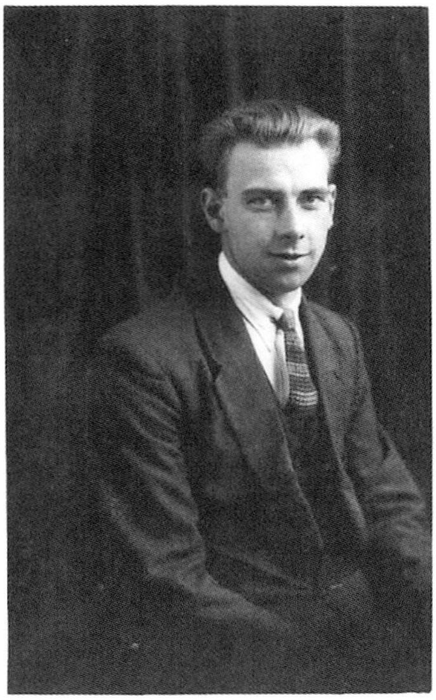

Ben Brassington aged about 25 on 14 June 1928 by Gale's Studio's Ltd – the date is stamped on the back

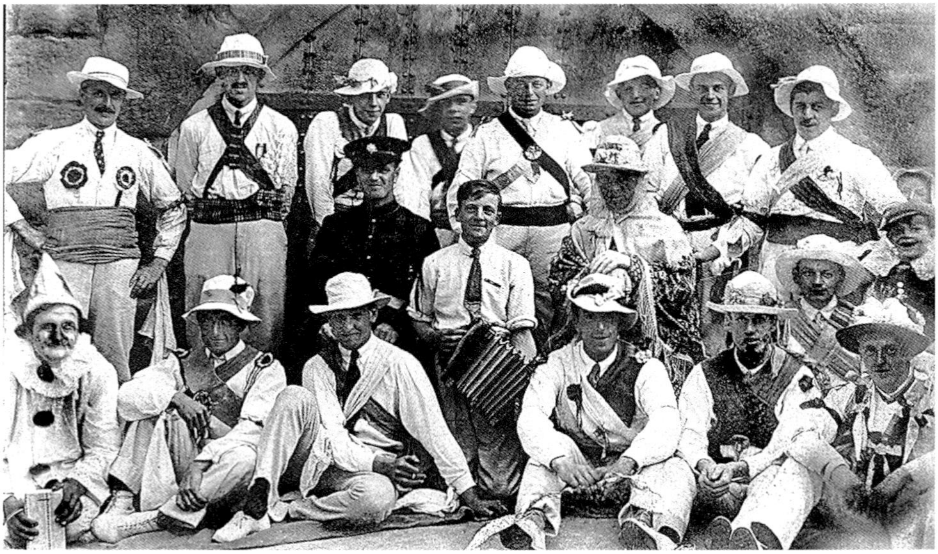

Winster Morris Dancers Outside Market House c1920s – Ben Brassington is on the back row (the penultimate man at right). The other dancers from left to right were: Back Row – Joe Taylor, next 4 men unidentified, Ray Marshall, Ben and Herbert Stone. Middle Row – Sam Moseley (King), Joe ("Pea") Rains (Musician) and Jess Burton (Queen). Front Row – Unidentified (pierot), Bill Foxlow, Charlie Dowling, George Walker, next 2 men unidentified and Dan Ingman. Image reproduced by courtesy of Eileen Crowder

hen races for that matter. As I was writing this text (January 2010) I googled *"Aldwark Hen Races"* and *"Hen Races"* to get some background information – up came a reference to Bonsall World Championships in 2006! I watched a video of a race – amazing how distracting the internet can be.

Ben was a member of Winster Harmonic Society. Members (including Ben) were pictured outside the Burton Institute in

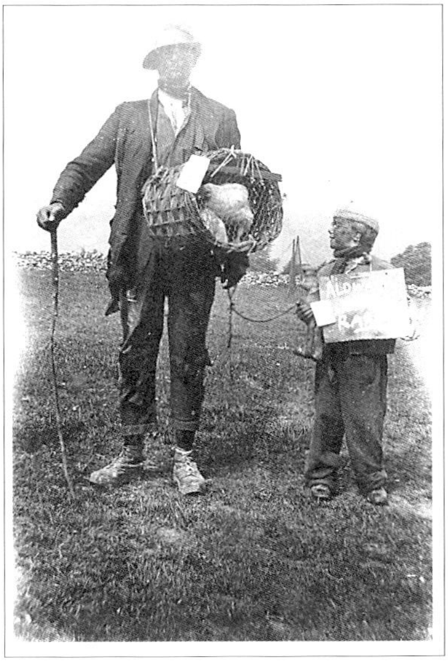

Possibly Ben Brassington at Aldwark Hen Races in 1920/30's. The identity of his young assistant is unknown

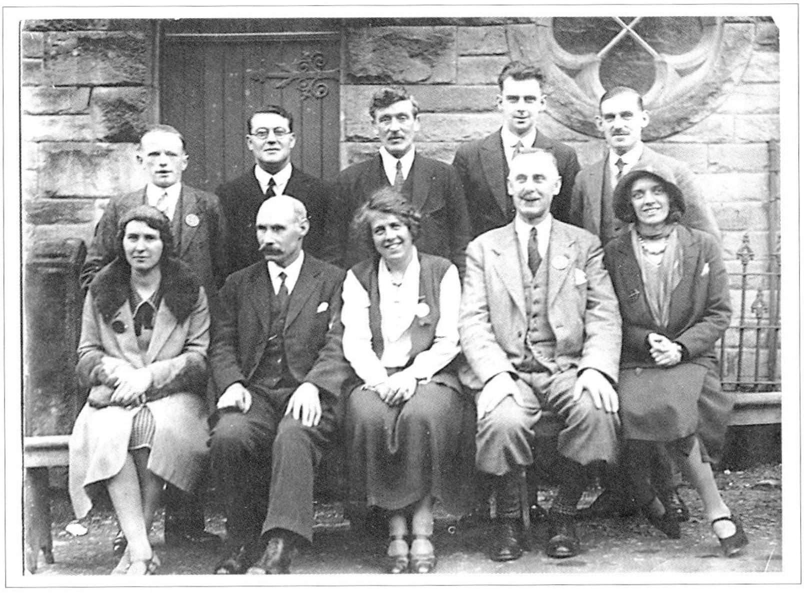

Harmonic Society Outside The Burton Institute 1931.
The people pictured were associated with a Music Festival held in the Institute. Ben Brassington is the man second from the right on the back row. Others from left to right were: Back Row – H. Bacon (Assistant Secretary), H. Holliday (Director of Competitions), S. Hodgkinson (Secretary), Ben Brassington and W. Boden (Treasurer). Front Row – Miss K. Thomas, Ernest Heathcote (President) – he also published topographical postcards of Winster which are discussed elsewhere, Miss Gertrude Beresford of Ilkeston (Musical Director), J. Taylor (Chairman) and Miss Williams

support of an article about a Music Festival held in the Institute which appeared in the *Derbyshire Times* on Saturday, 21st November 1931. Ben is again the penultimate man on the back row at right. The photograph is also of interest as it includes Ernest Heathcote (1873 – 1953) the man on the front row at left. We will meet him later when I discuss his publication of Winster topographical cards.

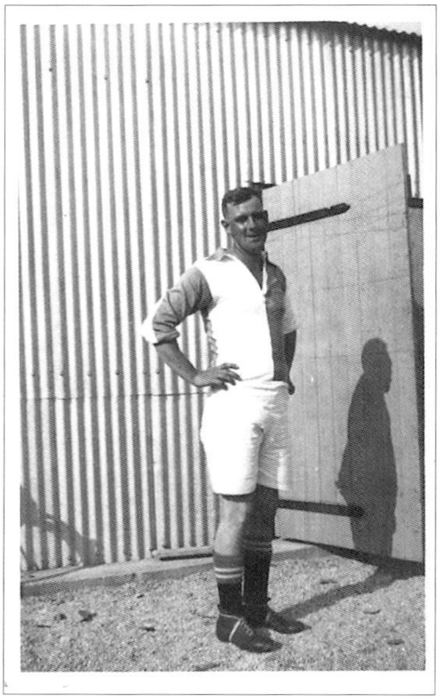

Ben Brassington in the late 1940s

The last card of Ben included here shows him dressed as a footballer sometime after 1945 when he was in his late 40s. Ben's son, Eric, recalls:

"Ben was about 6ft.2ins tall and he was always a goalie but had played on the wing when required but that must have been in his very early teens. When he left Rolls Royce after the war he worked for Firth Derihons near Rowsley and they had a team. He did not play regularly then but turned out for the odd charity match and I think this shot must have been taken at one of these matches. They may well have been playing Enthovens in an inter works game."

This image has a regular card back and is stamped "*748*" on the back right.

Hannah and Lydia Stone and A Mystery

Both of these cards have the characteristics noted previously of Marshall's work – the vegetation and the paving slabs. Hannah and Lydia Stone were sisters: Lydia is the woman holding a paper in her hand and Hannah is probably the seated woman. Both women were lacemakers and might be wearing examples of their own work. Hannah was born in Winster in 1879 and in 1901 she married Ernest Newton. In 1911 she was living with her husband and their three daughters in Winster. Lydia, was born in Winster on 4 August 1889. In 1911, aged 21, she was living at home in Winster with her parents, Henry and Mary, and was single and employed at home on domestic duties. She remained single all her life and died in 1974. This card is marked on the back in pencil *"Lydia Stone"* (standing). The other card was also part of the Eric Brassington collection. Sadly, Eric could not suggest a possible identification for the two women in this card. Both photographs were clearly taken at the same location and might have been taken at about the same time.

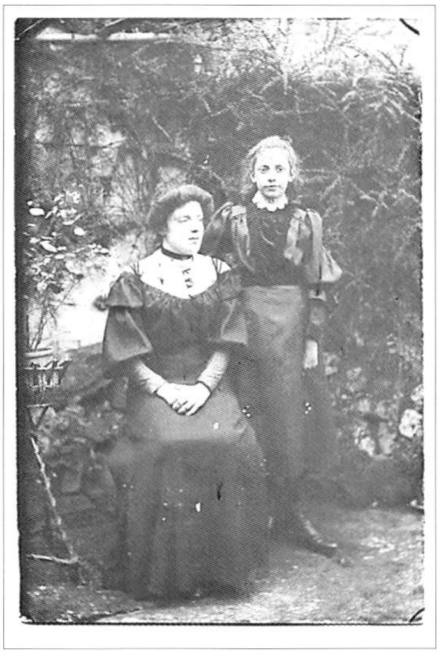

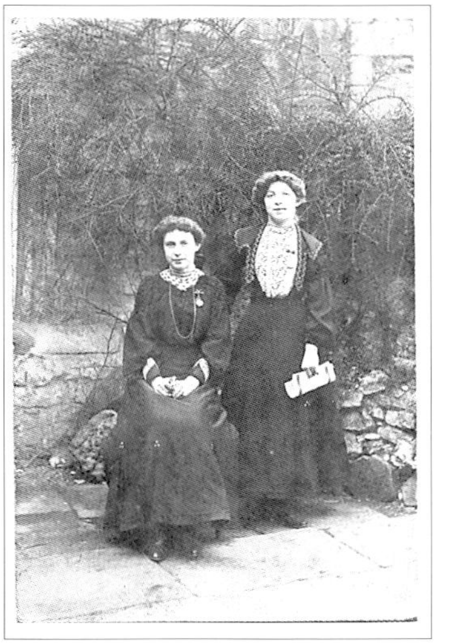

Hannah (b. 1879) & Lydia Stone (1889 - 1974)

The next two cards are probably by Marshall too – again the vegetation and the paving slabs. Both are dated 1911 in ink on the back with the names of the young men.

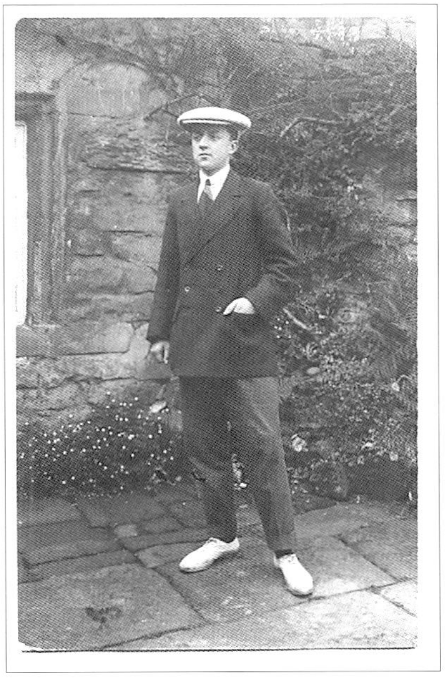

Joe Spencer in 1911

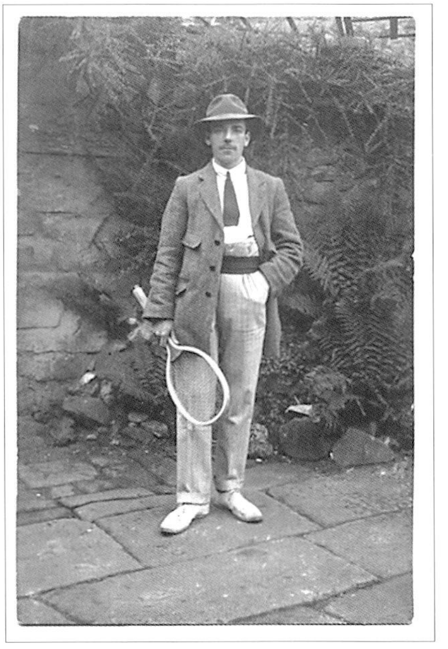

Frank D. Longden in 1911

CHAPTER 4

MORE PEOPLE POSTCARDS

The cards in the previous chapter are those where I am confident that Marshall was probably the photographer. In this Chapter are some collections of postcards associated with particular people.

Some Gregory People

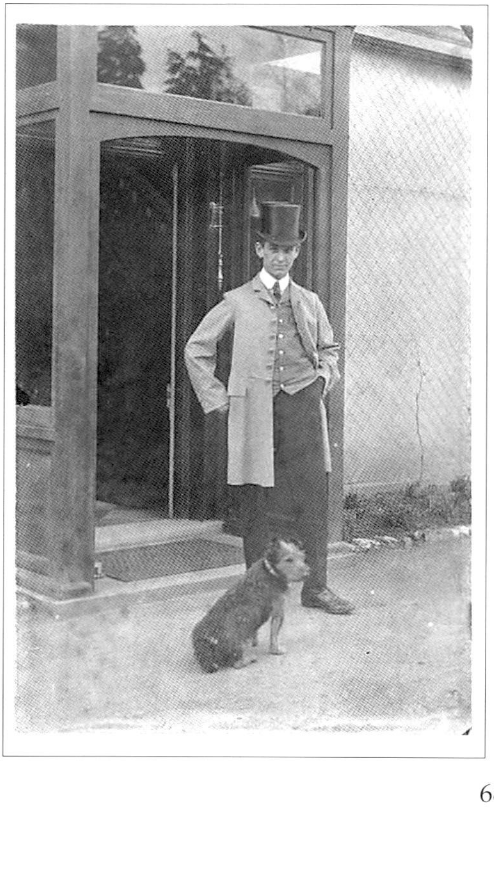

The unused card of the Groom resplendent in top hat and tail coat is probably Thomas Gregory (1864 – 1926) outside Oddo House. The name of the dog is unknown. Thomas is buried in Winster Churchyard along with his wife Emily (1868 – 1919).

The next three cards give me particular pleasure because I knew many of the people pictured, particularly those in the wedding group.

Probably Thomas Gregory (1864 - 1926) outside Edwardian Oddo House

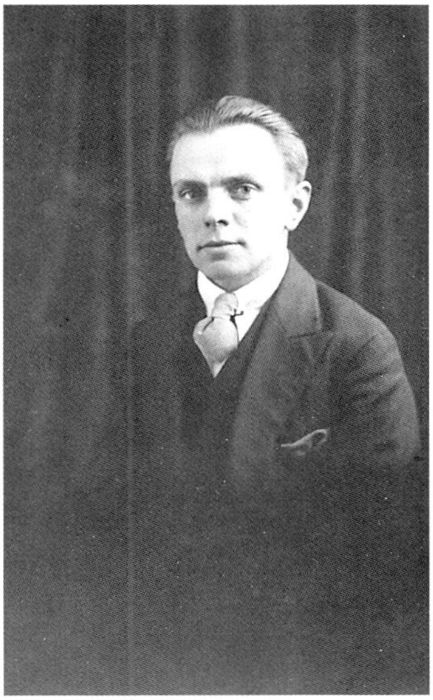

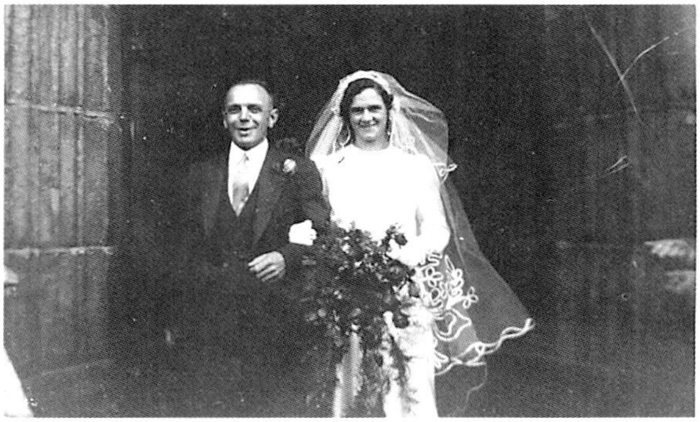

Tommy Gregory & Annie Slaney outside Youlgreave Parish Church, 1941

Thomas Gregory by Gale's Studios – 14 June 1928

The portrait of Thomas Gregory (1904 – 1977) known as *"little Tommy"* by my father, is by Gale's Studios and has an inked date stamp on the back – 14 June 1928 when Tommy was 24. In 1911 he was living with his parents and two brothers, William Henry and George Gregory on East Bank. In 1941, at the somewhat late age of 37, he was married at Youlgreave Parish Church to Annie Slaney (1908 – 1988). Tommy worked with my father at Longcliffe Quarry and I remember him well from the 1950s. Strange, but I have no memory of Annie. The couple had a daughter, Monica. The card of the couple on their Wedding Day is unused and by an unidentified photographer.

Tommy is also seen on the card of the wedding group at his brother George's wedding to Nancy Staton in 1933. Again this is an unsued card by an unidentified photographer. The wedding was at the Methodist Chapel, East Bank, outside of which the group are pictured. George Gregory (1906 – 1982) was for many years the Queen of Winster Morris Dancers. He was a prominent figure in my Winster childhood and I knew his wife, Nancy (1910 – 1989) too. She was one of my Sunday School Teachers during the 1950s at the Methodist Schoolroom opposite Doctor Stoker's surgery at Bank House, West Bank. In 2009 the Schoolroom had been converted into a private residence and I was fortunate to be allowed a peek inside by the then owner. No internal features of the schoolroom were left but the visit revived happy

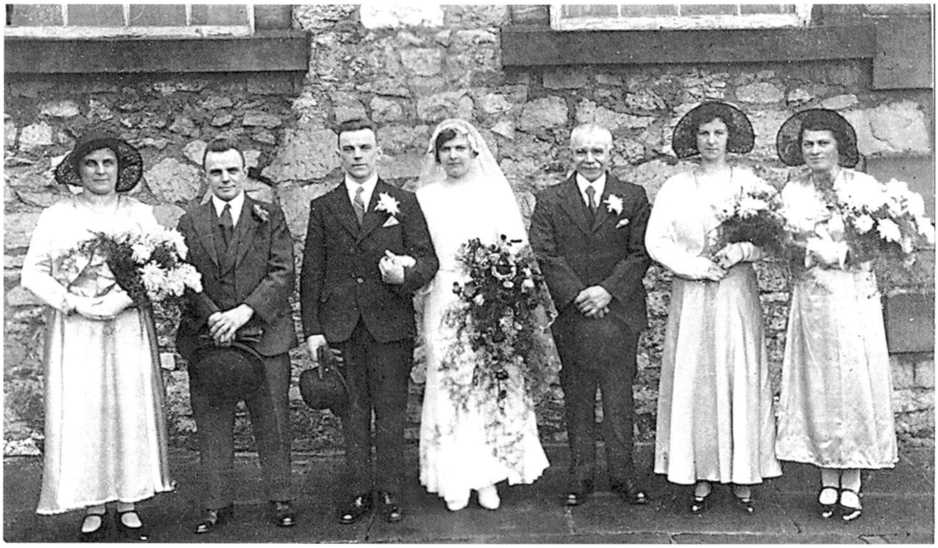

George Gregory & Nancy Staton outside Winster Methodist Church, 1933. From left to right – Lilian Gregory, Tommy Gregory, Groom, Bride, Francis (Frank) Staton, Doris Heath and Olive Slack

memories of Nancy and her other Sunday School teaching colleagues. I recall her as a kind, polite, charming woman ill-suited to controlling children but no doubt she was sorely tried at times by myself and other children. Seeing her leading children in prayer has left me with an indelible memory of her which I recall as I write these few words. She and George were stalwarts of the Methodist Chapel, East Bank. I bought a car from George in the early 1960s – it was an Austin 10 which would now be worth a small fortune if I still had it in running or other order. George married Nancy (her name was actually Sarah Ann but she was always known as Nancy) and they lived on East Bank. They had no children. George worked for Lehane, Mackenzie & Shand at Rowsley. There are Memorial Plaques to both George and Nancy inside the Chapel.

The other people pictured in the wedding group are:

Lilian Gregory (1901 – 1981). She was George and Tommy's sister. In 1937 she married Samuel Hodgkinson (1873 – 1949). Lilian too was also one of my childhood Sunday School teachers. Before that, in the late 1940s/early 1950s she had a small shop on East Bank, that part which leads to The Flat. I was often sent there as a child for household items. On one occasion I was sent from school with a written message from George Noton (1902 – 1973), the Headmaster, for Mrs Hodgkinson, as I knew her. I recall knocking on her house door (next door to the shop), delivering the message and waiting whilst she read it. I cannot recall at all what the message was about or if I returned to school with a reply.

Francis Staton (the bride's father) **(1878 –1960)** was born in Winster and in 1909 married Eliza Haywood Slack (1886 – 1973) who was also born in Winster. In 1911 the couple, and their daughter Nancy, aged 11 months, were living in Woolley's Yard. I wonder why the bride's mother was not included in this photograph? Was she ill and did not attend the wedding? Mr. and Mrs. Staton were living on East Bank in 1955.

Doris Heath (1915 – 1999) was married in 1939 to James Victor Dakin (1915 – 1994). In 1955 this couple were living at Vernon Cottage, Main Street. Later I recall them living down Pump Lane (Woodhouse Lane). The final person in the group is Olive Slack.

William Henry Gregory (1899 – 1956)

We met Henry (as he was known) before when discussing the Newton sisters: he was married to Ada Newton and cards illustrating the couple's wedding in 1926 are illustrated in Chapter 3. I knew him during my childhood but not well. In the 1911 Census he was recorded with his parents and siblings, Lilian, aged 9, Thomas, 6, and George, 4, on East Bank.

These first two cards were sent to Henry from Altrincham in 1908 and 1910 by his aunt, Lucy Gregory (1873 – 1933). Lucy was born in Winster and never married – she is buried in Winster Churchyard and has a memorial there. In 1911 she was living with her widowed mother, also on East Bank, and was described as a Housemaid Domestic. The first card was posted on 24 September 1908 and reads:

"My Dear Henry, I hope you will like this P.Card. I think it is a very pretty one. You must write and tell me if you like it . Give my love to Dad and Mum & Lily & Love & Baby & dearest love for your dear little self from Aunt Lucy."

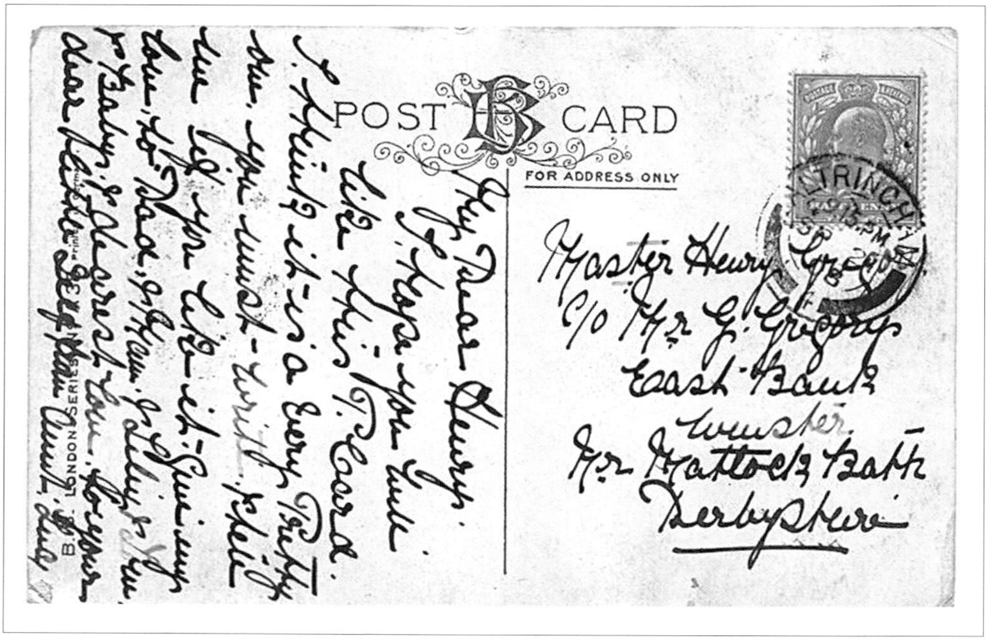

A Message from Aunt Lucy – 24 September 1908

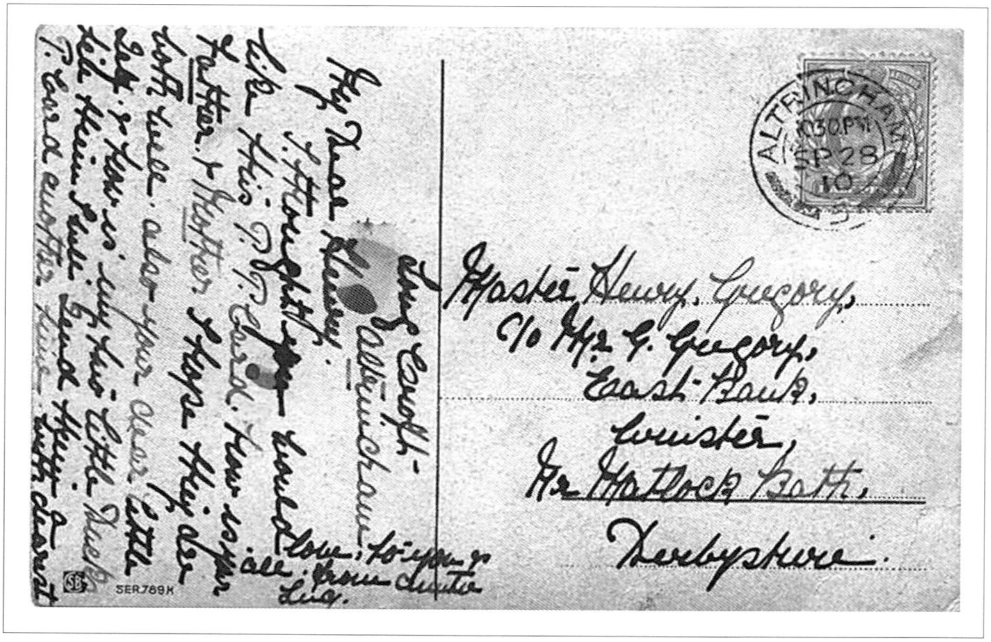

Another Message from Aunt Lucy – 28 September 1910

The picture side of this card (not illustrated) is a printed image of a child with a dog and the legend *"He won't bite!"* at bottom right. The card was published by BB London Series No. A38 and was printed in Germany. The second card was posted on 28 September 1910. The message reads:

"Long Croft
Altrincham
My Dear Henry, I thought you would like this P.P. Card. How is your father and mother. I hope they are both well also your dear little self & how is my two little ducks tell them I will send them a P.Card another time. With dearest love to all. From Auntie Lucy."

The picture side (not illustrated) is colour printed showing three young demure females dressed in blue, red and green flowing dresses bearing the verse *"Faith Hope and Charity, meek and lowly, pure and holy, chief among the "blessed three.""*

Both cards were posted in September two years apart – was Lucy visiting relatives / friends in Altrincham? Did she go there for a holiday? The next three cards show Henry during his Great War (1914 – 18) Service.

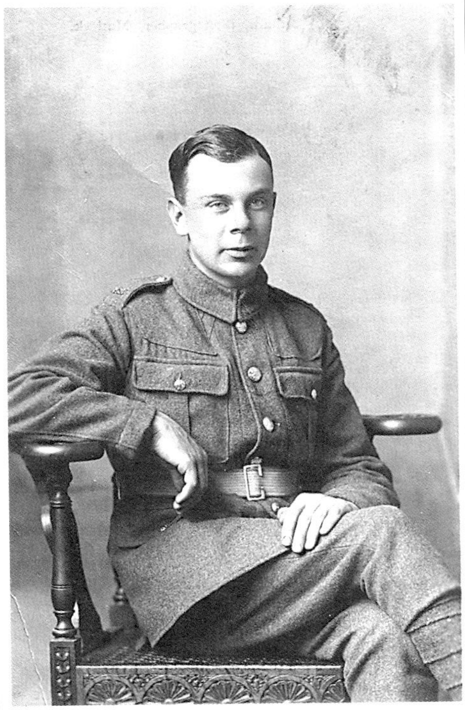

The first is a fine formal portrait by W.N. Statham, Photographer, Matlock. The second shows Henry fifth from the left on the back row. Henry wrote a note (not illustrated) on the back of this card which reads:

"This is a photo of our Section took at Guimerville. I thought I would get a couple & send them to you. I expect you will find me among the boys."

Henry Gregory by W.N. Statham, Photographer, Matlock

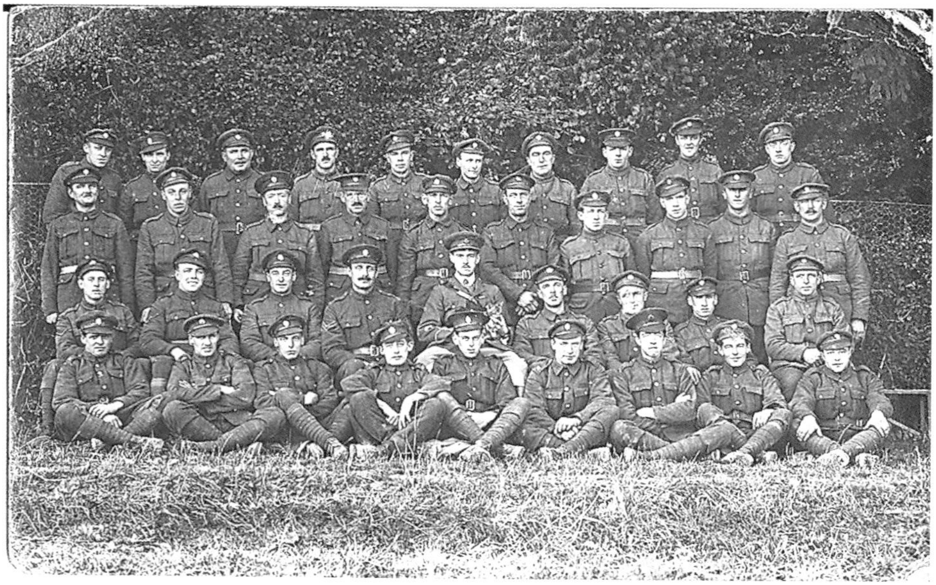

Henry Gregory (5th From Left on Back Row) at Guimerville, northern France

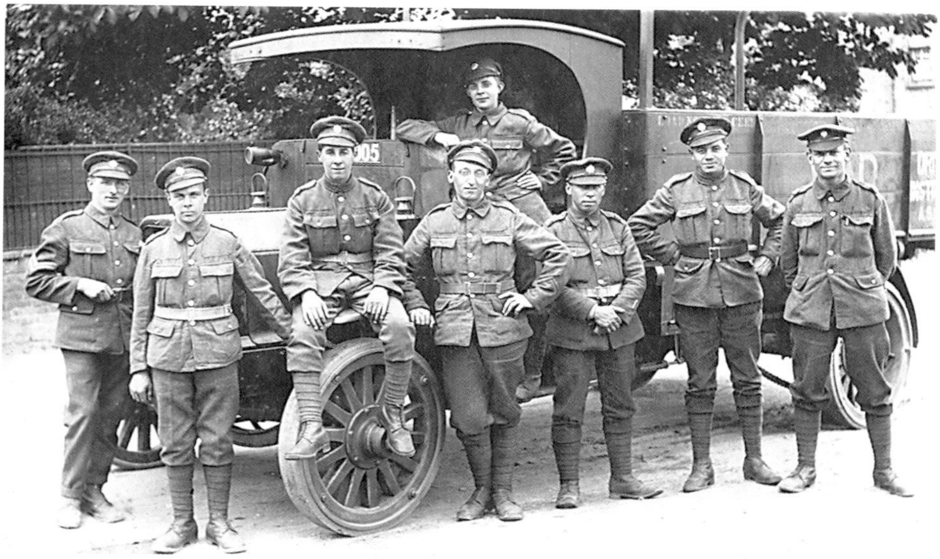

Henry Gregory 2nd from left

Guimerville is in northern France. Henry was lucky – he survived the Great War. He and Ada did not have children – he died at the relatively early age of 56 in 1956 and Ada died in 1988, at 88. There is a memorial to the couple in Winster Churchyard.

The following card was sent to Henry and Ada on 25 August 1926 at 58 Albert Road, Blackpool, where they were spending their honeymoon following their Winster wedding on 19 August. The message reads:

"Dear Henry & Ada, Hope you are having a good time over there, it's lovely here this week. Show this your Mother when you get back & ask her if she knows it at all.Love from all to you both. Auntie E.B."

In March 2010 58 Albert Road had become 58-62 Albert Road and was known as *"The Blackpool"* (a hotel near the town centre). It had formerly been known as Kenberry Hotel.

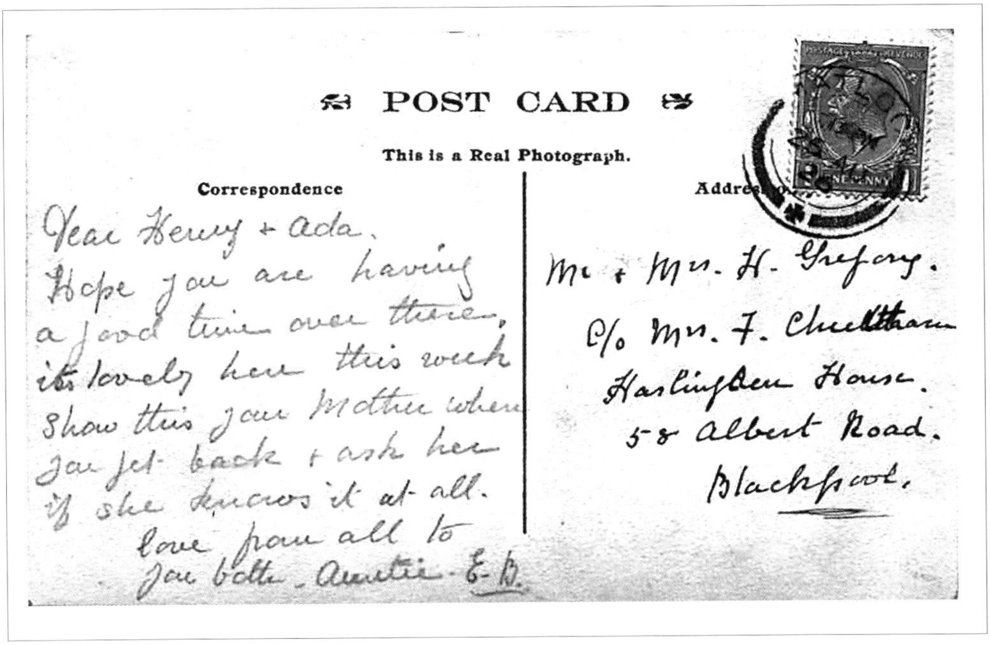

This card was posted to Henry & Ada Gregory on 25 August 1926 to their Blackpool Honeymoon Hotel

The Youlgreave Brassingtons

When I started to write this book the cards in this section were not destined to be used as I then concluded that their relevance to Winster was minimal. They were all part of the substantial Eric Brasssington collection. Eric's grandfather, Joseph Albert Brassington (JAB, whom we met earlier) was a Youlgreave man and Eric had drawn my attention to this group of cards as images of some of JAB's sisters and other relatives. JAB had eleven siblings. I reviewed the cards when the collection initially came into my possession but, for some reason, I had then overlooked the importance of at least three of them to Winster. Now that I look back the importance of the three cards seems obvious. As this book progressed, I had been immersed in writing, studying various cards, and doing research to support the text. The bulk of the early part of the work was concentrated, amongst other various tasks, in trying to identify possible Marshall people cards. I had got to the point where I thought that that part of the task was behind me when I casually reviewed these cards again as I drew breath before moving on to another Chapter. Eric had grouped these cards together for me in an album and something in Eric's arrangement of the cards caught my eye – in fact when I noticed it, I was both surprised and annoyed that I had overlooked it. This then led me to a decision to include the majority of these cards. It must be increasingly rare for family collections of cards to survive. Why break them up? Their interest and significance is surely of more importance when they are kept together so that added pleasure is derived from considering the cards as a group rather than treating them on an individual basis. And so I decided to include all these cards of JAB's sisters and other relatives.

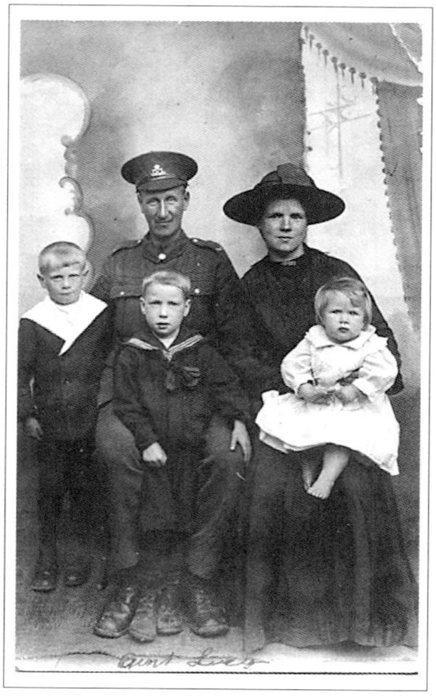

A Marshall postcard c1917/18 John & Lucy Marshall with three of their children from left to right possibly Ben, Fred & Alice

This was the first card which caught my attention.

Consider first the backcloth of the card of the soldier with his family – then go back and compare it with the backcloth on the image of Winnie Brassington at p34 in Chapter 3 it is identical. We know that Winnie's card was published by Marshall as it is stamped on the back to that effect: so this image of the soldier's family was probably taken by Marshall too c1917/18. Why hadn't I noticed the backcloth in the two cards before and "*put two and two together*" much earlier? This backcloth was likely bought from a photographer's supplier and, of course, the identical backcloth may have been used by different photographers in different areas. It is conceivable that, as well as being used by Marshall, it may have been used by a local photographer operating in the Youlgreave or Bakewell districts. My guess, though, was that the soldier's family postcard was taken by Marshall too. This then led me to look more closely at other cards in the same part of the collection. But first – what have I been able to discover about the soldier and his family. Eric had told me that JAB had a sister named Lucy. You will see that the soldier's card has been marked Aunt Lucy at the bottom. Who was she? Who was the soldier and the children too?

Lucy Brassington (c1889 – 1945) was born in Youlgreave. In 1910 Lucy married John Leonard Marshall (c1889 – 1964) who was born in Winster. In 1891 John was at The Workhouse, Bank Top, with his parents, Henry and Alice, and his sisters Sarah and Lizzie and his brother, Ernest. By 1901 John's family had moved to the Market Place – John was then a carter on a farm. He was then still living with his parents and Elizabeth (Lizzie), Sarah and Ernest and one other sister, Florence. Edward Hadfield, aged 76 and born in Winster, was living with the family as a boarder on his own means. In 1911 Lucy and her new husband, John, were living at Stanton in Peak. John was then a quarry carter (gritstone). The couple had a 10 month old child, Fred, born in Youlgreave, who was living with them. Lucy and John Leonard had eleven children of whom we probably see these three with them in this card – Alice (1916 – 2008), Fred (1910 – 1997) and Benjamin (1911 – 1985). John's cap badge is probably that of the South Staffs Regiment.

Another card which so dramatically caught my attention includes a younger Lucy along with her sister, Nellie. This too is a Marshall card – look at the flags and the vegetation behind the young women and then go back and compare it with those discussed also in Chapter 3 Nellie was born about 1885. Lucy, who is standing next to her sister, is not wearing a wedding ring so it probably predates 1910 the year of her

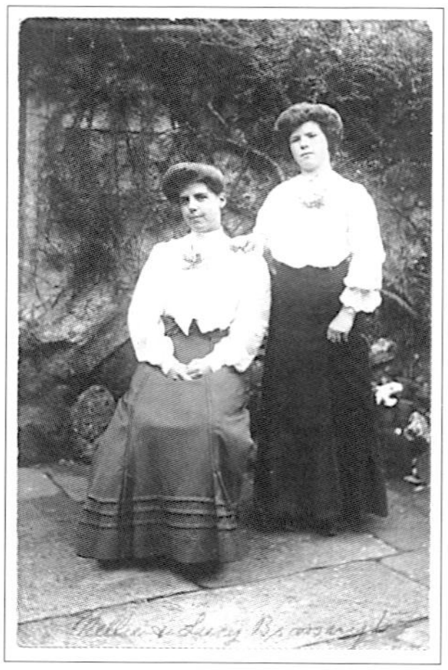

A Marshall postcard before 1910 – Nellie & Lucy Brassington

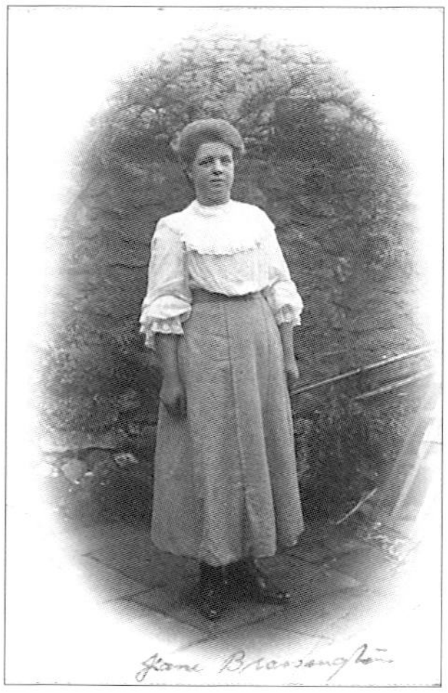

A Marshall postcard – Jane Brassington

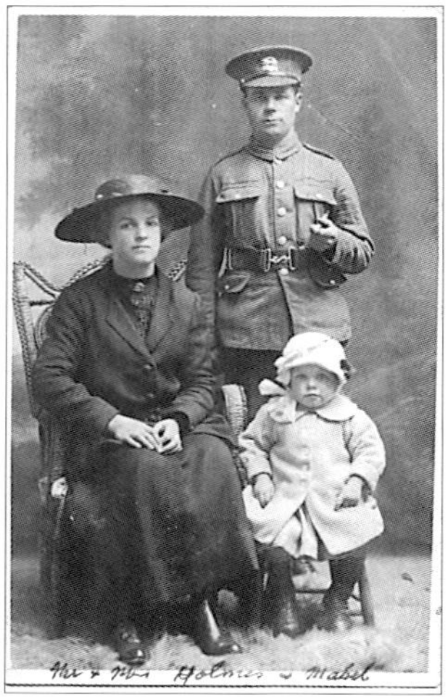

Pte John Holmes with his wife, Jane (nee Brassington), & daughter Mabel c1916

marriage to John Leonard Marshall.

The above card of Jane Twigg Brassington (b. c1892) (another of JAB's sisters), is also by Marshall. Again we see the flags and the vegetation on the wall. In 1913 Jane married John William Holmes (c1887 – 1918) who was born in Stanton in Peak and who was killed in action during the Great War. When John enlisted he and his family were living at Bradford, Youlgreave. He was Private 51753 of the 15th Cheshire Regiment at the time of his death although he had enlisted into the Sherwood Foresters. On 22 October 1918 Jane was awarded a pension of 20/5d a week for herself and one child. That child was Mabel Holmes who was born in Youlgreave on 14 November 1914. The family are pictured with John in uniform c1916 in the latter of the above three cards. It is not known where this photograph was taken – it was clearly taken in a studio but who knows where?

The card of Jane and her daughter, Mabel, is by W.N. Statham, Matlock, and I nearly missed this too. I held the card under a strong light, moved it around and the light caught the photographer's logo at bottom right – it is now well nigh invisible in daylight. This card probably dates from the early 1920s. The card of Mabel as a young woman is helpfully marked in ink with her name and on the back it has an ink stamped date:

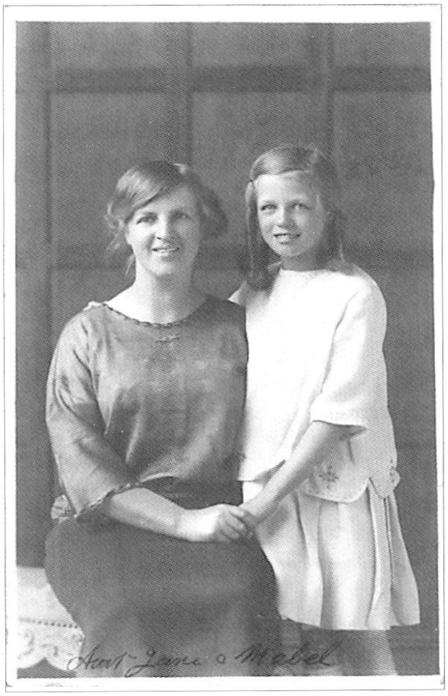

Jane & Mabel Holmes – early 1920s

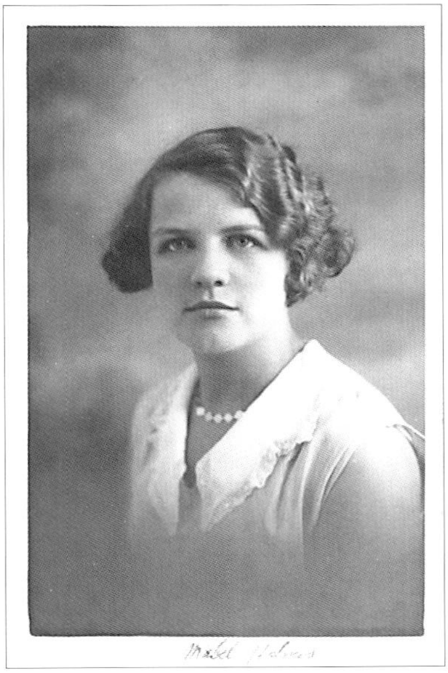

Mabel Holmes,19, by Jerome

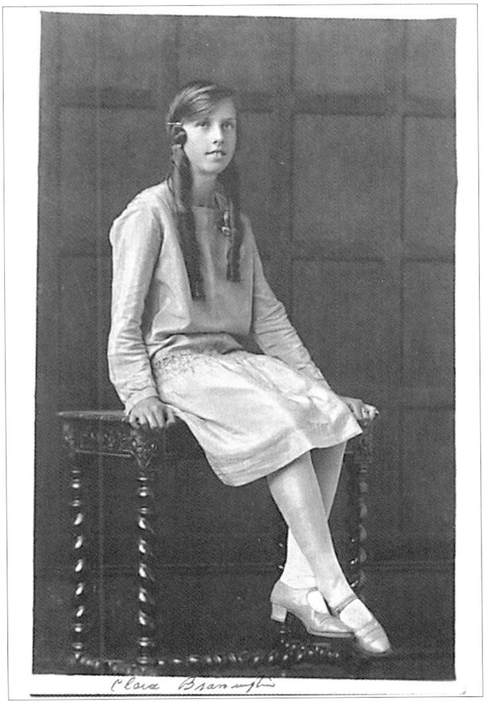

Clara Brassington
by W.N. Statham

24 September 1933 when Mabel was 19. The photographer was Jerome who had *"branches everywhere."*

The card of Clara Brassington is also by W.N. Statham, Matlock. She is pictured in front of the same panelling as were Jane and Mabel Holmes. Clara was probably a relative of JAB too. I cannot trace her with any confidence – in this card she looks to be a young teenager c1920s.

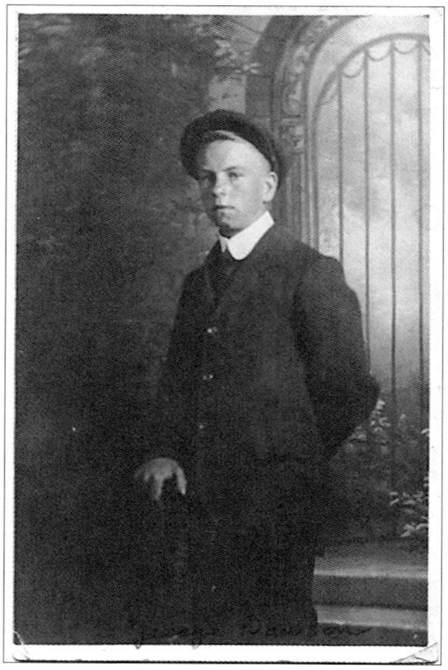

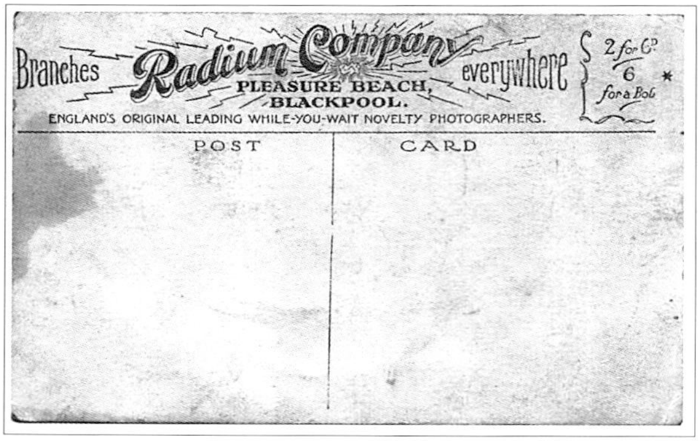

Back of previous card

George Dawson at Blackpool Pleasure Beach

The card of George Brassington Dawson (GBD) (1907 – 1974) was taken by the Radium Company on the Pleasure Beach, Blackpool, probably c1920 – the back of this card may be of interest too. GBD was JAB's nephew: his mother being Jesse Brassington, JAB's sister. Jesse Brassington was born in about December 1882. In 1905 she married Thomas Dawson born in Biggin in about 1879. In 1911 the couple were living with their family at Friden Cottages, Hartington, and Thomas was

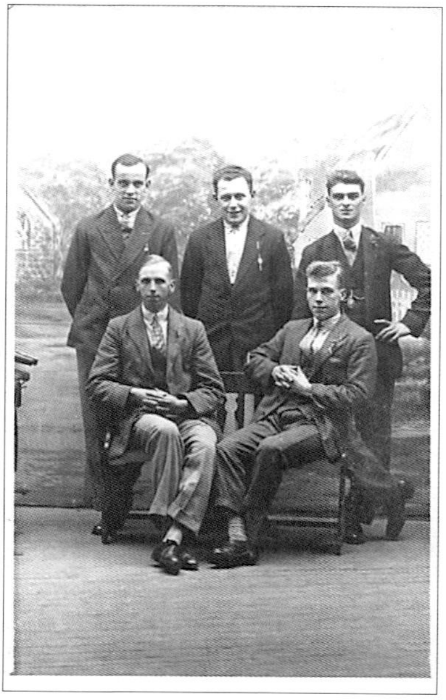

Albert Brassington & Friends at Blackpool 1928 by Charles Howell

Albert Brassington at Blackpool on 5 September 1928, aged 20, by Ellis Wolstenholme, Wellington Studio

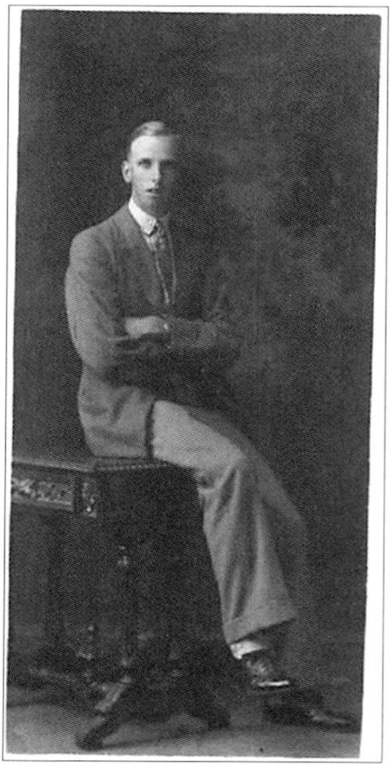

a labourer at a brick works, almost certainly the one at Friden. The couple had three children of whom GBD, who was born at Old Whittington, married Ivy M. Holmes in 1934. Ivy probably pre-deceased GBD in about 1962.

Albert Brassington (1908 – 1994) was JAB's cousin, the son of George Brassington, JAB's brother. In 1911 the family lived in Youlgreave. Albert is seated at left pictured with his friends (identities unknown but probably other Youlgreave young men) during a trip to Blackpool on 5 September 1928 when Albert was 20. This card has *"Charles Howell, Official Photographer Pleasure Beach, Blackpool"* printed on the back. We know the date of this trip from the smaller photograph of Albert (not a card) which helpfully has his name written in ink on the back with a printed photographer's stamp which reads:

"Only address
Ellis Wolstenholme
Wellington Studio
Opp Central Pier
Blackpool"

This stamp is itself overstamped with the date 5 Sep 1928. Albert is wearing the same clothes in both photographs.

Who Was Alice Garside?

Before we leave the Youlgrave Brassingtons, we need to ponder the identity of Alice and her place in this collection. This image has *"Parisian Studio, 118 Liverpool Road, Patricroft"* printed on the unused back. Patricroft is near Eccles, Manchester.

The original card is one of my favourites. The darkness of the setting against the white of the girl's dress is immediately apparent on the original. The card has clearly been in an album for some time as album marks are visible at the corners and the card has suffered from *"foxing"* (the damage caused to an old image by contamination over time). At the bottom right of the original is written in a clear hand: *"Alice Garside."* She was in the Brassington album(s) with no notes or information about her. Who was she? What happened to her? What was her place in the Brassington wider family? These questions about this charming image were too pressing to remain unanswered and demanded some research. This was an intriguing task and remains incomplete but you might be able to add to it.

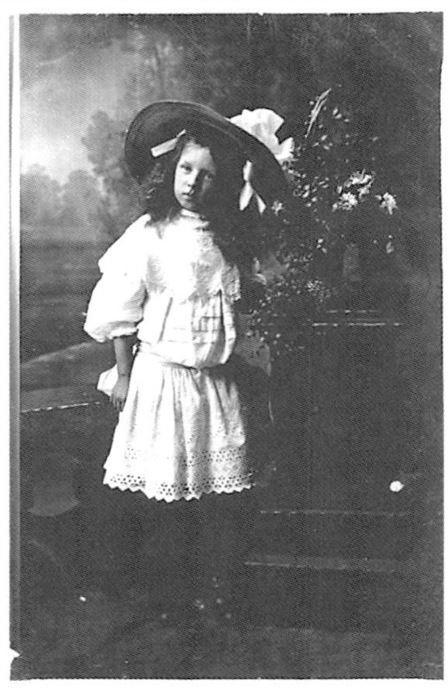

Alice Garside c1917 by Parisian Studio, 118 Liverpool Road, Patricroft

JAB had a sister, Georgina Dorothy Brassington, born in Youlgreave, who married William Garside. In the 1911 Census this couple had a child, Alice, aged six, living with them at 69 Phillip Street, Patricroft. So I speculate that this picture may be of Alice taken when she was about 12 years old, c1917. I uploaded Alice's image to Flickr in the hope that someone might recognise her and be able to provide more biographical information about her life. Within hours of the image being uploaded a man in Australia e-mailed me with more information about Alice which firmly put her amongst JAB's relations and fills a gap in Eric's family tree. Hurrah! My Australian informant told me that Alice might be the Alice Sullivan (née Garside) who was born on 4 August 1904 and who died in 1989 in the Salford District. If this is the right, Alice married Arthur J. Sullivan in 1922. The couple may have had two children, James A.G, born 1923, and Margaret, born 1926. James probably married Eva Horner in Barton-Upon-Irwell District in 1943. Can any reader now fill out Alice's story? Have Alice Sullivan's descendants already preserved a copy of this card or if they read or are told about this book are they overjoyed to discover that this charming image of Alice has survived into the 21st century?

JAB and his wife clearly treasured this lovely picture of their niece. Did Alice ever visit her uncle and aunt in their home on East Bank? Most likely she did in which case she has a connection with Winster. So, please look closely and kindly on these images – there must be dozens out there – just like this one of Alice. They are too precious for our heritage simply to be discarded. The internet gives us the opportunity to "*solve*" some of these "*old photo*" puzzles and to leave a record which others may value.

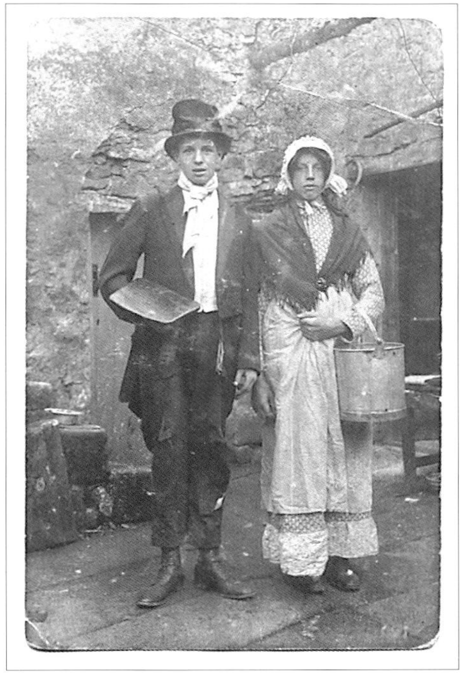
Douglas Hawksworth & Charlie Hardy c1910 in Fancy Dress

On the back of this card written in ink are the names Douglas Hawksworth & Charlie Hardy. Also, but this time written in pencil and parts of it just legible is:

"Look at Douglas with the stool and Charlie with his wig on. I dressed him? and got your…."

The pair may be Douglas Hawksworth (1895 – 1960) and Charles Robert Hardy (1894 – 1978). The photo is probably dated c1910 and shows the boys, both born in Winster, in fancy dress. In 1911 Douglas lived on West Bank with his parents and three brothers. Douglas' Army records show that he enlisted at Matlock on 6 July 1915 and was discharged the following day as *"Not being likely to become an efficient soldier."* His name is on a framed list of men who served in the Great War 1914 – 1918 which hangs in Winster Parish Church. So even men who served in the Great War for one day only are commemorated. In 1911 Charlie lived with his parents and sister. His occupation is given in the census as *"labourer above ground"* probably at a lead mine.

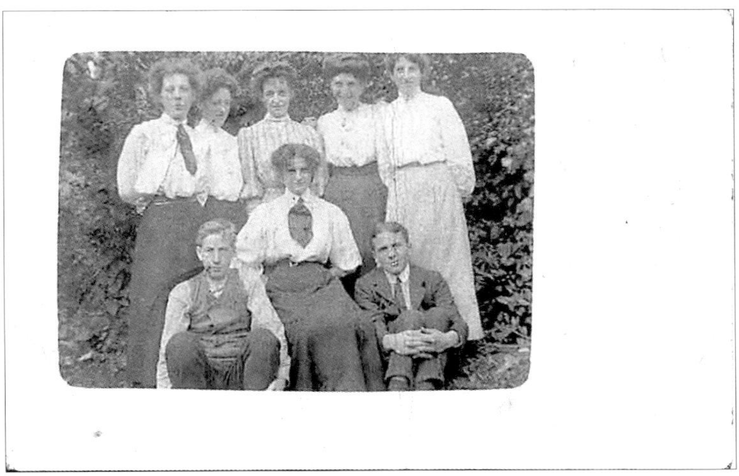
Woolley's Yard before 1906

The above card is included chiefly as it is rare (at least so far as this book is concerned) – it is a regular "*Golden Age*" size with a small photograph which is why I have shown it complete. On the back it is endorsed in ink: "*Winster A Group of Friends Seated front left Wallace Boam right Victor Rowland. (ladies unknown).*"

Wallace Boam (1891 – 1972) (if it is him) married Agnes Ethel (maiden name unknown) (1901 – 1968) and both are buried in Winster Churchyard where they have a memorial. Wallace was active in village life, particularly during my childhood in the 1950s. Victor Rowland I cannot trace.

Some Wild Family Cards

In June 2010 (when I thought I was nearing the end of writing this book) I came into possession of some of the papers left by Joan Freda Priestnall nee Wild (1916 – 2010) by courtesy of the executors of her Estate. There was an interesting selection of Winster related cards amongst these papers two of which were important additions to my collection of Marshall cards and others which identified for the first time (for me at least) that an Edwardian postcard publisher (W.S. Scott of Chesterfield) worked in Winster. I had never previously seen images of events in Winster endorsed with Scott's imprint on the back. Thus I had "*discovered*" another photographer responsible for some of the many Winster event cards which hitherto were the work of an unknown (to me) photographer and possibly Albert Marshall. So Scott was responsible (along with Marshall and, who knows, others yet to be "*discovered*") for some of these unidentified Winster cards. The two Marshall cards have been incorporated elsewhere in the appropriate Marshall Portrait section. The temptation to include some of the Wild cards in this work was too great to resist.

One of the documents passed to me by Joan's executors was the marriage certificate of her parents dated 10 April 1901. There were also photos of people with just names on the back. I noticed that Joan's parents were married at Wadsley, Yorkshire. The names of the witnesses linked up with the names on the backs of some of the other photos. But why did this Winster couple choose to be married outside Winster? The Census for 1901 was taken on 31 March 1901 and both Joan's parents were recorded as living in Winster at that time so why did they marry in

Wadsley just 10 days later? Neither of the two witnesses who signed the register were members of the parents' families (Wild and Roper) – their names were Walter Samuel Mottram and Nellie Oldfield. Did the Winster members of the Wild and Roper families attend the Wedding? Did they travel to Wadsley from Winster for the ceremony? Was there a family rift over the marriage? Another original birth certificate amongst the papers provided the obvious answer – and an age-old one at that. Joan's mother, Beatrice Amelia Roper, was 8 months' pregnant on 10 April 1901 when she and John Wild were married – less than a month later (on 6 May 2010) the couple's first child, Harold Beverly Wild, was born at East Bank, Winster. The birth was registered on 14 June 1910 and Beatrice was the informant who gave her address at East Bank. So the couple were living separately in Winster before their marriage and during the first eight months of Beatrice's pregnancy (hence the census records recording them at separate Winster households); then they went to Wadsley where they had friends or connections, before returning to Winster to set up home together on East Bank. A reasonable guess was that either John was friends with the witness Walter Samuel Mottram or that Beatrice was friends with the other witness, Nellie Oldfield.

In the 1901 census Nellie Oldfield was employed as a Cook (Domestic) in the home of the Rev. & Mrs. Parkin, The Vicarage, Church Lane, Wadsley, Nr. Sheffield, Yorkshire. The Rev. Parkin officiated at John and Beatrice's wedding in his Parish Church at Wadsley. Question answered. That also explained the many other photographs included with the documentation from Joan's executors, including one of The Rev. Parkin (marked on the back *"Rev. Parkin, Wadsley Vicarage, Sheffield A true Christian"*). If only these people had a stronger connection to Winster, I would have have included many of these images here. Walter Samuel Mottram and Nellie Oldfield were themselves married in 1904 and the 1911 census records them at 55 Dykes Hall Road, Sheffield.

But where was Beatrice when the 1891 census was taken, when she was about 15 – I cannot trace her? So how did she meet up with Nellie Oldfield? This and other intriguing questions raised by the other photographs remain unanswered so it will be as well to return my concentration to the cards which are specifically linked to Winster.

But first, a little about the Wild family.

John Wild (1877 – 1953) was the quintessential King of Winster Morris Dancers. This photograph of him in the garden of his home at Vernon House, Main Street, was probably taken in the early 1920s when he was in his mid 40s. His daughter, Joan Freda, wrote on the back:

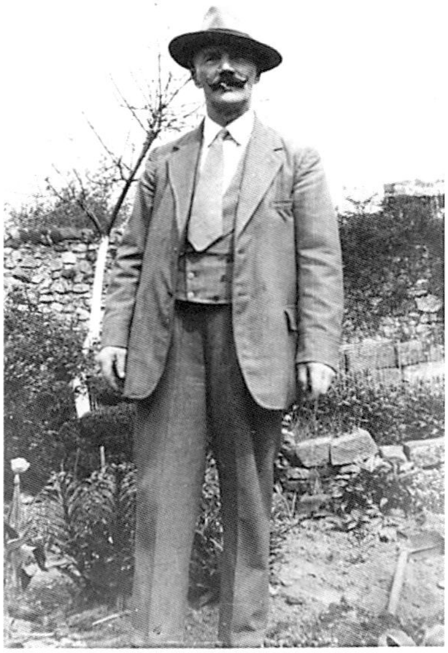

John Wild c1920s in the garden of Vernon House, Main Street

"My father – John Wild. Most splendid of men. In the garden at Vernon House, Winster, when we were all together."

One of the following cards shows Joan in about 1918 aged about two. Joan's mother as noted earlier was Beatrice Amelia Wild nee Roper (1876 – 1960). The Roper family have been farmers in Winster since the late c19 and are still farming in Winster in 2010. Both Joan's parents were born in Winster. Joan firstly married George D. Revell in 1952 and then one Priestnell whom I have not yet traced. Strange, he ought to be easy enough to find. For many years Joan was one of the organists at Winster Methodist Church even when she no longer lived in Winster. In the early 1960s she was employed by Derbyshire County Council at the then County Offices on Smedley Street, Matlock, and was in charge of the telephone switchboard.

Before moving to Vernon House, the Wild family lived at Sunny Bank, Wensley Road. The 1911 census captures Joan's parents there with two sons, John Normanton and Harold plus a Nurse/Baby, three boarders and a General Servant (Domestic). The house must have been crowded. Another of the following images is the message side of a card sent to Mrs. John Wild from Sheffield on 14 August 1911. The message reads:

"Dear Auntie, I arrived safely at home about 8'o'clock this morning without any mishap. I got a little wet with the dew. I shall see Mr. Longden tonight & will ask him to come with me again. I think he will do. We shall come on the 26 August all being well but I shall be writing again. Your affect. Nephew Joe."

I wonder if this Mr. Longden is the man illustrated on the cards on with Joe p67?

It is as well to note that the picture side of the card is a real photograph of a crowd of uniformed children in what may be a football ground. I wonder? So, I've just taken a break from writing this text to google appropriate words/phrases in case something turned up – it didn't. Neither the picture nor the back identifies the location or the photographer. I assume (probably wrongly) that it might be Sheffield from the postmark and that the Spencer family (see below) were based in Sheffield. Someone has written in ink in capitals on the picture side "*A Living Union Jack* (on Empire Day)". It is a big crowd and I leapt to the clue that it might be a Sheffield football ground. A Sheffield/Empire Day/Union Jack postcard collector may read this and exclaim: "I wish he had shown us the picture!" But it's not included here as only the message is of interest to Winster.

If you look at the image yourself (you'll have to turn this book to one side) you will probably ponder over the signature which I now interpret as "*Joe.*" It seems almost childlike compared with the beautiful handwriting of the rest of the message. However, Joe was probably Joe Spencer a member of the Spencer family (headed by Reuben and his wife Mary Jane nee Roper sister to Beatrice Amelia Wild) recorded in the 1911 census at 149 Walkley Lane, Sheffield, although I cannot trace any of his vital records.

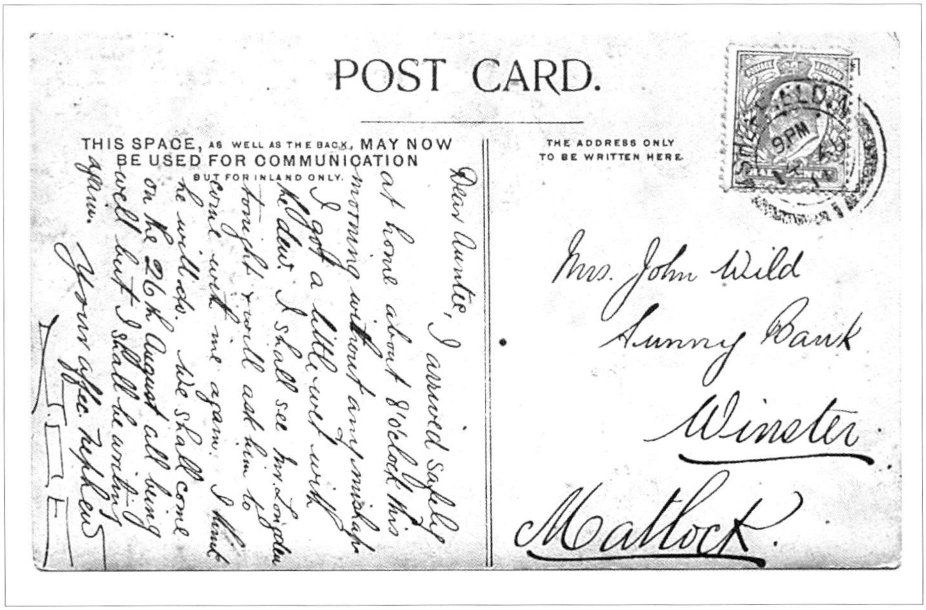

Posted 14 Aug 1911

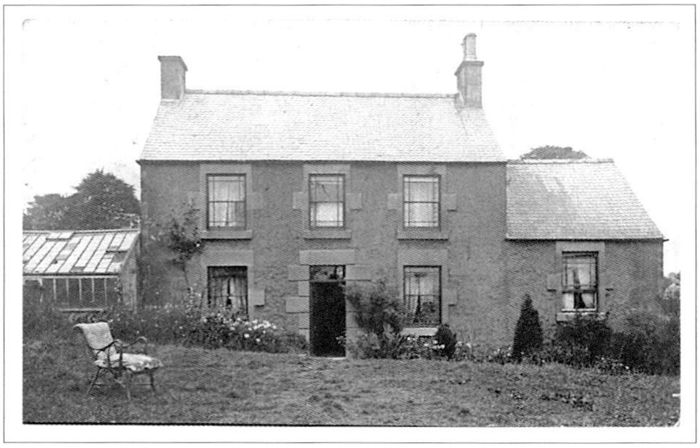

Sunny Bank, Wensley Road

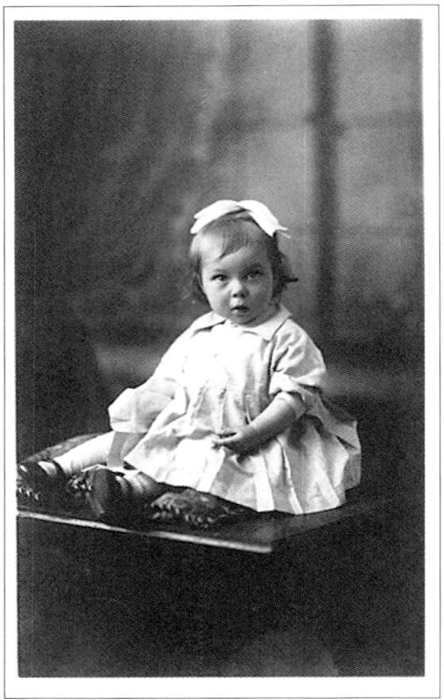

Joan Wild c1918 aged about 2

The card at bottom left is endorsed in ink on the back: *"Cousin Joe Spencer on left and friend on a visit outside Sunny Bank, Winster, 1911."* The final card of the group shows Joan, second from left on the front row (between the lad and the man), as a young girl in a 1920s Wedding Party outside the Burton Institute on West Bank. Unfortunately, I have been unable to identify the Wedding but readers may be able to offer some assistance. I think it might be a Boam wedding.

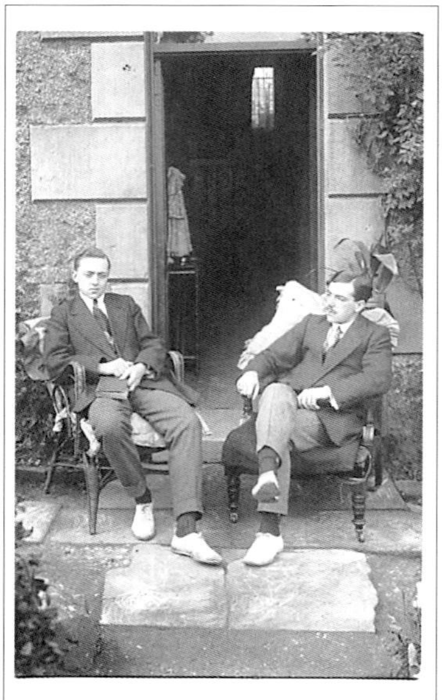

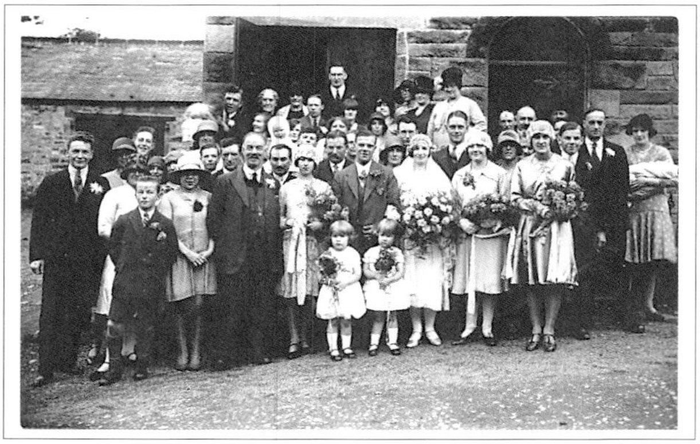

Wedding Group c1920s. Bride & Groom unknown

Joe Spencer on left and friend outside Sunny Bank

Four Men With Cigarettes

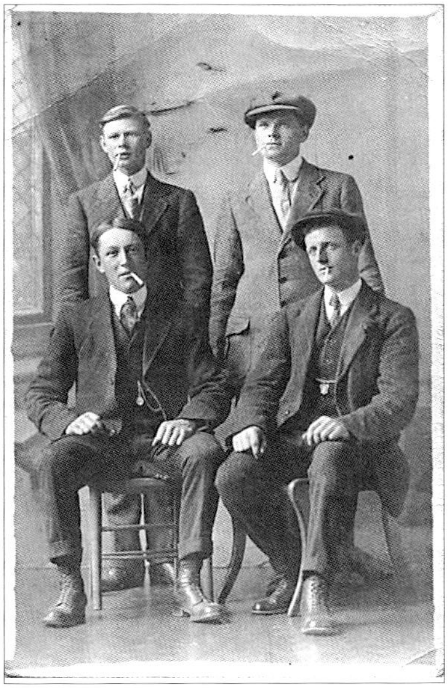
Four young men with cigarettes

This card interests me on two counts: the four young men smoking cigarettes and, secondly, it has a link with Winster. My, how times have changed. It is inconceivable in 2010 that a group of young men would want to be photographed by a professional photographer in his studio (note the backcloth) with cigarettes in their mouths. The back is endorsed in ink: *"Seated front row – left Norman Stone (married Mary Dale). Standing back row left ?Wood – Carson All From Elton."*

Normanton Stone (1892 – 1966) was born in Elton and died in Winster. In 1923 he was married in Winster Parish Church to Mary Dale (1893 – 1985). In 1955 the couple lived on Main Street.

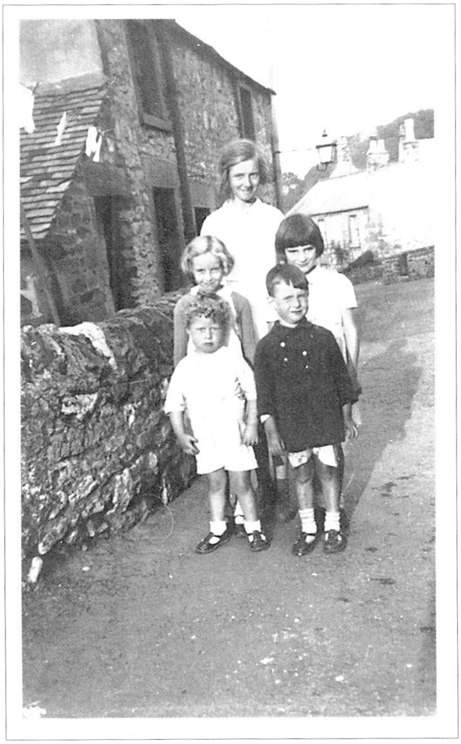

Five On The Flat – Late 1930s

This charming group of 1930s children seem to have been carefully posed by the unknown photographer. The tall girl at the back may be Annie Maskery, the blonde girl at left is Eileen Brassington but the other girl is unidentified. The two lads at the front are Malcolm White and Eric Brassington (in dark shirt). Eileen and Eric lived at Woodland View just out of shot at right – Malcolm lived in the house at left beyond the wall (known in 2010 as Orchard Cottage). No doubt the other children lived close by.

CHAPTER 5

JOSIAH GREATOREX (1874 – 1957) & FAMILY

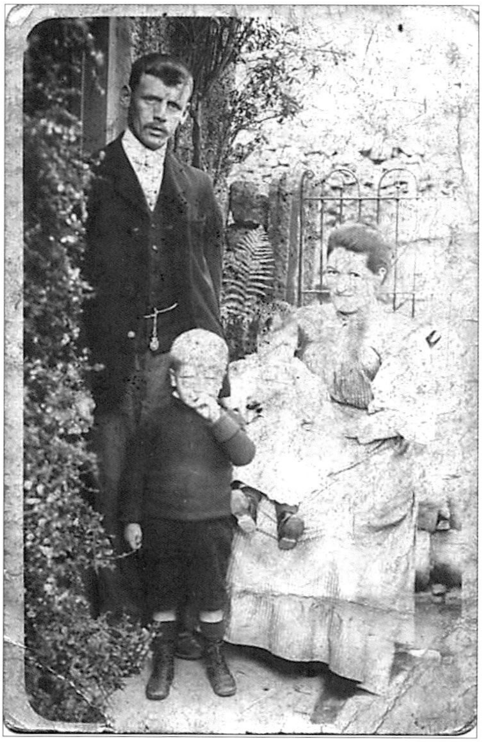

Josiah & Jane Greatorex & Family
Outside Wesson Cottage c1911

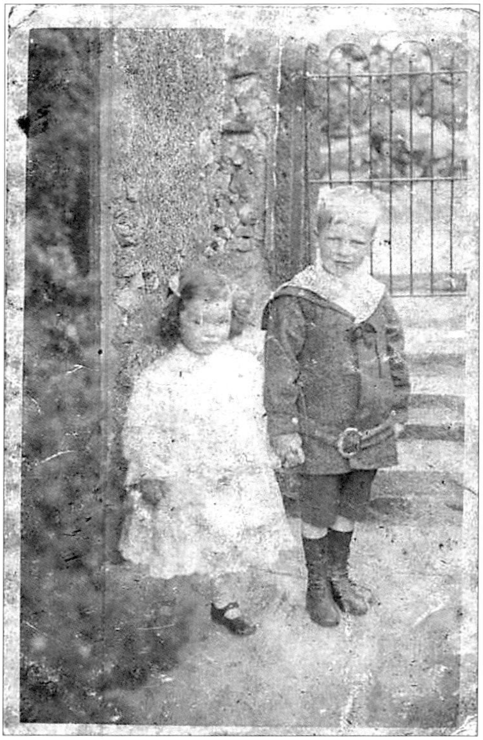

Edith & Arnold Greatorex
Outside Wesson Cottage c1912

These first two cards picture my paternal grandparents, my father and my aunt. The remainder of the Chapter also includes cards associated with all the members of my grandparents' family (and my sister). I hesitated in including these cards; they seem so personal but, on balance, I have decided that they should be included. Irrespective of their association with me, they belong in a book devoted to Winster postcards: a book which attempts to convey the fun and pleasure in preserving them; and tries to convey how important they are now (and might be in the future) in preserving the work of Edwardian photographers and recording some snippets about former Winster residents. As these people were members of my own family the next decision for me was how much accompanying text I should write to place the people and the cards in context. I then resolved that the text should be minimal. There is much that I could write about my grandfather and my parents but this is not the place to record those memories. So, just enjoy the cards and the notes.

Wesson Cottage, West Bank, (where Josiah and his family lived) is best approached on foot. From the top of East Bank take the unmade road across Wesson Common and the Cottage is the first building facing you on the left. From the Market House in Main Street ascend East Bank and take the right fork leading to The Flat. At the far end of The Flat find the footpath to the left of the house which closes this cul-de-sac (incidentally the *"house where I was born"*) and follow the path up the hill. Wesson Cottage is at the top on the right. The Cottage was originally two cottages and came into the possession of Josiah Greatorex through his mother. It was sold by Josiah's Estate following his death in 1957 and was bought by Mr. and Mrs. Rodger. Margery Rodger was a well-known Winster historian of her time.

Josiah was a lead miner at Mill Close Mine. In 1905 he married Jane Bradbury (1873 – 1947). She was born in Rugeley, Staffs, and had relations in Wensley and was living there at the time of her marriage. The couple had three children, Arnold, Edith and Stanley. One of the cards above shows two members of the family outside Wesson Cottage but one child is missing: either Edith or Stanley. Note the typical pocket watch and Albert chain worn by Josiah. He still wore a waistcoat and watch and chain during my childhood in the 1950s. This fascinated me: he would snap open the back of the watch and let me see inside and I marvelled at how it worked and how small and intricate the mechanism seemed to be. Josiah's watch and chain were presented to me by my parents many years after his death and I still have them and intend, in turn, that they be handed down to a younger Greatorex descendant of Josiah.

A glimpse of the lives of these people is seen here in cards. First, a few cards associated with Josiah and Jane and then some associated with their children.

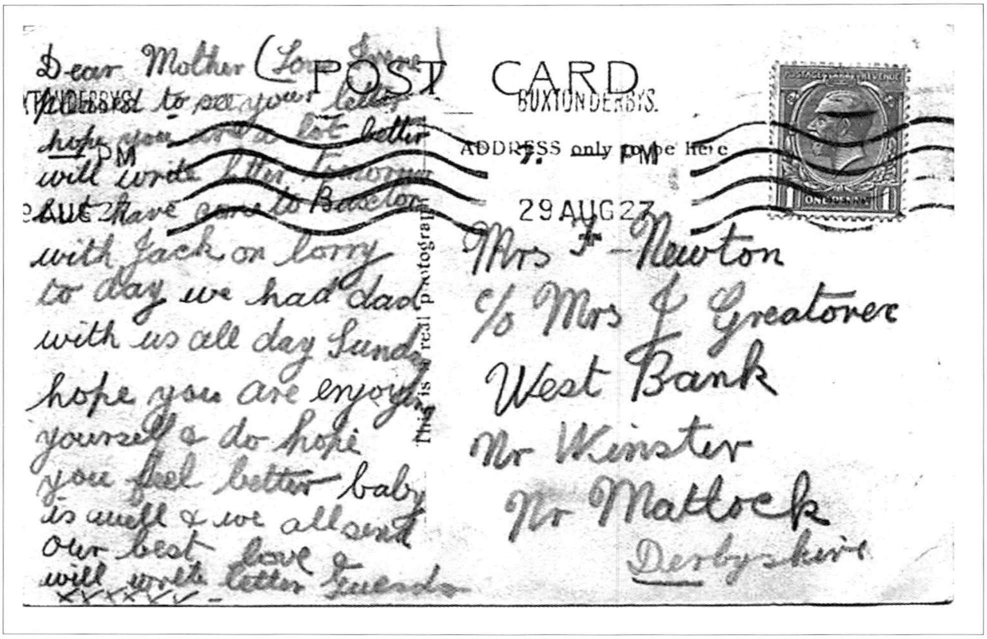

On 29 August 1927 Irene Newton (1902 – 1978) sent a card to her mother, (Josiah's sister Edith Eliza) who was staying at Wesson Cottage. Irene's father, Thomas Newton, was born in Winster in 1867 and had moved to Staveley, Derbyshire, before the 1881 Census to work in the coal industry. Irene's parents were married in Matlock in 1901. In 1911 the family were living at 14 Hartington Road, Spital, Chesterfield.

The picture side is a real photo *"General View of Buxton"* by an unidentified publisher. The message reads (with my notes added in brackets):

"Dear Mother, pleased to see your letter will write tomorrow but have come to Buxton with Jack (Holden, Irene's husband – they married in 1925) *on lorry today we had dad with us all day Sunday hope you are enjoying yourself & do hope you feel better baby is well & we all send our best love and will write letter Tuesday love Irene."*

Another of Josiah's sisters was Emily Smedley (b 1868) who had married Thomas Smedley (b1869) in 1889 – they lived at Church Street, Matlock. Emily too sent Josiah and Jane a card on an unknown date.

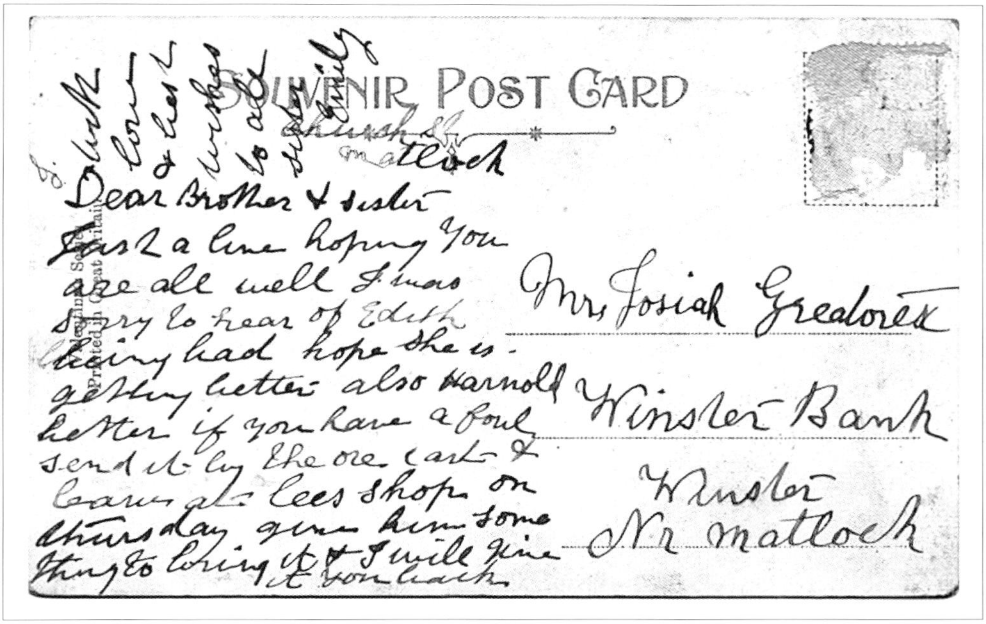

"If You Have a Fowl Send It By The Ore Cart"

A vandal has removed the postage stamp but it was posted after 1907 as the message refers to her niece, Edith, who was born in that year. The picture is a coloured view of Wingfield Manor Nod. 17462 by Valentine's. The message reads:

"Dear Brother & Sister, Just a line hoping you are all well I was sorry to hear of Edith being bad hope she is getting better. Also Arnold better if you have a fowl send it by the ore cart & leaves at lees shop on Thursday give him something to bring it & I will give it you back. With love and best wishes to all sister Emily."

Another of Jane's nieces, Annie ?, sent Jane two cards on 17 March 1924 and probably on 14 June of the same year (the year of the cancellation strike is illegible). The first card is a real photograph of Bolsover Castle (The Pelham Series) published by Boots Pure Drug Co. Ltd. and was posted from Old Whittington, Chesterfield.

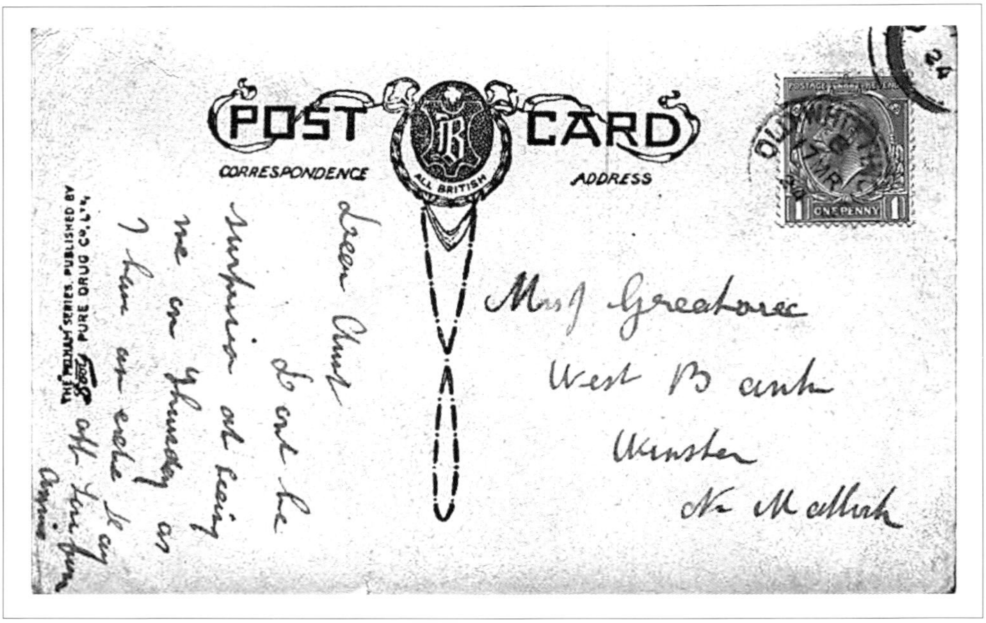

Dear Aunt From Annie 17 Mar 1924

The second card is another real photograph – this time of Chesterfield Parish Church, S.W. by an unknown publisher. It too was posted from Chesterfield.

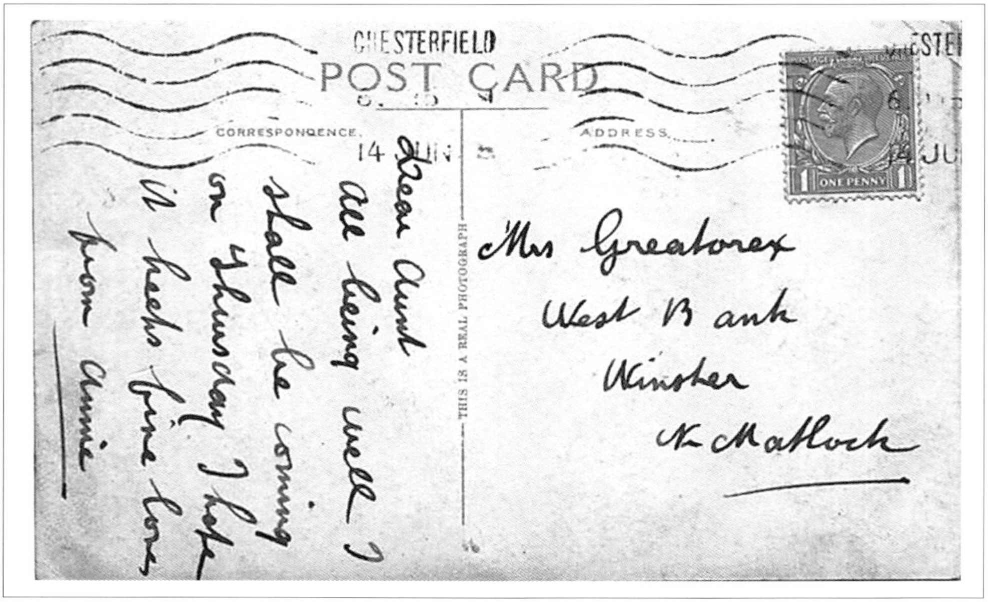

Dear Aunt From Annie 14 Jun 1924

Arnold Greatorex (1906 – 1989)

Arnold lived most of his life in Winster. As a youth he worked for a butcher and then at a quarry in Birchover. Most of his working life was spent at Longcliffe Quarries, Brassington. During World War II he served in Winster's Home Guard. He was active in village life as a morris dancer; as secretary of the Odd Fellows Friendly Society and as a darts player. In 1929 he was married in Bonsall to Harriet (Etta) Jane Gratton (1907 – 1999). The couple lived for a short time at Cromford but soon came to Winster where, at various times, they lived on West Bank, The Flat and at 10 Leacroft Road. They had five children. The couple both died in Winster and are buried in Winster Cemetery.

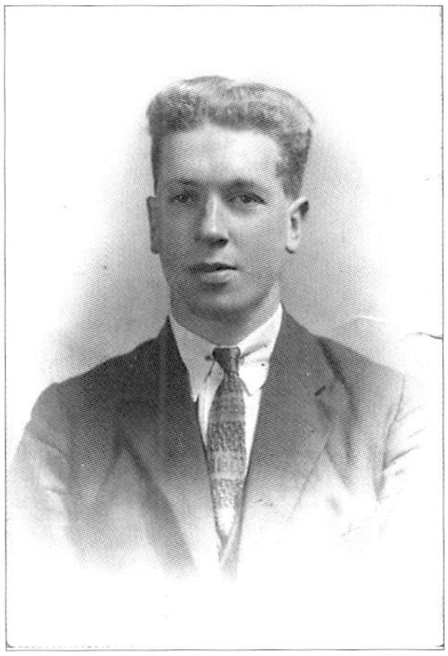

Arnold Greatorex aged c18 by J.V. Drake, Matlock

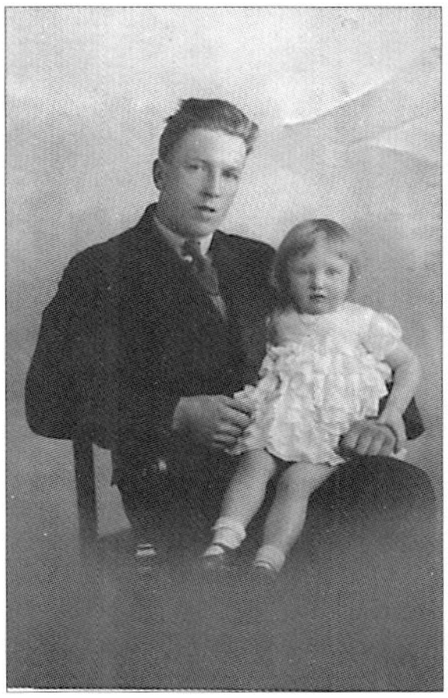

Arnold Greatorex & his daughter, Joan, c1933

The card of Arnold shows him aged about 18. It is by J.V. Drake, Matlock. For many years a framed enlargement of this image adorned Arnold's bedroom. In the other card Arnold's daughter, Joan, is shown on his knee. This is by Jerome and has a date stamp on the back: *"1 Apr 1933."* Joan was born in Wirksworth in 1931 and was still living in Winster in 2010. She sent a card to her Auntie Joyce Greatorex nee Dakin of Birchover (1916 – 1999) and Uncle Stanley on 7 August 1947.

It is a printed sepia view of Matlock Road, Ambergate, with a single vehicle in the far distance. The card was published by Raphael Tuck & Sons Ltd and is marked *"Copyright Age. 38"* at bottom left of the picture.

Joan might have been to Duffield to visit one of her relations (probably one of her mother's sisters).

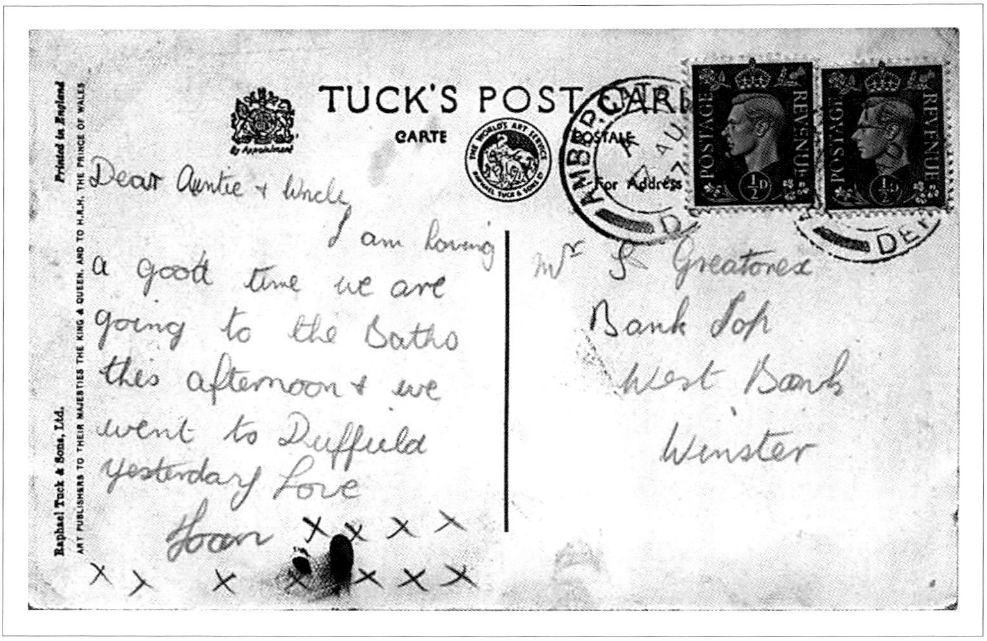

Message to Aunt and Uncle 7 Aug 1947

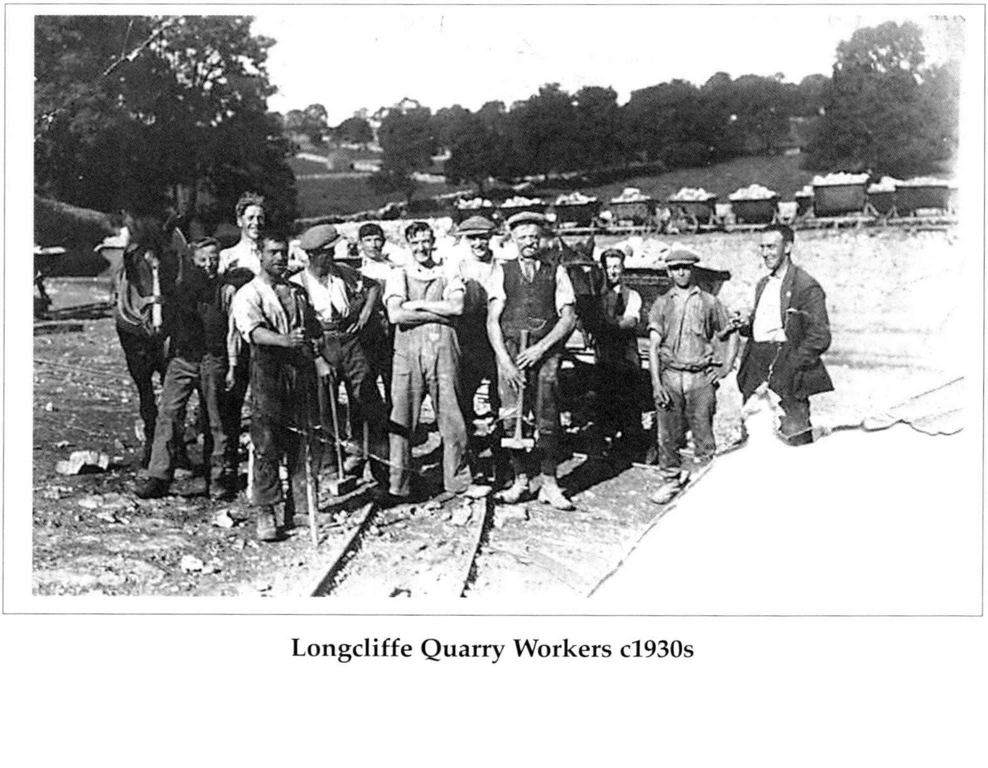

Longcliffe Quarry Workers c1930s

The damaged card of the group of quarry workers was taken at Longcliffe Quarry in the 1930s. Arnold is the tall figure second from the left at the back. Note also the horse power still being used in the quarry at this time. Arnold worked at Longcliffe for over 40 years until his retirement in 1971. At various times three of his sons also worked for the company. Following his retirement Arnold was a regular at Longcliffe reunions, usually held around Christmas time. In a photograph (not illustrated here) of one such reunion in the 1970s Arnold is the only Winster man pictured. The group undoubtedly captures some of the men in the 1930s card. One of the men, Les Allsop, is pictured holding a print of the card displayed for the camera and no doubt the subject of many nostalgic memories amongst the party who also included Jack Allsop, Denis Humphrys, George Newton, Mr. Tranter and Fred Hyde.

Edith Ann Greatorex (1907 – 1971)

Here Edith was captured by Charles Howell, Official Photographer, Pleasure Beach, Blackpool. The card is ink stamped on the back *"28 Aug 1933"* when Edith was about 26 years old. Edith was born at Wesson Cottage. She was married twice: first in 1936 to Alfred Andrews of Elton (with whom she had one son) and then to Reg. Jones. She was for many years the landlady of the Duke of York Pub, Elton.

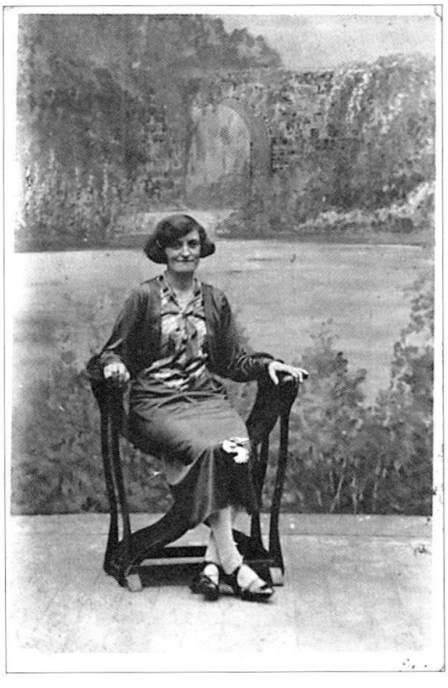

Edith Ann Greatorex aged c26 at Blackpool 1933

In 1921 Edith was the recipient of a card from her cousin, Irene Newton. The picture is a real photograph of the Hippodrome, Nottingham, No. 656 (Colonial Series) by C. & A.G. Lewis, Sherwood Street, Nottingham, and was posted on 16 June 1921 from Mansfield. The Hippodrome is in the background beyond the imposing figure of, I presume, a statesman or then local worthy atop a plinth. To the left of the Hippodrome is a building with a sign denoting the Car & General Insurance Corporation Ltd and to the right is a sign for "Rufford." Real photographic cards by Lewis are prized by some collectors.

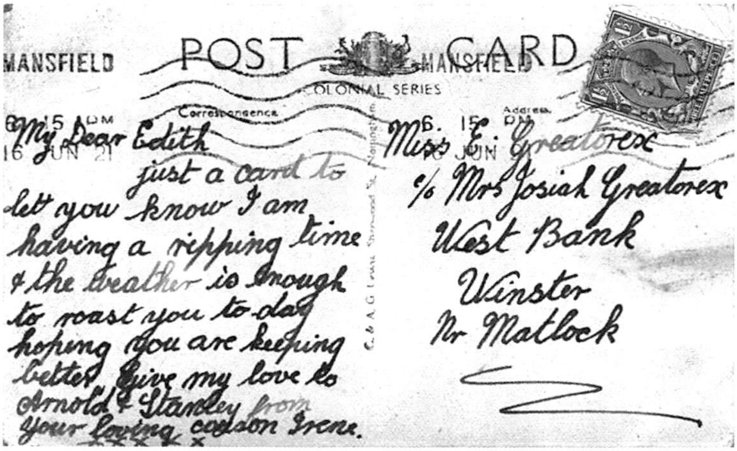

My Dear Edith From Irene 1921

Irene's message reads:

"My Dear Edith, Just a card to let you know I am having a ripping time & the weather is enough to roast you today hoping you are keeping better. Give my love to Arnold & Stanley from your loving cousin Irene."

On 9 October 1928 Edith might have been visiting relatives at Chesterfield. She sent her mother a card on this date being a real photograph of St. Mary's Church, Chesterfield, by an unknown publisher.

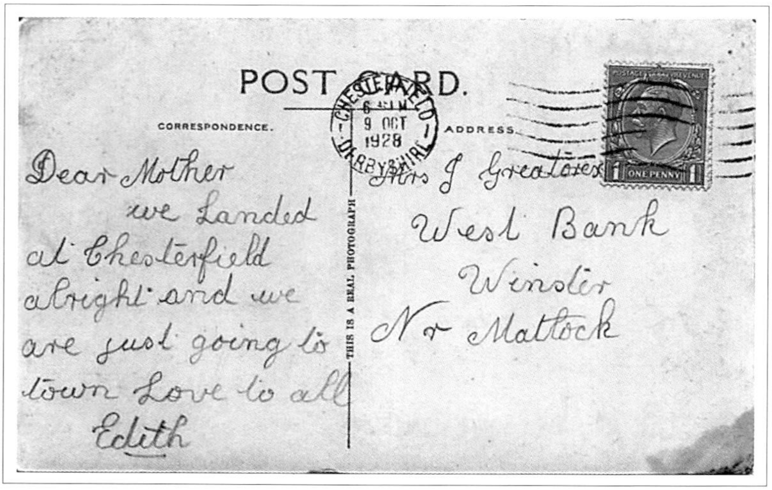

Dear Mother From Edith 1928

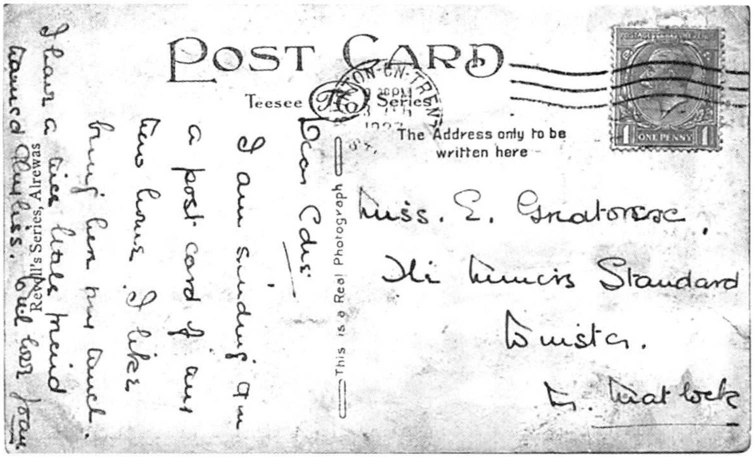

Dear Edie From Joan 1927

In 1927 Edith was sent a card addressed to her at The Miner's Standard, Winster. Was Edith working there? Again, this is yet another real photograph – this time of The Paul Pry Inn, Alrewas, Staffs, (Revell's Series, Alrewas. Nod. 129-19 at bottom left of picture.") The message is intriguing:

"Dear Edie I am sending you a post card of my new home. I like being here very much. I have a nice little maid named Phyliss. With love Joan."

Making a *"new home"* in a village Inn and with a maid too. This might interest local historians of Alrewas. The card is signed "Joan". Who was she?

In the early 1930s Edith may have been *"in service"* at the home of Dr. John and Mrs. Agnes Mary Fletcher at Green Gates (also called The Dower House), at the west end of Main Street. Dr. John Fletcher was born on 25 February 1870 in Manchester and died at Green Gates in 1955. Somewhat confusingly he had a brother who was also a medical doctor. Dr James Fletcher practised medicine in Winster whereas John was probably retired (or not practising) when he lived in the village. Mrs. Fletcher was born Agnes Mary Coates in about 1879 at South Darley. The couple were married in Winster in 1900.

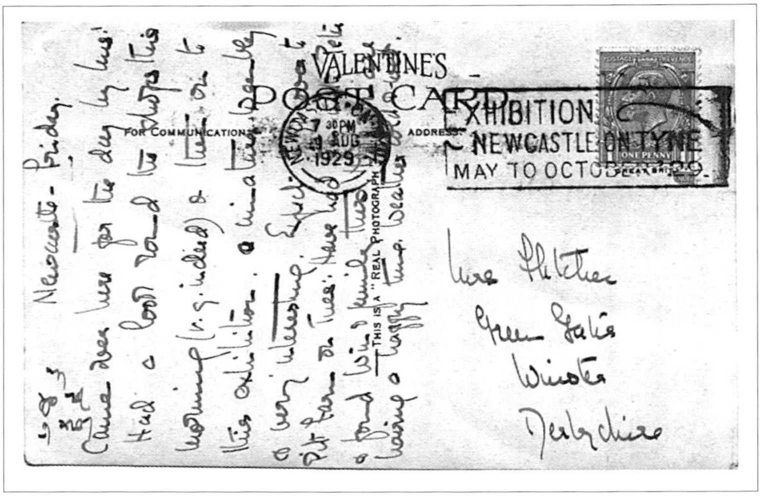

To Mrs. Fletcher From Newcastle 1929

On 9 August 1929 an unknown person sent Mrs. Fletcher this card.

The picture side is a real photograph of the main entrance, North East Coast Exhibition 1929 at Newcastle Upon Tyne. It is Nod. 206,225 JV and was published by Valentine's. The message reads:

"Came over here for the day by bus. Had a look round the shops this morning (v.g. indeed) & then on to this exhibition. A minature Wembley & very interesting. Expect ?? Pit Farm on Tuesday: have had ?? Peter and found Win and family there. ?? are having a happy time. Weather cold and wet. Love to all."

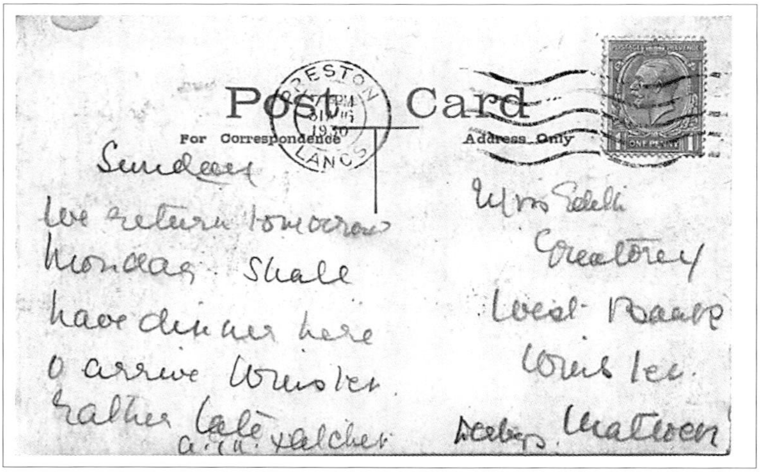

On 31 August 1930 Mrs. Fletcher was in Preston and sent Edith a card.

"We Return Tomorrow" from Preston 1930

The picture is a real photograph of the Trough of Bowland by an unknown publisher and is Nod. 20. The message reads:

"Sunday We return tomorrow Monday. Shall have dinner here and arrive Winster rather late. A.M. Fletcher."

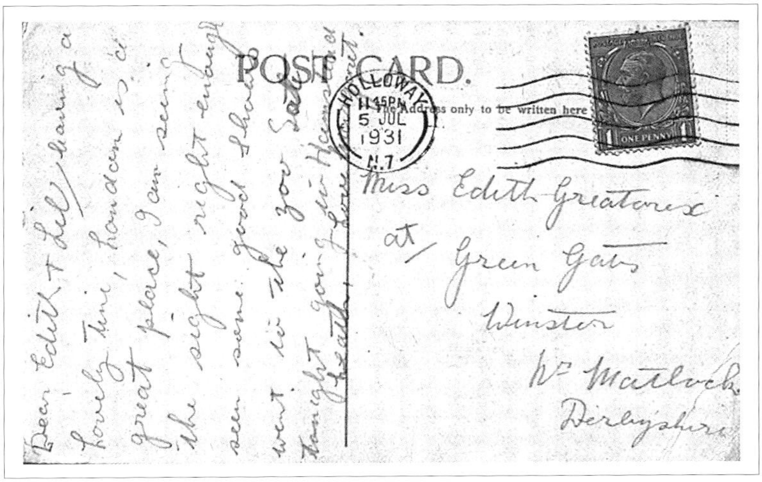

Dear Edith & Lil 1931

About the 5 July 1931 Edith was sent a card by possibly two friends, one appears to sign herself Harriet but I cannot decipher the other name. It is a printed colour card of Trafalgar Square, London, by an unknown publisher. The message reads:

"Dear Edith & Lil having a lovely time, London is a great place, I am seeing the sight right enough seen some good shows went to the zoo Sat tonight going in Hamstead Heath. Love ? Harriet."

Finally, in this section, Edith was sent a card posted on 14 July 1932 from Falmouth, Cornwall. It is a black and white photograph of Mullion Cove and is Nod. 17809 by A.H. Hawke, Helston. There is no message: I suppose the picture itself conveys the unspoken message which is: *"I have visited this place and thought of you so am sending you this card."*

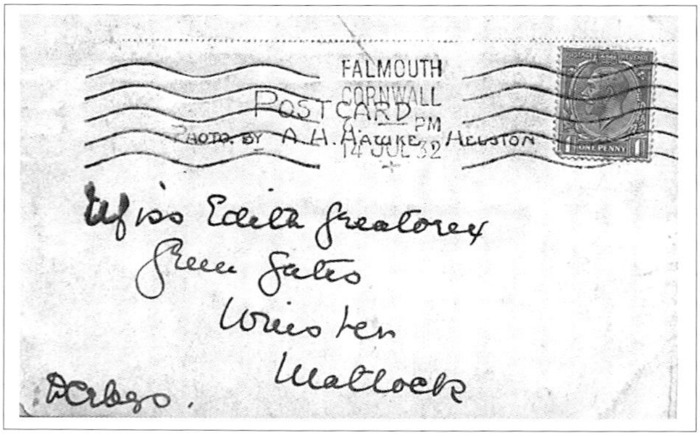

To Miss Edith From Cornwall 1932

Stanley Josiah Greatorex (1911 – 1979)

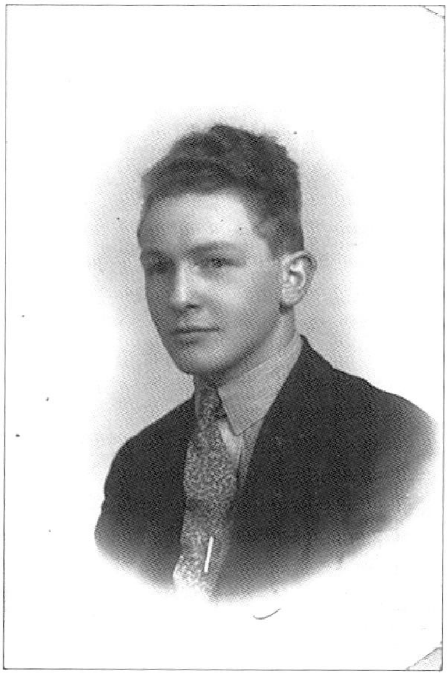

Stanley Josiah Greatorex by Statham's of Matlock

Stanley was born in Winster: in 1937 he married Joyce Dakin in Birchover and settled there. The couple had one daughter. Stan worked at Enthoven's, South Darley.

The last two cards in this Chapter are associated with my brother, Alan Greatorex.

The second card is a link with Alan's National Service during the 1950s.

During World War I conscription (National Service) of young men into the armed forces was introduced. It was also introduced again in 1939 at the start of World War II and lasted until 1960. In 1954 Arnold Greatorex's eldest son, Alan, was conscripted. Later another of his sons was also conscripted but his two youngest sons "escaped" National Service after it was abolished. In 1954 Alan was aged 18 and was summoned to start his National Service at Catterick in Yorkshire. This was probably the first time that he had made a journey of this length by public transport and was probably also his first introduction to being away from home and family. The journey from Winster involved a bus to

Matlock, a train to Derby and then another train to head north. At Derby Alan took the opportunity to send a card home (the family lived at 10 Leacroft Road) and he reported:

"Everything OK so far catching the 12.45 for Darlington then on to Richmond then bus for Catterick."

This journey undoubtedly took most of the day.

The image is a printed photo of Victoria Street, Derby, by Valentine's Nod. G2643. The damage to the card was caused by it being stuck into an album from which it has been rescued.

Alan lived in Winster until 1958 when he married and left the village.

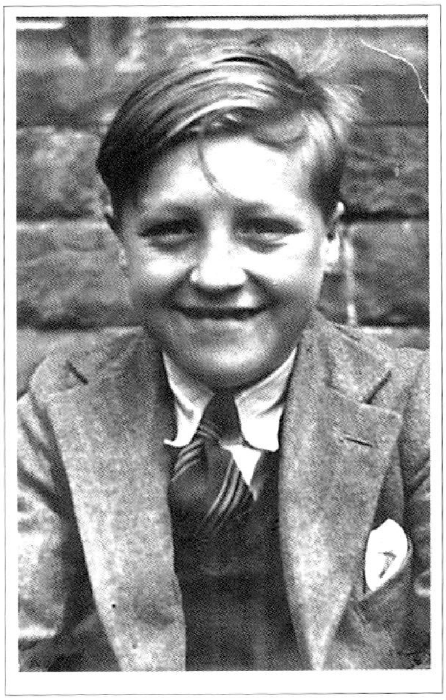

Alan Greatorex at School – 1940s by Bricklebank, Grimesthorpe Road, Sheffield

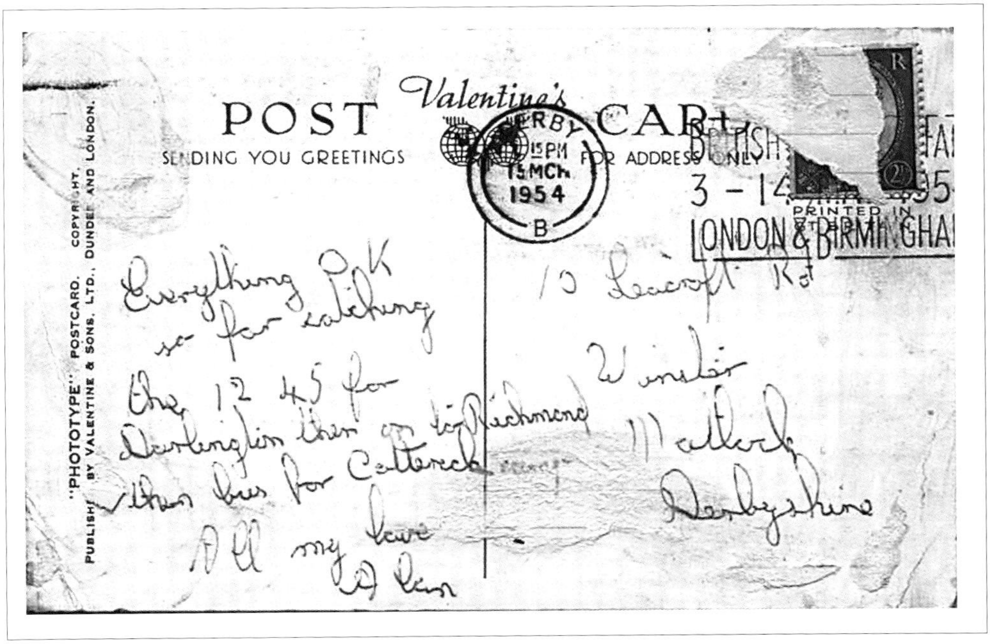

Off on National Service – "Everything O.K." at Derby!

CHAPTER 6

BILTON HOUSE & THE GREATOREX SISTERS

All of the following six postcards have associations with Bilton House, Harrogate, and Sarah Hadfield Greatorex (1883 -) and her half-sister, Bertha (1872 -1965). The sisters were in service together in the early part of the 20th century at Bilton House. In October 2009 Bilton House was occupied by The Registrar for Births, Marriages & Deaths. In the early 20th century the sisters' family home was at The Homestead, East Bank, and they had three other sisters and two brothers.

Bertha was the older of the two: she never married and died in Winster

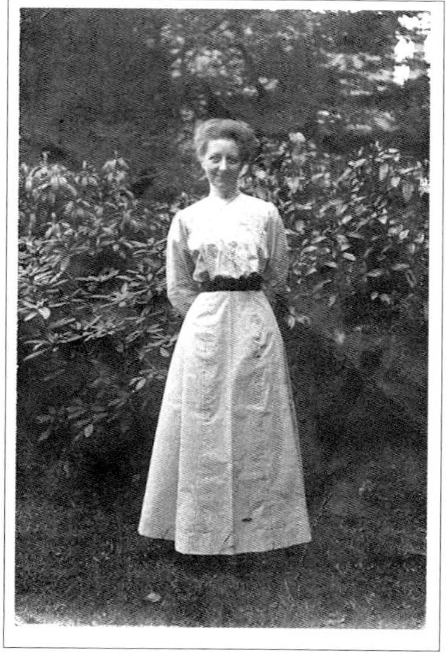

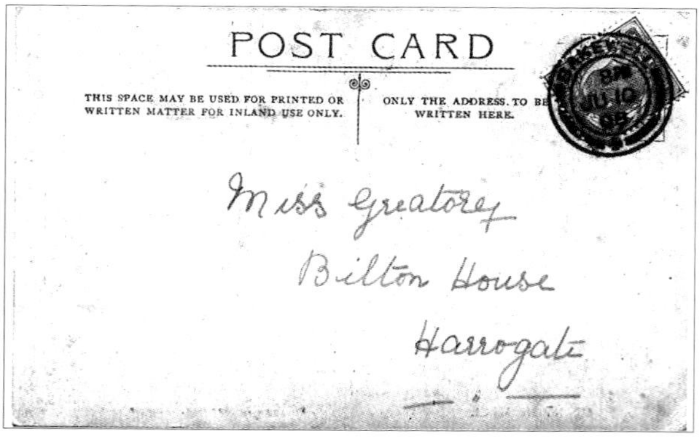

The message side of a Marshall view of Stanton Hall. Posted 10 June 1908. See also p33

Bertha Greatorex (1872 – 1965) as a young woman

in 1965. In the year of her death she was photographed as the then oldest Winster resident with an infant relative who was the then youngest Winster resident.

Sarah Hadfield Greatorex (her mother's maiden name was Hadfield) was also born in Winster. At age 18, in 1901, the Census records Sarah as a servant for Earl Halsbury in London.

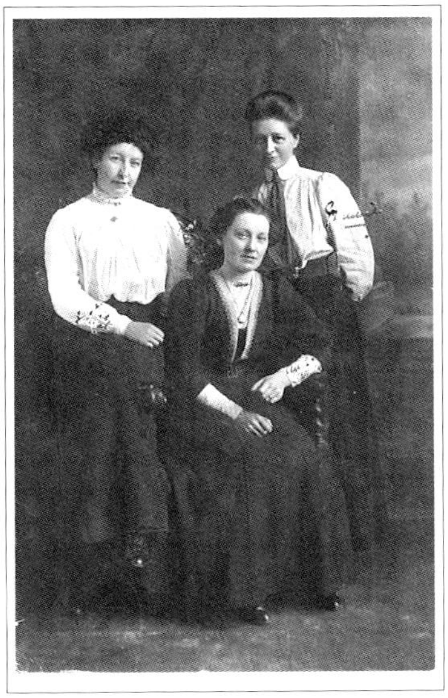

Greatorex Sisters – From left to right Ann Elizabeth (later Boam) (1888 – 1972), Kate Ethel (later Potter-Marsden) (1886 – 1946) or Sarah Hadfield (later Rodman) (b. 1883) and Bertha (1872 – 1965)

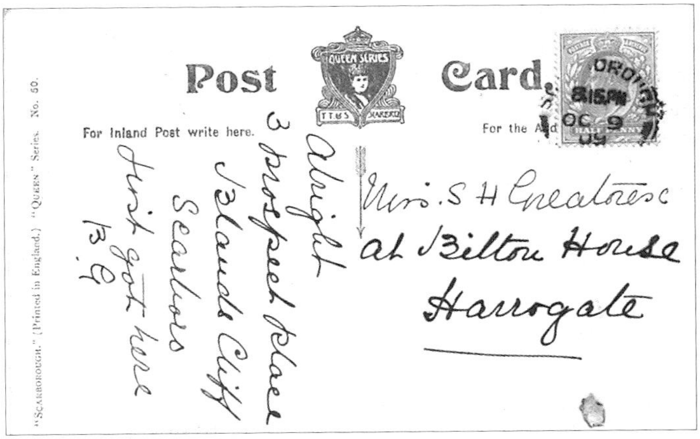

The message side a view of "The Giant Wave, Scarborough"

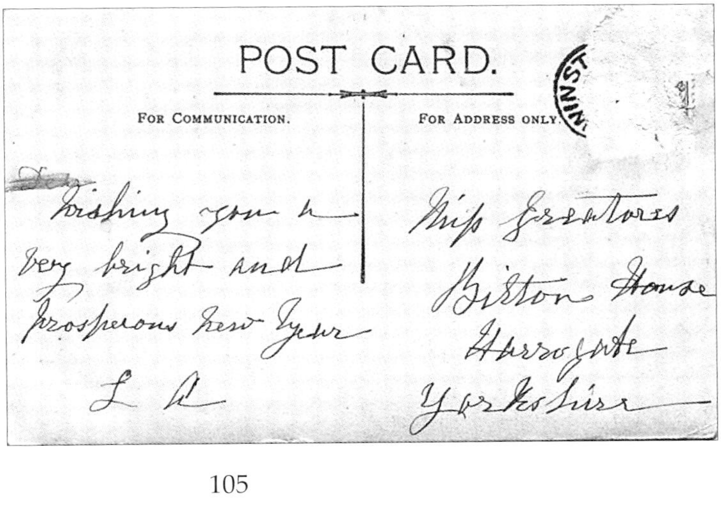

The message side of a Winster Multi-View by Marshall

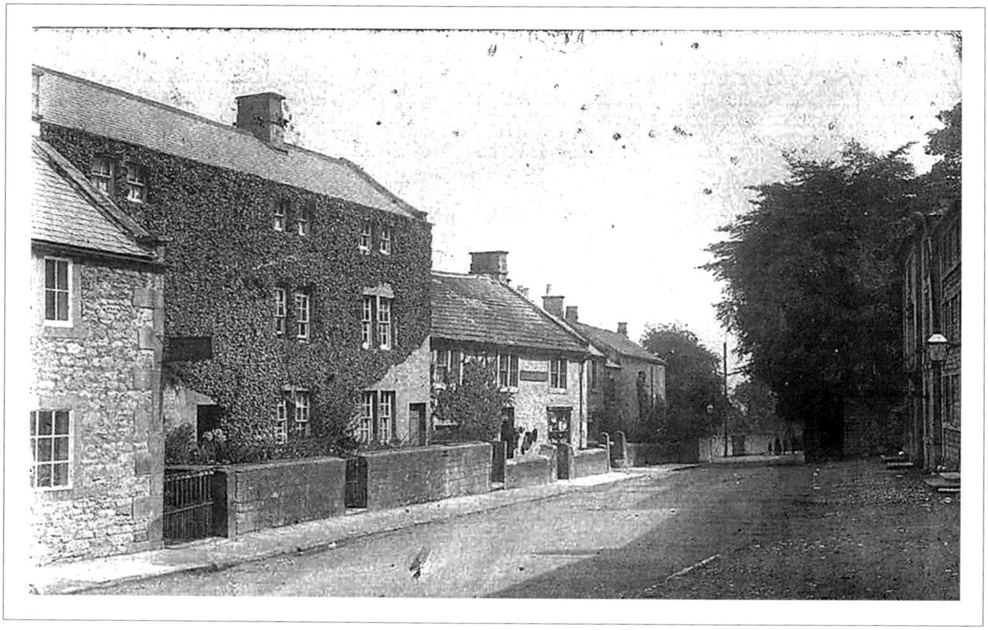

East Main Street – 1909

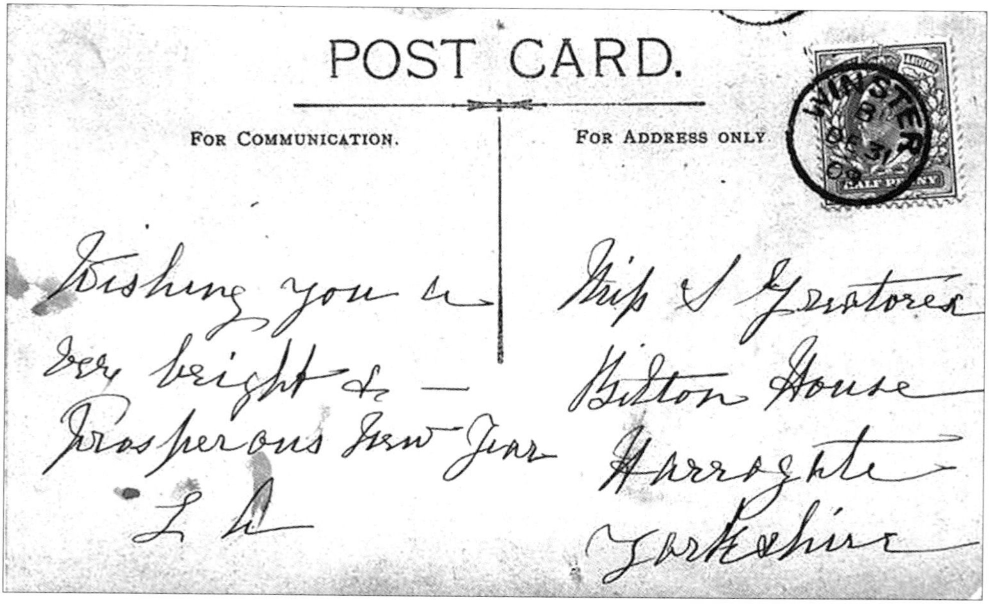

The message side of a view of East Main Street posted from Winster on 31 December 1909

In 1911 the Census captures both sisters working at Bilton House as cook/domestic and parlourmaid respectively. The head of the household was a widow, Ellen Mary Fawkes, living on private means who, incidentally, was born in Spondon, Derbyshire. In addition to Bertha there were three other parlourmaids in the household along with Mrs. Fawkes and her daughter and a male visitor from London. On 11 September 1911 Sarah was married at St. John's Church, Winster, to George Henry Rodman whom she had presumably met during her time at Harrogate.

The card of the three young women is a studio portrait by Thos. A. Cornall, Station Studios, Harrogate. Someone has written on the arms of the three subjects (probably clues to their identities) but, unfortunately, it is illegible.

In chronological sequence the cards are dated:

10 June 1908 – This is the back of a view of Stanton Hall by Marshall – you can see it on p.33. It is simply addressed to "Miss Greatorex, Bilton House, Harrogate." The card was probably sent by Sarah (b.1883) to Bertha.

9 October 1909 – This card was sent by Bertha to Sarah. The picture side (a coloured view of "*The Giant Wave, Scarborough*") is not illustrated here – interesting it is not! My thanks are due to Kath Cassey who recognised the handwriting of "*B.G*" as that of her relative, Bertha.

Undated – This is the back of a Marshall Winster multi-view – you can see it on p.17. Note immediately that a vandal has removed the postage stamp and with it the date of the cancellation strike. Compare the handwriting of the message side of this card with the message side of the card posted on 31 December 1909. The only difference is that the dated card was sent to Sarah Greatorex whereas the other card was simply addressed to "*Miss Greatorex*" without an initial. The cancellation strike on both cards appears to be the same. Was the card which now lacks the stamp/cancellation strike meant for Bertha Greatorex? Both these cards were sent by "*L.A*" or is it "*L.G.*"? I have pondered at length who this might have been. None of Sarah's sisters' first names begin with the letter "L" so we can rule them out. Sarah was related to the Gregory family of Winster who lived on West Bank. "*L.G*" might have been Lucy Gregory who was born on 28 May 1873 and who died on 23 March 1933 and is buried in Winster Churchyard.

31 December 1909 – Both the picture and message side of this card are of interest to Winster. The picture is a real photographic view of East Main Street but there is no identification of the photographer. At left was the sweet shop run by Sarah Ann Wilson (nee Hardy) who was born in 1882. Her husband, Frederick George Wilson (1880 – 1939) was a joiner and undertaker and he ran his business from the adjacent part of the building just out of shot at left (in 2010 called Carpenters Cottage and then still occupied by his daughter). Sarah and Frederick were married in Winster Parish Church on 16 October 1902. Their sons worked in the business with their father. There is a sign hanging from the gable wall but, tantalisingly, it is illegible on the card. Further down the Street at about left centre of the card was Gilding's Ironmonger's shop run by John Gilding (1888 – 1968) with the assistance of his wife, Alice Emmeline (nee Smith) (1898 – 1989). Again, there is an illegible shop sign. This shop was active well into the 1950s. In the far distance a wall is visible on the left fronting Wensley Road – this wall lasted until the early 1950s when it was demolished to provide a green frontage to the Leacroft Road Estate the front row of which facing Wensley Road was completed by the late 1940s.

CHAPTER 7

FRIENDLY SOCIETIES

Winster had a number of Friendly Societies of which the Buffaloes, the Foresters and the Odd Fellows were prominent. They played an important role in the social and economic life of the village in the late 19th and early 20th centuries. They were (and still are) mutual aid organisations protecting their members against hardship. The Friendly Societies Act 1875 made provision for auditing as well as registration and by the late 1870s about 27,000 Lodges were registered. The Societies and their Branches (called Lodges in the case of the Odd Fellows and Courts in the case of the Foresters) were governed by Rules which provided for the rights of members but also what was expected of them. For instance, in 1864 the "*anniversary*" of the Odd Fellows in Winster was the subject of a Rule which required every member, except the sick and those residing more than 5 miles from Winster, to attend the anniversary or to send a proper substitute and all members were expected to walk to church. If this Rule was not draconian enough it went on to prescribe that "*no part of the expenses to be taken out of any funds of the society*." Thus the members were expected to pay for their own anniversary meal. It seems that the Odd Fellows anniversary was celebrated in mid-Summer at the same time as Winster Wakes. On 8 July 1863 the *Derby Mercury* reported:

"*Winster. The Wakes – This annual feast was kept up as heretofore with unusual energy; a large number of relations and friends from a distance were brought once more together, and the enjoyment of it was uninterrupted by any unpleasant disturbance. The Odd Fellows Club was held at the Crown, where a substantial and luxuriant dinner was provided by the landlord, Mr. Joshua Burton; 80 members sat down to it, and the Youlgrave band, which has much improved, added to the enjoyment of the cheerful feast. This club is now a thriving one, with every prospect of progressing."*

Joshua Burton (1830 – 1891), the landlord, mentioned in the *Derby Mercury* report was married in 1861 in Winster Church to Phoebe Shaw (1833 – 1898) of Bradnop, Staffs. Joshua died at High Lees, Lea, Derbyshire, and his wife at Lenton Boulevard, Nottingham. The couple had four children. The family were buried in Winster Churchyard where a magnificent, well-preserved headstone marks their burial plot.

The importance of the Friendly Societies' Anniversary Feast, and the attendant celebrations associated with it, is eloquently described in typical Victorian prose in a report in *The High Peak News* for 12 July 1873. It is worth quoting at length:

"On Monday the Win Tor Court of the Ancient Order of Foresters held at the house of Mr. Boam, the "Shoulder of Mutton Inn" its annual feast. The members having assembled formed themselves into a procession, and headed by their new and magnificent banner and by the Birchover Band marched along the principal street to the venerable old market house, and then returned to church where an appropriate sermon was preached. Divine service being over the procession was re-formed and preceded as before by the banner and the band, marched up to the "Shoulder of Mutton." Here a sumptuous dinner was laid in the club room which, thanks to the liberality of the landlord (Mr. Boam) had been considerably enlarged, to this the Foresters at once repaired. The chair was taken by Mr. Jewitt, of Winster Hall, supported by Dr. Cantrell and other visitors; and the dinner, which was served in excellent style was done ample justice to by the company, numbering about sixty persons, who were present. On removal of the cloth the chairman gave the usual loyal toasts in effective speeches, which were warmly responded to. He next gave "Success to the Win Tor Court of Ancient Foresters," and in the course of his speech alluded to the increase in the number of members, the enlargement of the club room, the satisfactory state of the funds, and the small amount of sickness which had occurred since the last annual meeting. He also gave excellent and practical advice to the members both senior and junior, on matters touching the well-being of the Court. The other toasts were, "the health of the Chairman" (given with musical honours) to which he cordially responded; "the health of Mr. Hunt the district secretary of the Order," to which that gentleman responded; "the health of the Visitors," and "the health of Mr. Boam," in proposing which the chairman eulogised the dinner and the liberal spirit Mr. Boam had

displayed in enlarging the room. In the evening the club accompanied by the band and the beautiful banner, paraded the village, the band playing a selection of music at each of the principal houses. The same evening the Winster band also visited the principal houses and paraded the streets accompanied by some grotesquely dressed and masked figures. At dusk a brilliant and very extensive display of fireworks through the liberality and kindness of Messrs. A. and H. Brittlebank, took place at Oddo. It was one of the largest and best displays which has taken place in Winster and the evening being fine the effect was remarkably good."

Phew! This gives the impression that the members had a remarkably good day. The marking of the anniversary and the parading of the banner continued and has been captured on cards. I participated in a Wakes Sunday parade as a child in 1955 in support of the Odd Fellows banner and was captured by a photographer. Sadly, my copy does not have a postcard back! (See the image on p.117.)

The Friendly Societies influence declined as the State and trades unions and charities made provision for many welfare services which we now

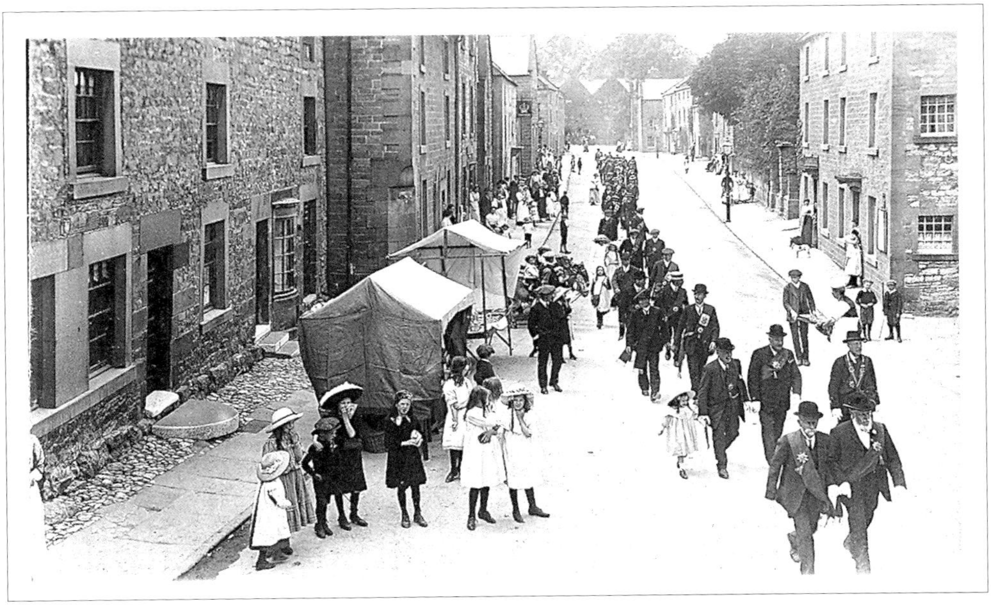

Men parading wearing Friendly Society regalia but no banners in evidence. Donkeys wait patiently at mid-left. Are the two men at mid-right carrying refreshments towards one of the stalls?
Postcard reproduced by courtesy of Eileen Crowder

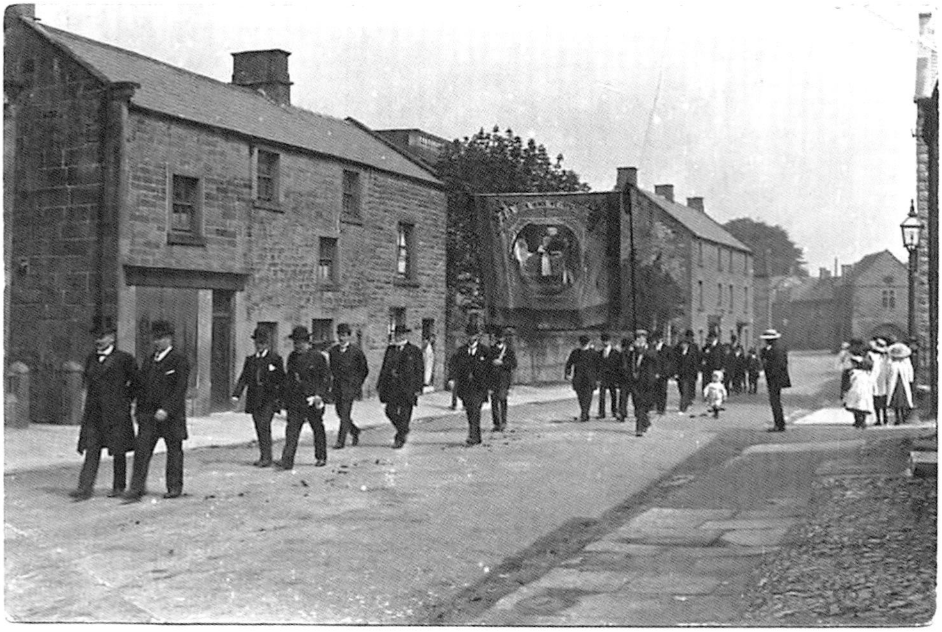

Foresters parading on Main Street

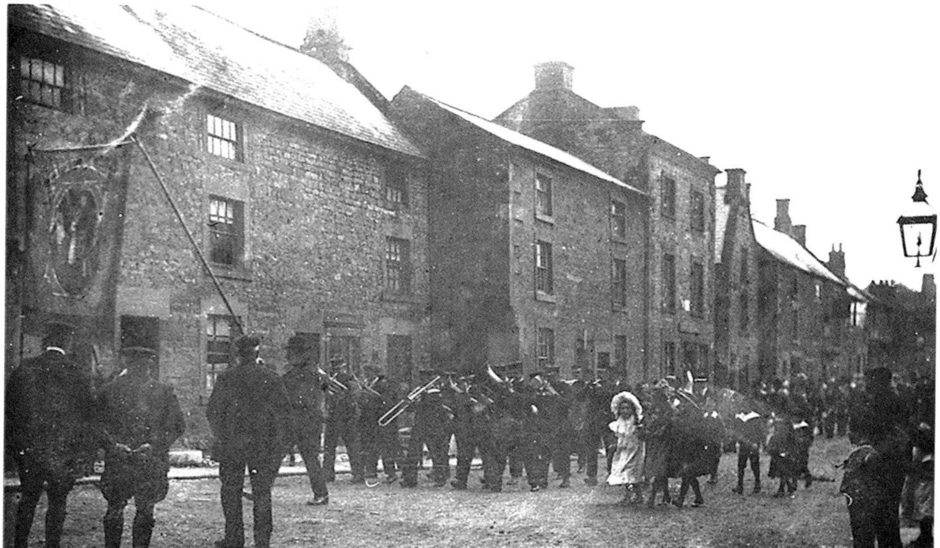

Foresters banner at left – the two men at left appear to be in military uniform

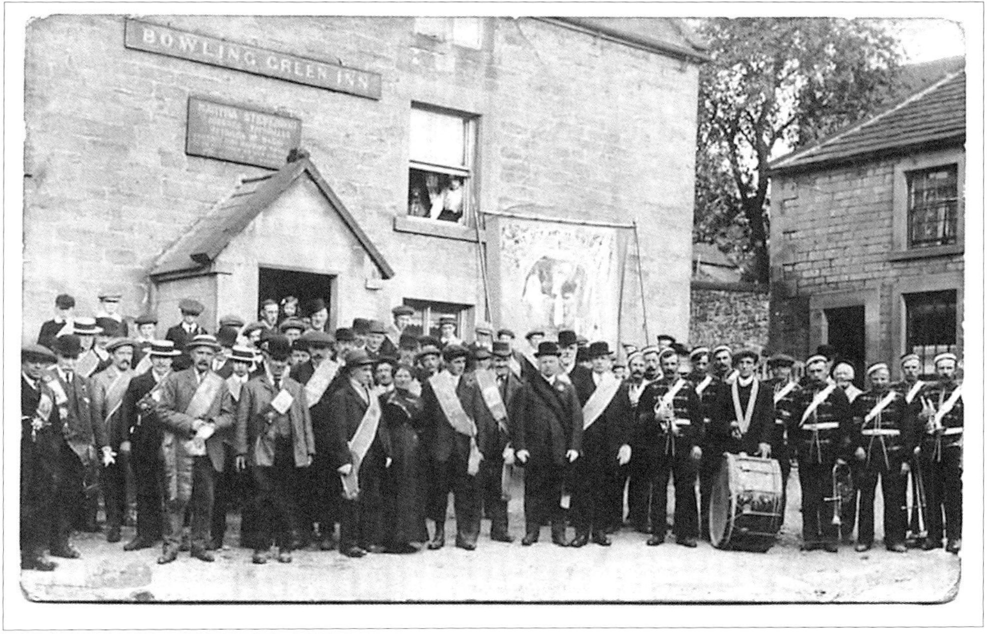

Foresters and a band outside the Bowling Green c1910.
The pub sign shows that Martha Stevenson was the landlady

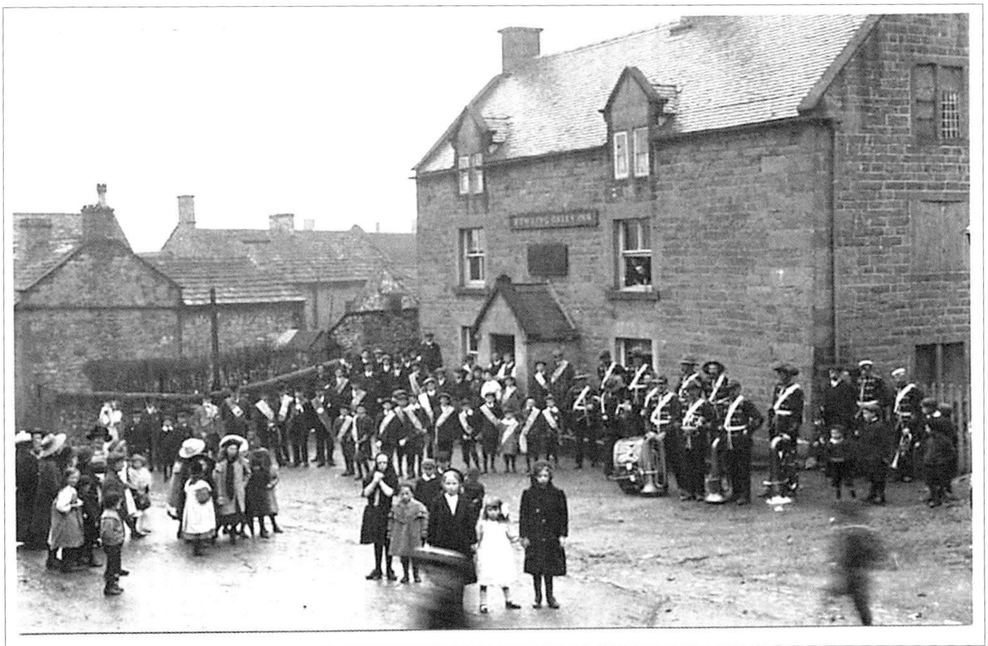

Compare this image (not a postcard) with the previous one. Was this image and the previous postcard image both taken on the same day?

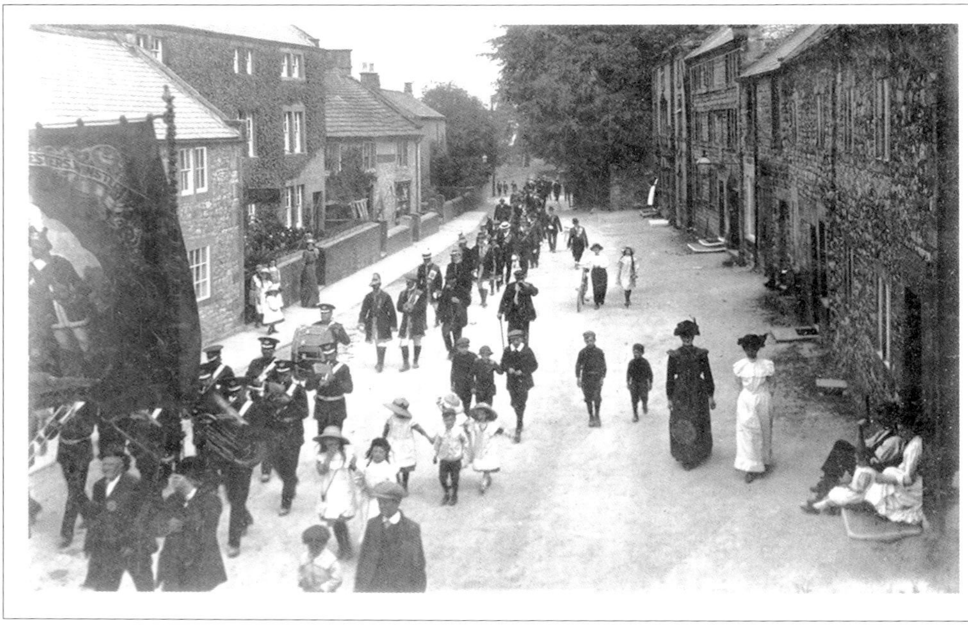

Foresters parading towards Market House along Main Street East. Note the signs outside the joiner/undertaker's and ironmonger's premises at left. A metal fence appears to run atop the wall outside Vernon House and Cottage at left

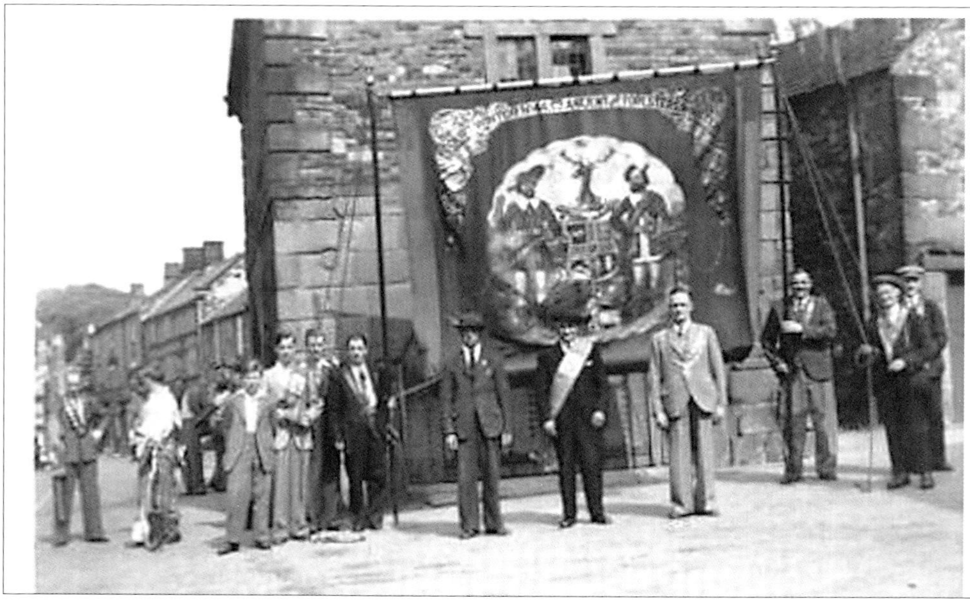

Win Tor Banner outside Market House in early 1950s. Cedric Ellis, Greg Boam, Bernard Stone, next 3 unidentified, Ben Brassington, Dan Ingman and Walter Bacon. Photograph reproduced by courtesy of Eric Brassington

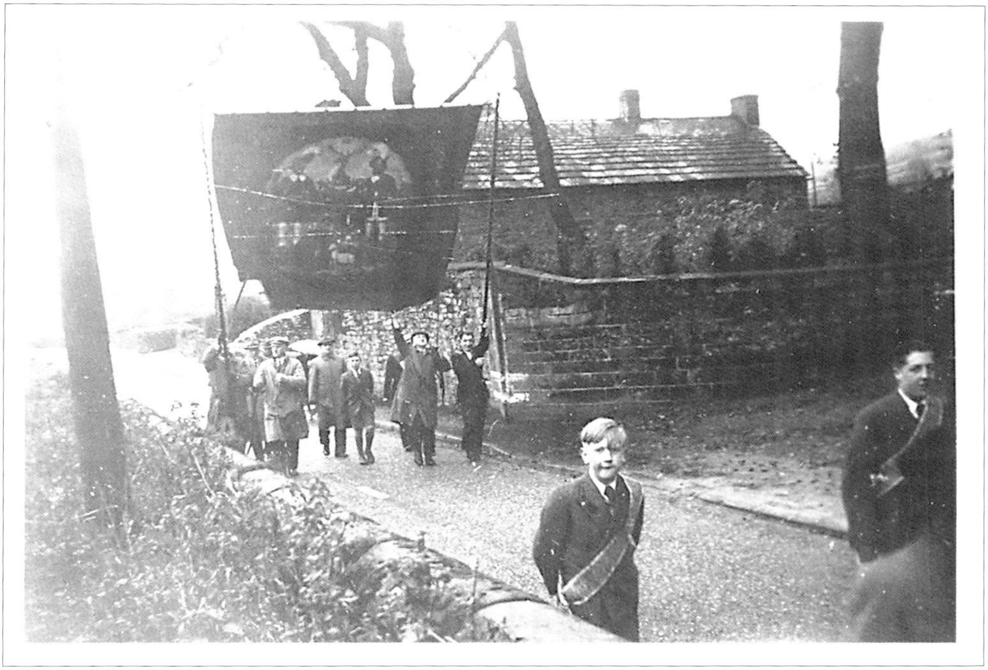

Win Tor Banner parading in Wensley Road 1950s. The boy immediately underneath the banner is Cedric Ellis, the man reaching upwards is Dan Ingman and the man at right carrying the pole is Bernard Stone. The boy at front right is Ron Greatorex and the youth at extreme right is Alan, Ron's brother (both brothers of the author).
Photograph reproduced by courtesy of Eileen Crowder

take for granted. However, although many of the small Branches have been incorporated into larger Branches, the Friendly Societies have survived into the 21st century and continue to provide limited financial benefits and welfare support for members and opportunities for them to socialise (or holiday) with other members.

The Foresters

The Winster Branch, (known as a "*Court*") was formed in 1864 as the "*Wintor Court No. 4453 of the Ancient Order of Foresters*" as part of the Derbyshire Central District of Foresters and met in the latter part of the 19th Century at The Shoulder of Mutton on West Bank where the landlord was John Boam. Meetings continued to be held there until 1898. The Court was still active in Winster in 2009 with meetings then held at the Bowling Green.

In 1901/1902 the venue for meetings was the Public Hall on West Bank (now the Burton Institute). For the next nine years to 1912 meetings were held at the Crown Inn on Main Street and then until 1939 at the Market House.

In 1871 membership numbered 32 and the average age of members was 36. Membership grew and by 1911 had reached 113; by 1939 it stood at 403. The day to day operation of the Foresters was in the hands of local court members of whom the secretary and treasurer were influential.

The identity of the founding secretary has not yet been traced but by 1871 the secretary was William Wild (1814 – 1886). He was a Draper living in Wood Lane and held office until 1881. He is buried in Winster Churchyard. Like many people in 19th century Winster, William was born in the village. Indeed, even as late as 1901 (the Census year) there were 567 people living in Winster of whom 405 (71.42%) had been born there.

From 1881 to 1885, Thomas Ingman (1837-1909) was secretary. He was born in Middleton By Wirksworth and lived in Winster from at least 1871 to 1901. Next, from 1885 to 1919, Thomas Henry Ellis (1861-1939) was secretary. In 1901 he lived on Main Street and was a railway clerk. Then in 1920 there was John Henry Barnsley who was probably born in 1851. He was followed in 1923 by T.H. Ellis again who had another long stint until 1939.

From 1889 to 1890, the treasurer was J. Stone and then for seven years to 1898 it was Edward Allen (1859-1914). He too lived all his life in Winster. From 1901 to 1913 the job was done by J. Bateman and from 1914 to 1939 (except 1920) it was J. Barnsley's turn.

The Odd Fellows

The Winster Lodge (Branch) had a grand name which intrigued me as a child:

"The Loyal Triumphant Hope Lodge No 1543, Wirksworth District, of the Independent Order of Odd Fellows, Manchester Unity."

As a child I wondered what an *"Odd Fellow"* was and am still inclined to the view that it is an unusual name. It leads to the confusion as to the correct spelling? It is "*Oddfellow*" as used on the official web site in February 2010? It seems to have been a problem down the ages: in 1863 the local press used "*Odd Fellows*" and the printed 1872 rules of the Winster Juvenile Friendly Society also referred to "*Odd Fellows*" but then in 1949 Winster used "*Oddfellows*" on the printed balance sheet and as late as 1973 "*Odd Fellows*" cropped up again in printing tickets for attendees at the national Annual Conference. My preference throughout is to use "*Odd Fellows*" for no other reason than whimsy.

The Winster Lodge was established in 1838. My father, Arnold Greatorex (1906 – 1989) was a member from 1924 and was Secretary and Sick Paymaster from at least 1949 to 1977. My 1950s childhood memories are legion of him working in his spare-time on the Lodge's business. During the 1950s membership was in severe decline. My father kept informal minutes of meetings; often just a note of the date and venue (Bowling Green) and the numbers of members attending: some-

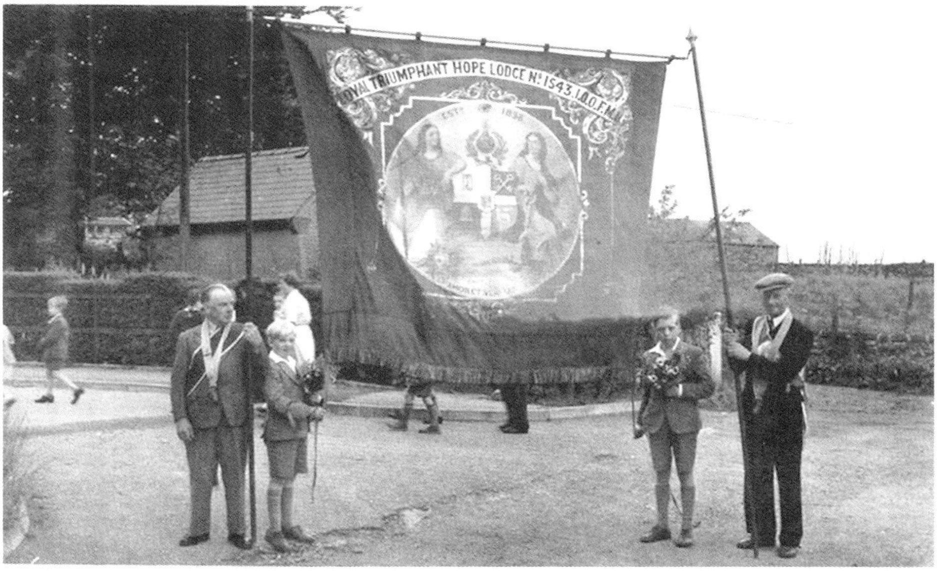

Odd Fellows Banner at bottom of Leacroft Road – Wakes Sunday 1955.
From left to right William Henry Gregory (1899 – 1956), the author, Kenneth Greatorex (1943 – 2003) and Arnold Greatorex (1906 – 1989). Arnold was the Odd Fellows Secretary and Sick Paymaster and the two boys his sons.
In the background the boy striding left is John Wint and the girl in the white dress is Janet Staton

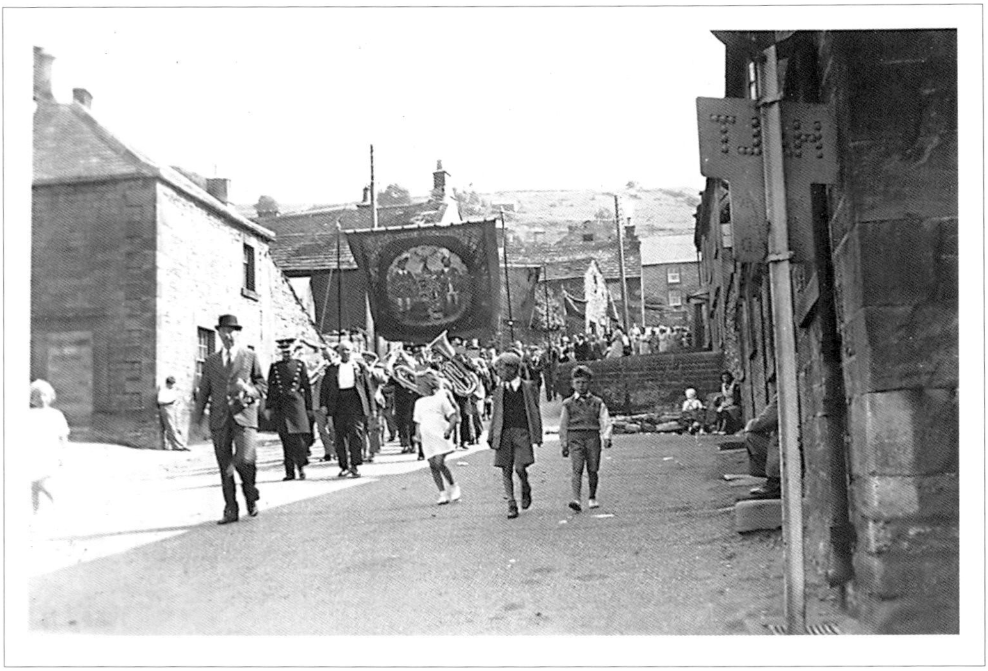

Parade down East Bank 1950s. Dr. A. D. Stoker (1909 – 1993) leads the parade followed by the Foresters' banner and that just visible behind was no doubt that of the Odd Fellows. The boy in the group of 3 children at centre-right is the author's brother, Kenneth Greatorex (1943 – 2003)

times 'two or three'. Occasionally there was a note of 'poor attendance', and once 'worse than ever'. It must have been a thankless task for him to try and keep the Lodge going. But times were a-changing. In 1977 the business of the Lodge was transferred to The Offspring of Hope Lodge No. 209 based in Matlock, which itself was transferred in 1987 to The Loyal Devonshire Lodge No. 396 in Bakewell, which in turn was transferred in 1990 to the Derbyshire Peak Lodge No. 10049 in Chesterfield. This latter now includes the interests of Winster's former Lodge and all those Odd Fellows Lodges in Winster's neighbouring villages which too must have suffered greatly from a loss of membership.

After my father's death in 1989 my mother told me about "3 or 4 old suitcases of Odd Fellow papers found around the house" and wanted to know what she should do with them. She knew of my interest in Winster's local history so I hastened to recover them from her. I then

only had time to glance at the contents but that was enough to convince me of two things; firstly, many of the papers were not just my father's personal Odd Fellow memorabilia but included papers which had historical significance, not just to Winster, but to the Odd Fellows movement. I would need plenty of time to review this material but decided that the task would have to wait until I had that time. It subsequently involved tracing the successor Lodges to Winster to establish the current Lodge now responsible for Winster's Odd Fellows heritage. In the meantime the old suitcases were stored in my own loft. Some years later I set about the task of reviewing all this material. I eventually traced Winster's successor lodge and surrendered the material to it having got an assurance that some of it would be deposited at Derbyshire Record Office for access by the public. I got the Odd Fellows permission to publish a single volume Register of Winster Members from 1838 (the year the Lodge was formed) through to 1914. This Register gave the name of the member, his age and trade and residence and the names of his proposer. I transcribed the Register and it was subsequently kindly published online by Dawn Scotting and could still be accessed online in February 2010 at
http://winster-ancestry.blogspot.com/2009/05/oddfellows-members.html
The original Register has been deposited at Derbyshire Record Office.

During the 76 years covered by the Register 280 men applied for membership. The dominant trade mentioned was that of Miner which is unsurprising. The earliest name recorded is that of Ralph Staley on 28 July 1838. Only a small number came from the professional classes. Mr Hampton, a Surgeon, joined in 1839, and Mr B[enjamin] Brittlebank, was made an Honorary Member in 1840. Joseph Thomas, aged 18, a pupil teacher and resident at Sabine Hay [near Mill Close Mine] joined in 1897; Albert Marshall, aged 18 and a printer, joined in 1910. We have already met him and his father many times in this book. A junior lodge, known as 'The Bowling Green Juvenile Friendly Society No. 13064 of the Independent Order of Odd Fellows, Manchester Unity', was established in July 1872. Accounts survive for the three years ending 4 December 1875.

Membership of Friendly Societies probably followed established family allegiance and there was rivalry over issues such as membership. An aspect of inter-lodge rivalry can be detected from the record of a special meeting of the Odd Fellows at the Bowling Green on 1 June

1880, where it was resolved by a large majority to remove the Triumphant Hope Lodge from the House of William Staley, Bowling Green Inn, to the house of John Taylor, the Angel Inn. Application was made by the Lodge on 4 September that year to the Officers and delegates of the Wirksworth District Committee for permission to 'remove' the Lodge in accordance with the above resolution, on the grounds that "*the younger part of our members say that they will go and enter into the Foresters sooner than be forced to come here*."

In dealing with the surrender of the papers to the Chesterfield Lodge I discovered that my own membership had lapsed. As a tribute to the work done for the Odd Fellows by my father and the historical legacy he had been a party to preserving (the first Register of Members amongst other documents), I was proud to re-join the Odd Fellows and once again became a member in 2004. Alas, I was unable to join the Winster Lodge (as it no longer existed) but am content to be a member of the Lodge which serves the area in which I presently live.

In pursuing my interest in Winster Odd Fellows I discovered that a book was being prepared by Daniel Weinbren supported by the Odd Fellows to mark the bicentennial (1810-2010). I drew Winster's Odd Fellows legacy to Mr. Weinbren's attention and was pleased that he subsequently included the Wakes Sunday 1955 image mentioned above in his book. My father would smile wryly if he knew that a brief mention of Winster's Odd Fellows was included in the official history of The Odd Fellows spanning 200 years.

CHAPTER 8

OUTDOOR EVENTS

This Chapter records some of Winster's Edwardian and later outdoor celebrations. The Maypole Dancing is c1907 and shows a scene at the back of the Market House. The group of *"Robin Hood"* characters probably dates to c1911.

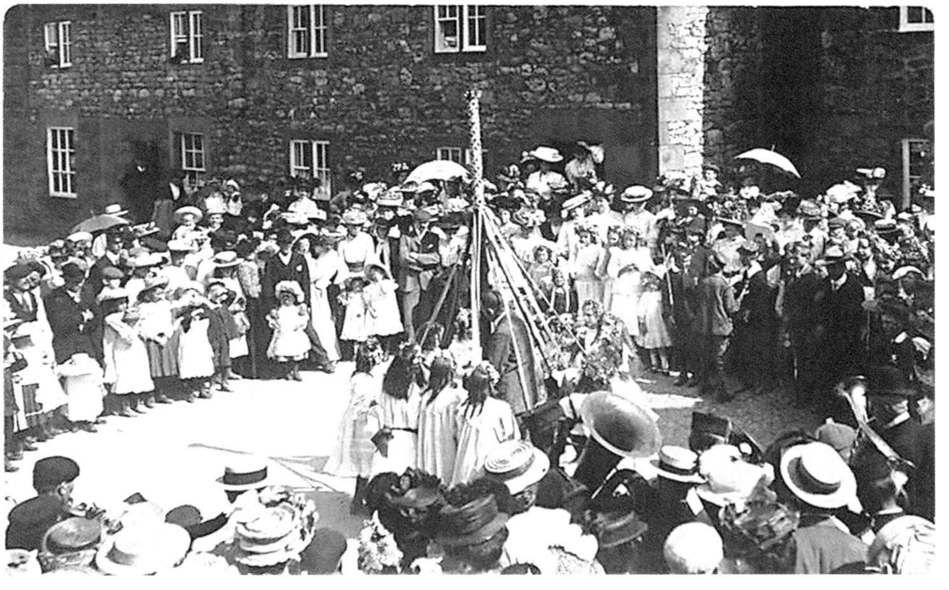

Maypole Dancing c1907 at back of Market House

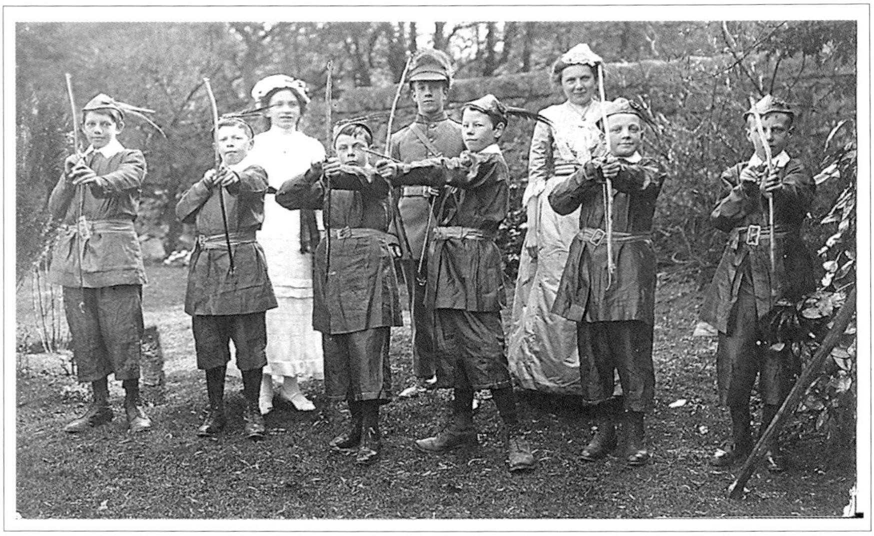

Six "Robin Hoods" c1911. The boy third from left is Wm. Henry Gregory (1899 – 1956) and the boy fifth from left is Joe "Pea" Rains

The *High Peak News* for Saturday, 12 July 1913, reports in detail Winster's Flower Queen Festivities for that year. The article is a teasure-trove for family historians as not only does it describe the events but it names the organisers and the participants including what the latter wore and the themes that their costumes depicted. For instance, the *High Peak News* reports that Mrs. Fletcher was the organising secretary and that the "*Apple Blossom Queen*" was Miss Dorothy Nixon.

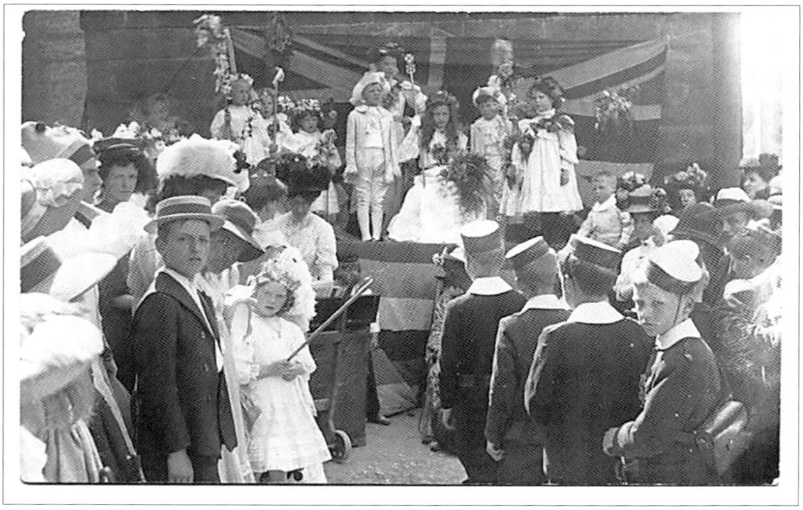

Crowning of Flower Queen (Carrie Walker) c1912 in Market Place

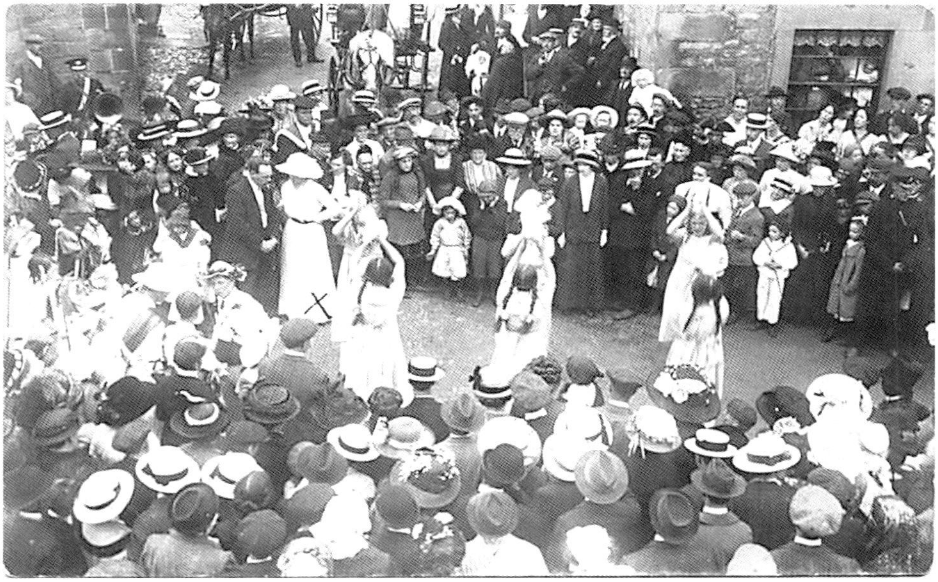

Flower Queen Festivities 1913. The woman in the dress marked X was probably Mrs. Emma Fletcher. Image reproduced by courtesy of Roland Corfield

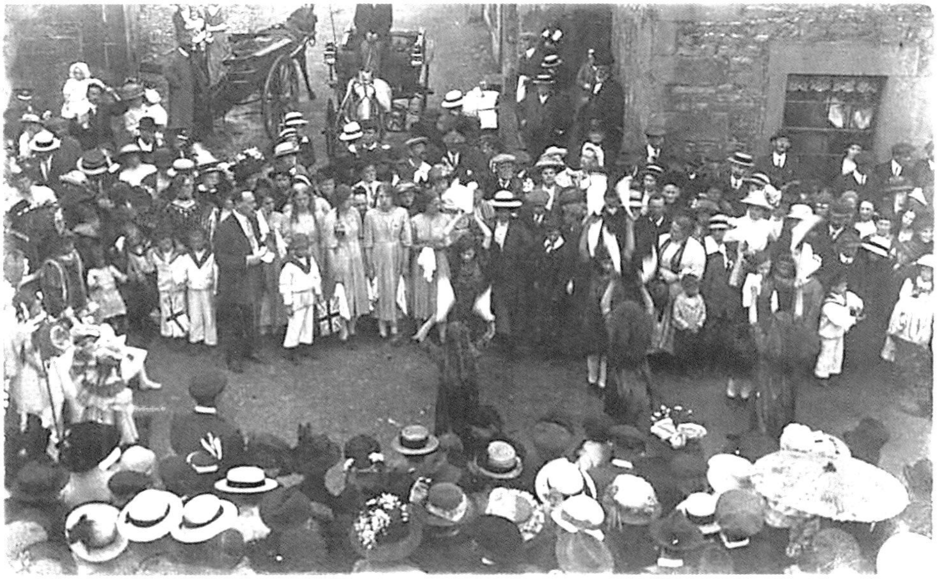

Flower Queen Festivities 1913 – Dancing in the Market Place. Image reproduced by courtesy of Roland Corfield

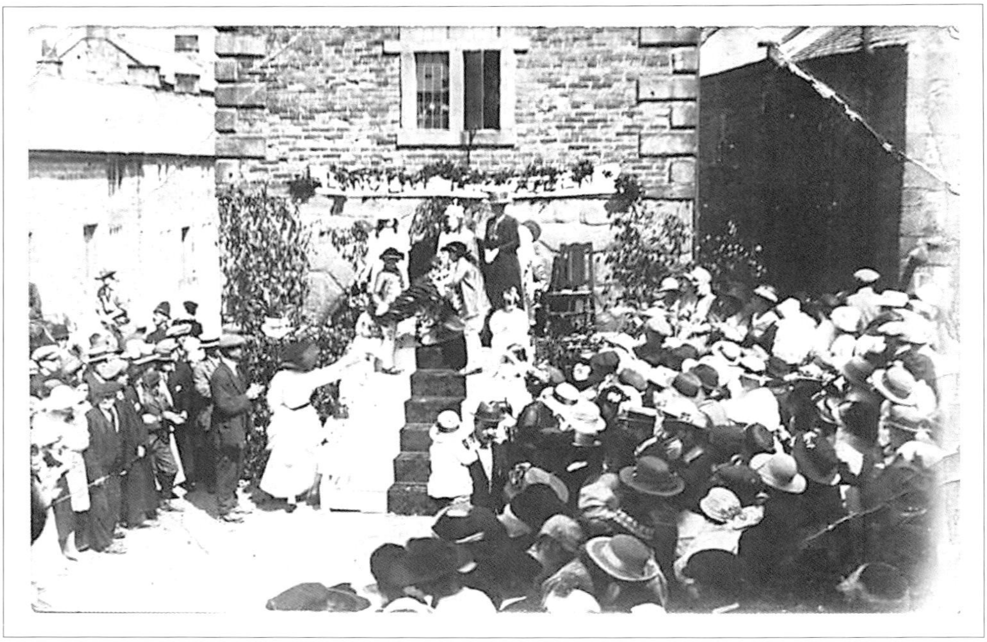

Flower Queen Festivities 1913

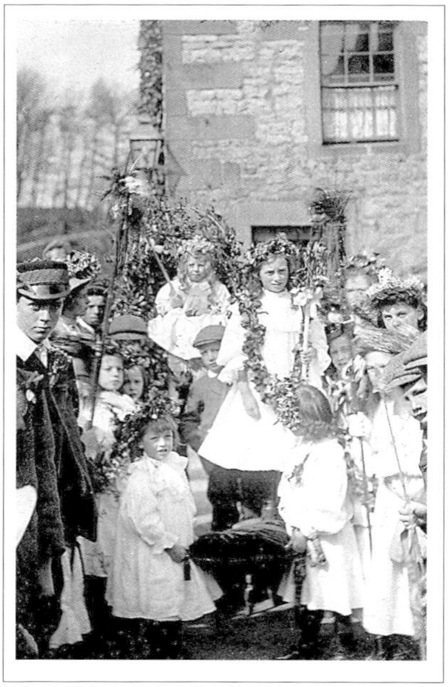

Flower Queen And Retinue – Possibly on upper East Bank

Look closely at the two cards showing dancers in the Market Place. They probably show scenes from the 1913 festivities and are remarkably similar but were taken moments apart. Both are views with horses and carriages waiting patiently at the bottom of East Bank. The first card shows a woman in a striking white outfit replete with equally striking white hat talking to a man. She is marked with a X at the bottom of her dress. On the back of the card someone has written in ink *"Happy Memories From E. Fletcher."* Is the woman marked with the X Mrs. E. Fletcher and is the man to whom she is talking her husband Dr. J.L. Fletcher?

Emma Fletcher (nee Greatorex) was born in Winster in 1877 and died in 1960. Her parents were prominent in Winster life at the close of the c19 – they ran a shop on Main Street and her father was landlord of the Bowling Green Inn.

James Lyon Fletcher (1868 – 1935) was born in Manchester. He married Emma in Winster in 1898. The couple had one child, Joseph Stanfield Fletcher. Dr. Fletcher was a medical practitioner in Winster. He had a brother, John Howard Fletcher (1870 – 1956) who was also a medical doctor and who also lived in Winster. Emma and James are buried in Winster Churchyard.

The *"Apple Blossom Queen"* was Dorothy Nixon, the daughter of Winster's then Vicar, the Rev. W.H. Nixon (1865 – 1941). Dorothy was born in 1899 and died in 1973 in Dorset. In 1924 she married John Saner. Dorothy's brother, William Eric Nixon (1897 – 1917) was a Captain in the Great War. He was shot down from his plane in France and killed, aged 19.

The Queen and her retinue are pictured in front of the Market House. The banner proclaims: *"Long Live The Queen."* On the close-up view of the "royal party" card someone has written on the back: *"Photo by A. Marshall & Son Winster."* The last card of this sequence intrigues me – *"Where was it taken?"* My guess is towards the top of East Bank unless you know otherwise. Incidentally, there are two postcard prints of this photo in the Eric Brassington Collection. One is a decidedly sharper image than the other and both have different postcard backs.

The last card in this Chapter (below) is of a Funfair at Bank Top. There are again two cards of this image in the Brassington Collection both utilising the same photograph but cropped differently and with different backs. The sharper image is the one illustrated here whereas the other has the name *"Laura Wilson Winster"* written in pencil on the back. I was intrigued by the part advertisement atop the ride: *"Twigdon's Grand Stud Of.."* so I googled the phrase in November 2009. Up came a reference to two families in 1901 with the surname Twigdon both roundabout proprietors operating in the Midlands.

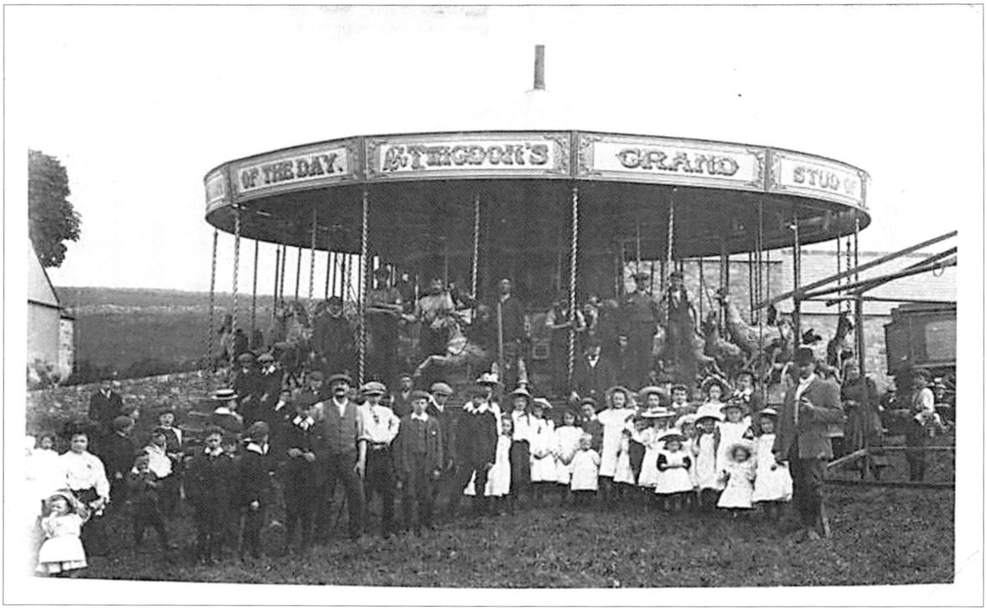

Twigdon's Funfair at Bank Top

CHAPTER 9

E.L. SCRIVENS

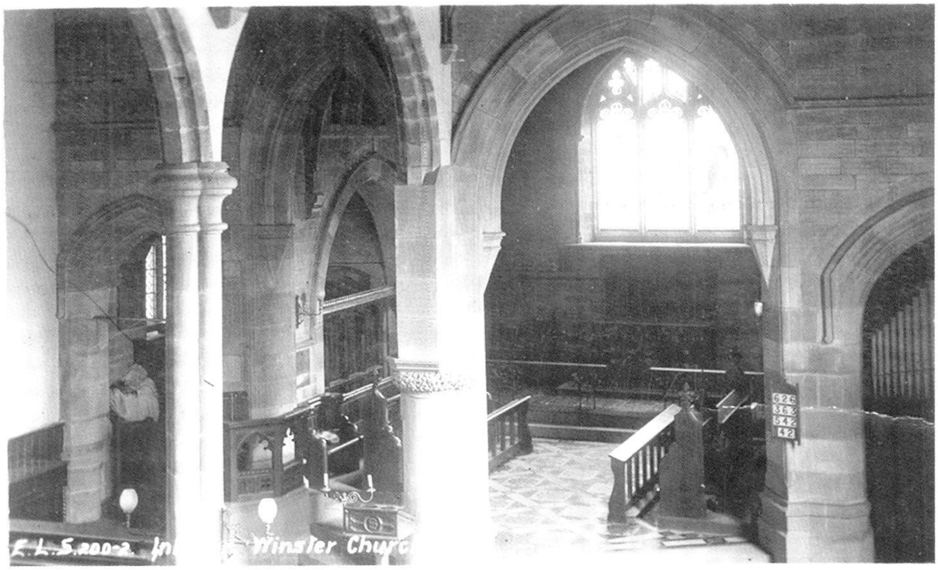

Winster Church Interior E.L.S. 200-2.
Reproduced by courtesy of Steven White

Edgar Leonard Scrivens was a Doncaster based itinerant photographer. He operated over a wide area and his real photographic cards are of the highest quality. He was active between 1909 and 1930.

In 1901, aged 19, he was living at home in Doncaster with his Mother and was a Bill Poster's Clerk. In 1905 he married Emily Gertrude Wilson. By 1911 he was still living in Doncaster, with his wife and a brother and sister. He was then aged 29 working as a photographic printing employer and his brother, Henry Morton Booth Scrivens, aged 16, was a photographic printing worker, probably employed by Edgar. At some time a limited liability company (E.L. Scrivens & Co. Ltd) was formed. Scrivens numbered his cards E.L.S. 200 – followed by individual numbers. There are 9 cards included in this Winster collection the first of which is numbered 200-2 and the last 200-23. That suggests that there may have been at least 23 cards of Winster or the surrounding area. If you have done the simple arithmetic, there are therefore 14 more Scrivens Winster cards yet to be *"discovered"* by me.

E.L.S. 200-4 – Main Street looking west & E.L.S. 200-5 – Main Street looking east. These two photographs were taken on the same day. A shop, the Post Office and The Crown (with a couple of beer barrels on the footpath) are captured as well as some people. The man and the children at left in No. 4 also appear in No. 5 – the pictures are clearly posed. Professional itinerant photographers and their equipment must have attracted much attention in rural Edwardian villages. Photographers knew that by including local people in their photographs they would be able to attract more interest in the subsequent postcard sales. This pair of images were taken before 31 January 1915 as that is the date

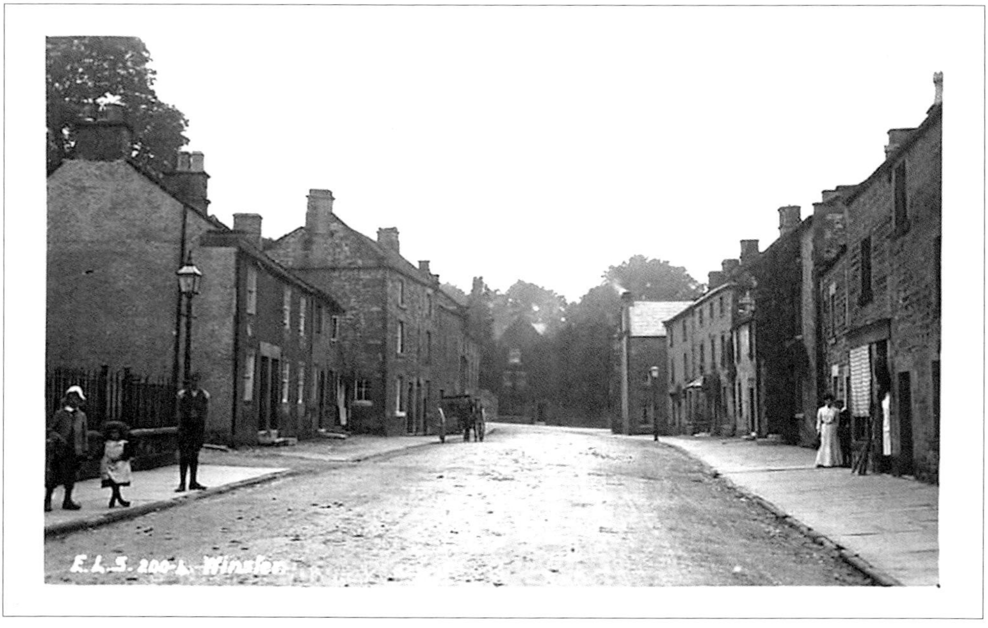

Main Street West E.L.S. 200-4

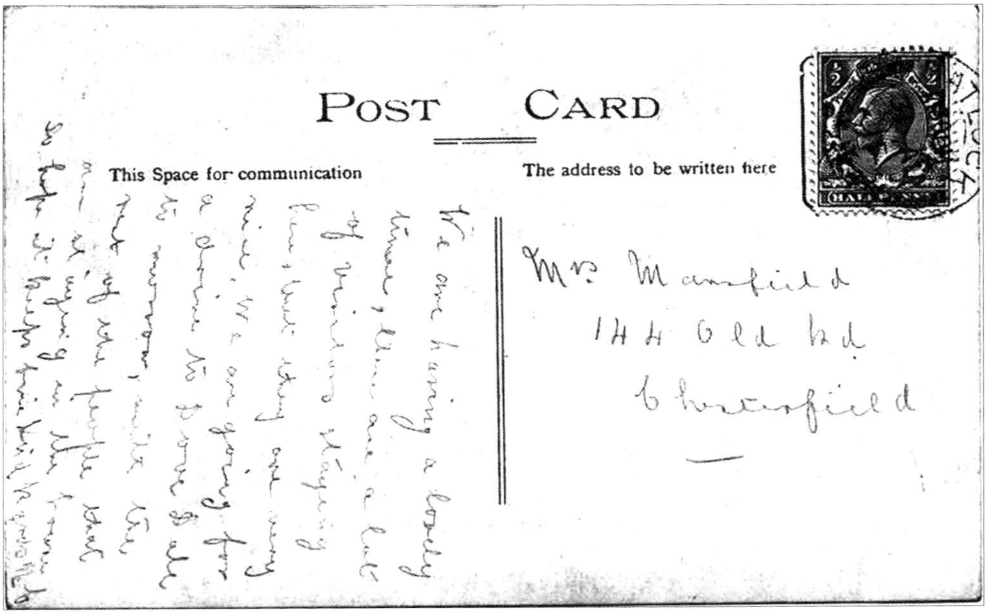

Back of E.L.S. 200-4 Posted From Matlock on 31st January 1915

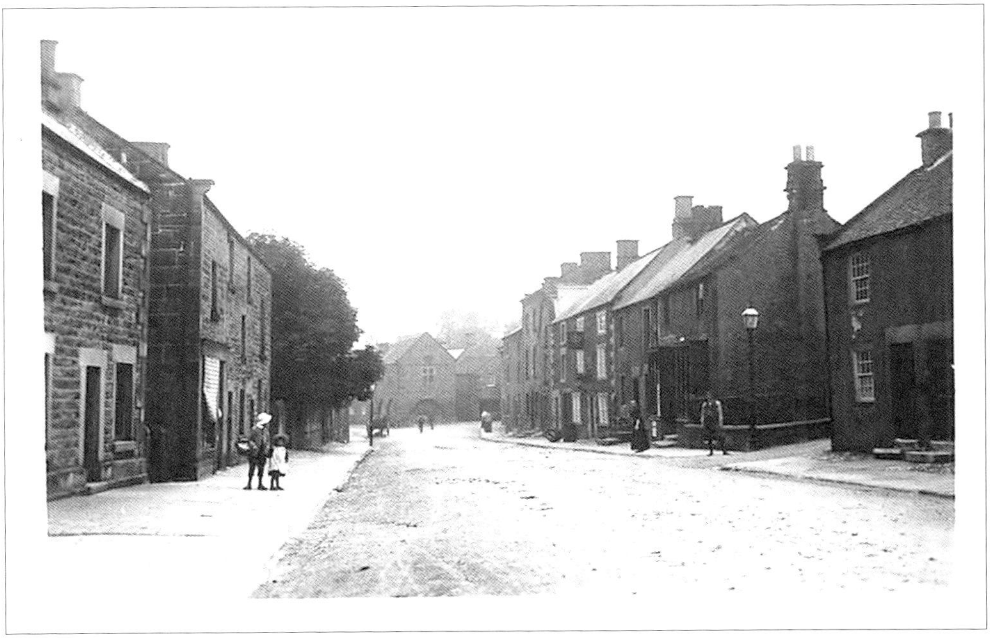

Main Street East E.L.S. 200-5

that No. 200-4 was posted from Matlock and is the earliest postal date of Scrivens cards discussed here. By way of contrast No. 200-18 bears a postal date of 1923. Is the postal date a reliable indicator of when the image was taken? No, it is not – it is a clue only – we have to look to other clues, such as the style of personal clothing and also the style of the backs of the cards and, of course, what research tells us about the business activities of the photographer. A copy of No. 200-4 for example, might survive with an earlier postal date than 1915 and a copy might survive with a later date, possibly as late as 1923 or even later. Some images of Edwardian photographers were published as postcards and then re-published years later still as postcards but sometimes with subtle changes to the images and having different backs. Nos. 200-4 & 5 are classic examples – they have different backs; one does not even identify Scrivens whereas the other is printed with the title of his limited company.

No. 200-4 was posted to Mrs. Mansfield, 144 Old Road, Chesterfield, and the message reads:

"We are having a lovely time, there are a lot of visitors staying here, but they are very nice. We are going for a drive to Dove Dale tomorrow, with the rest of

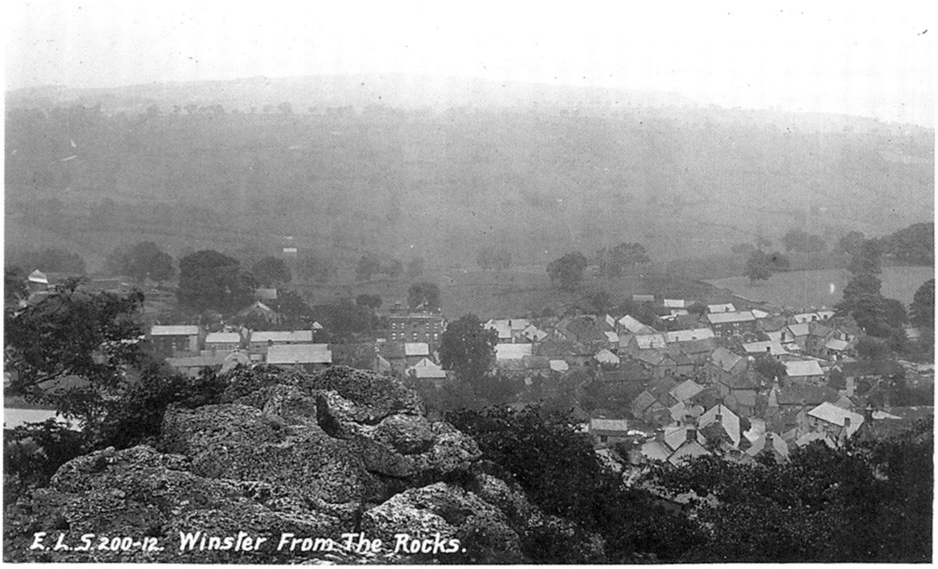

Winster From The Rocks E.L.S. 200-12. Reproduced by courtesy of Steven White

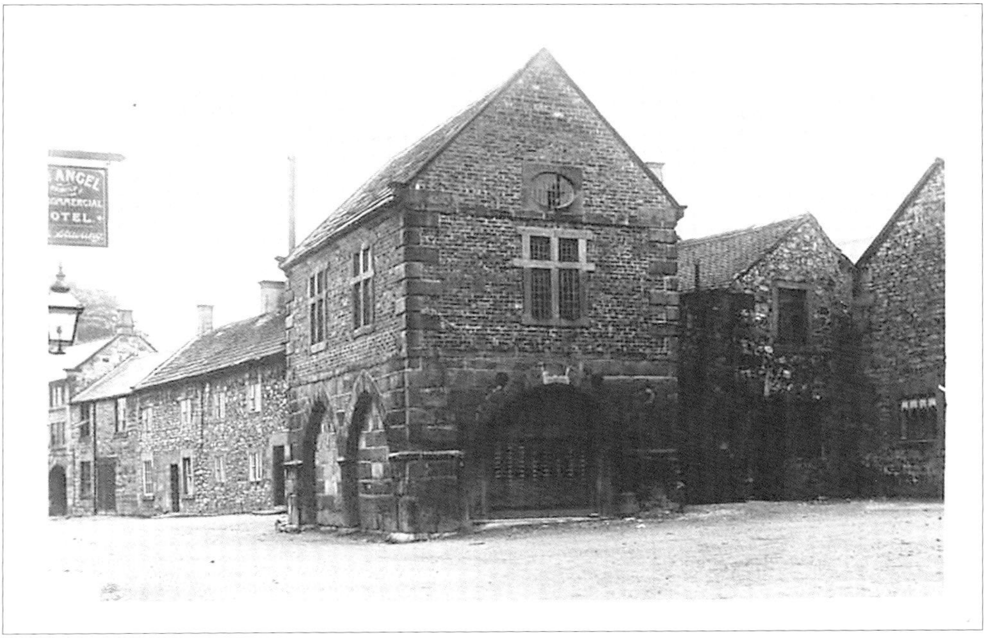

Market House E.L.S. 200-16

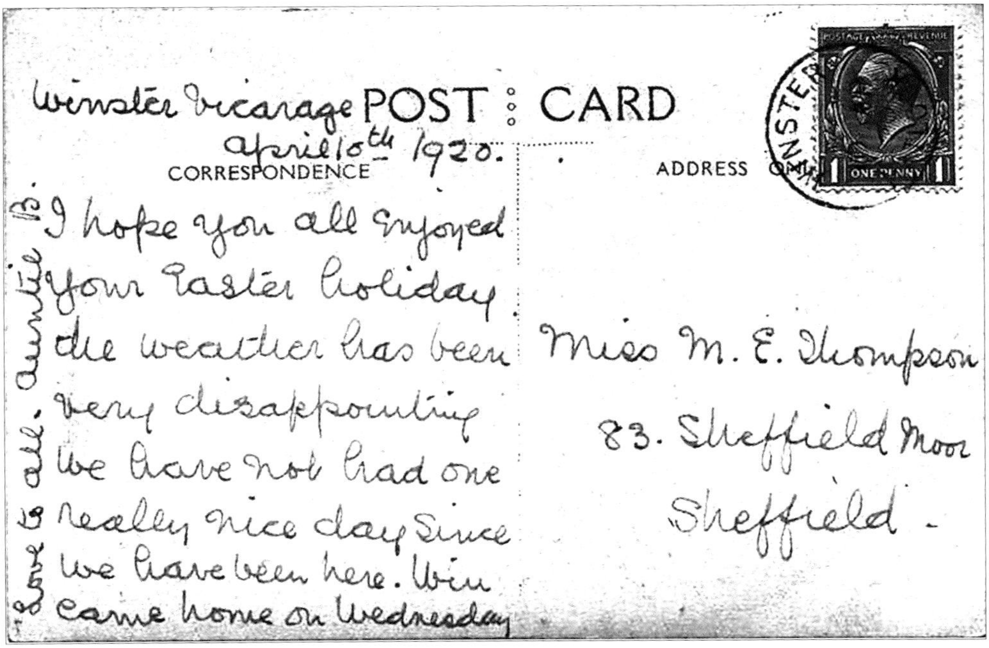

Back of E.L.S. 200-16. Posted from Winster on 10 April 1920

the people that are staying in the house, so hope it keeps fine. Kind regard. N.C."

We can speculate where the writer might have been staying – was it in a *"house"* in Winster or in Matlock?
No. 200-16 Market House is a gem – it has many of the characteristics that a postcard collector seeks. The picture speaks for itself – it is the back of the card which adds to the interest – posted from Winster to Miss M.E. Thompson, 83 Sheffield Moor, Sheffield, with a message from the writer at Winster Vicarage usefully dated 10th April 1920. It reads:

"I hope you all enjoyed your Easter holiday the weather has been disappointing. We have not had one really nice day since we have been here. Win came home on Wednesday. Love to all. Auntie B."

There is a fuller discussion of other postcards sent to the Misses Thompson in Chapter 11 – Ernest Heathcote (1873 – 1953). No. 200-18 was posted from Winster in 1923 to Mrs. Wakefield, c/o Mrs. Arthur, Toynton Villa, Scarborough Ave, Skegness, Lincs, and reads:

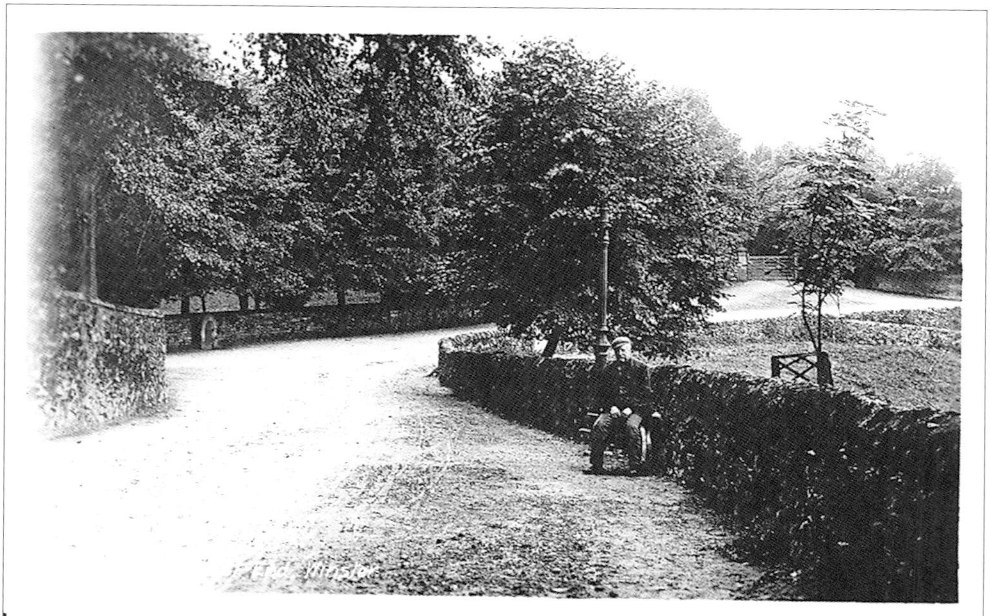

West End E.L.S. 200-17. The churchyard is behind the wall to the left, in the right upper distance is the entrance to Oddo House, behind the seated man is a lamp-post. Reproduced by courtesy of Steven White

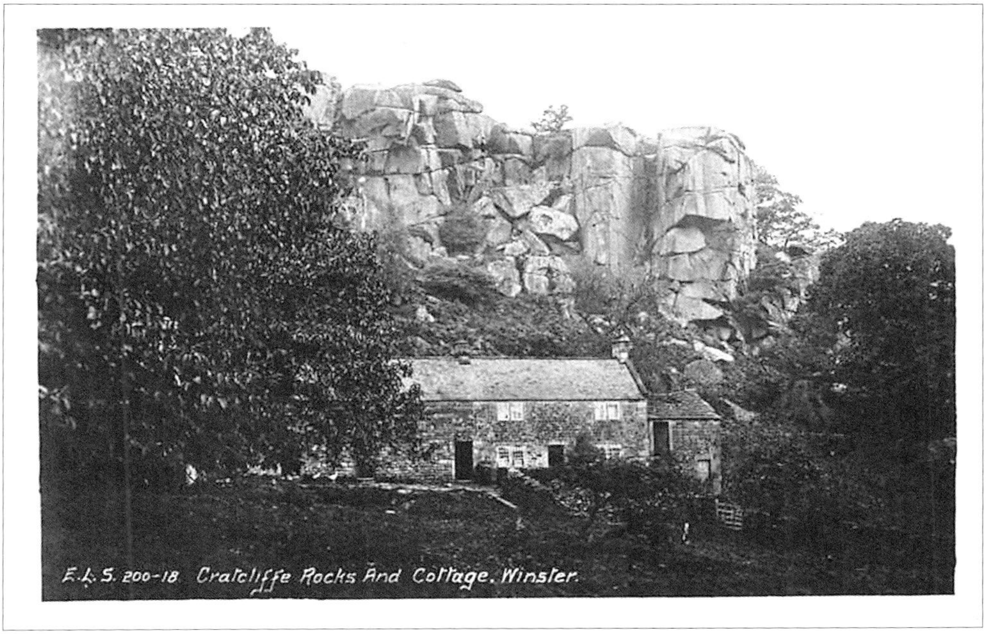

Cratcliffe Rocks & Cottage E.L.S. 200-18. The Rocks/Cottage lie outside urban Winster between the neighbouring villages of Birchover and Elton

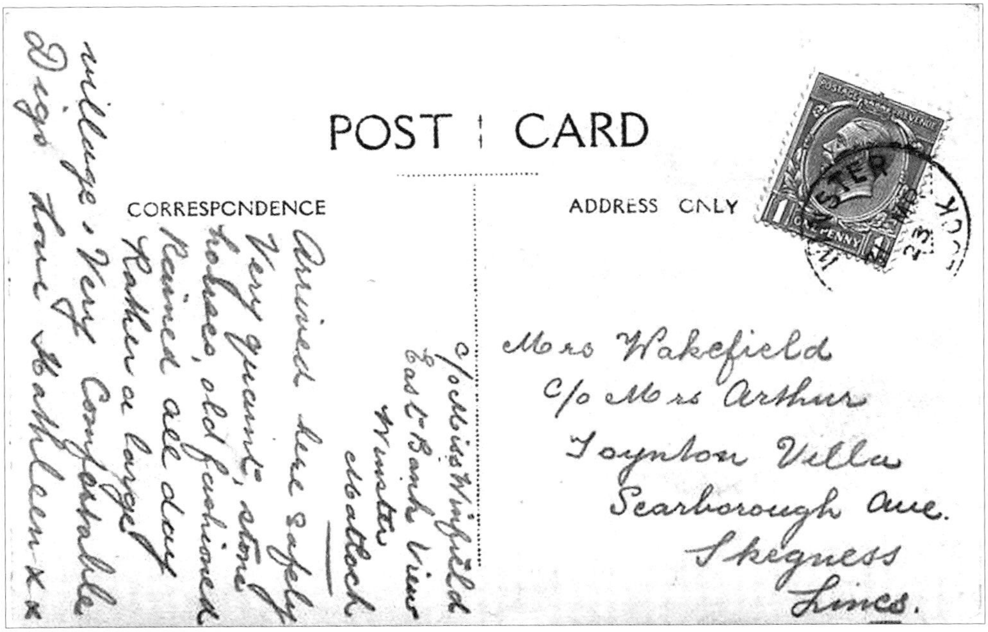

Back of E.L.S. 200-18 – Posted from Winster in 1923

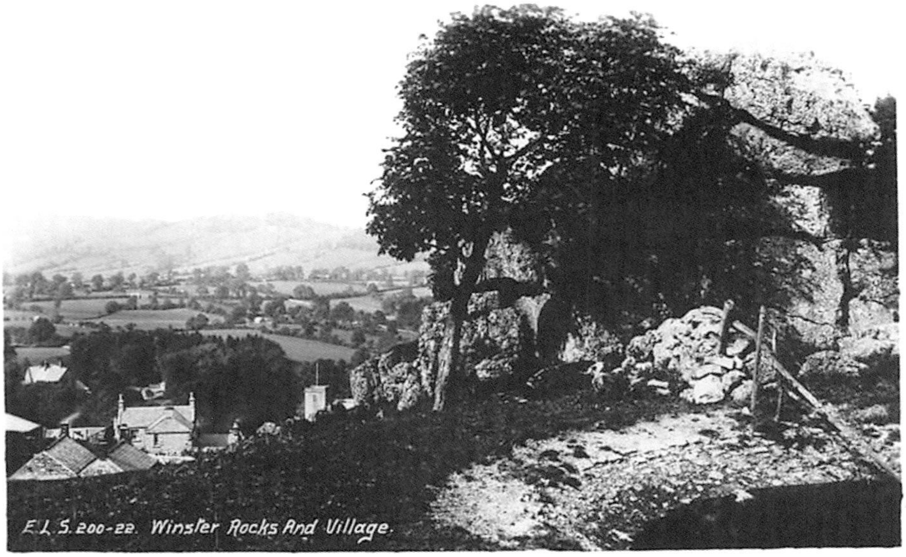

Rocks & Village E.L.S. 200-22

"c/o Miss Winfield
East Bank View
Winster Matlock
Arrived here safely Very quaint, stone house, old fashioned Rained all day Rather a large village. Very comfortable digs Love Kathleen."

This Miss Winfield of East Bank View was probably Eliza Winfield (b. about 1876) who later married F.J.A. Pollard in 1926.

No. 200-23 View From Winster Bank. Although not postally used the message on the back (not illustrated) reads:

"I hope you will like these views. Ask Ray to show you our house on this one. Mrs. H. Wagstaff."

Although there is no addressee on this card and the writer refers to *"these views"* it suggests that this card was enclosed with others in an envelope/package which was then addressed and sent to the unknown recipient.

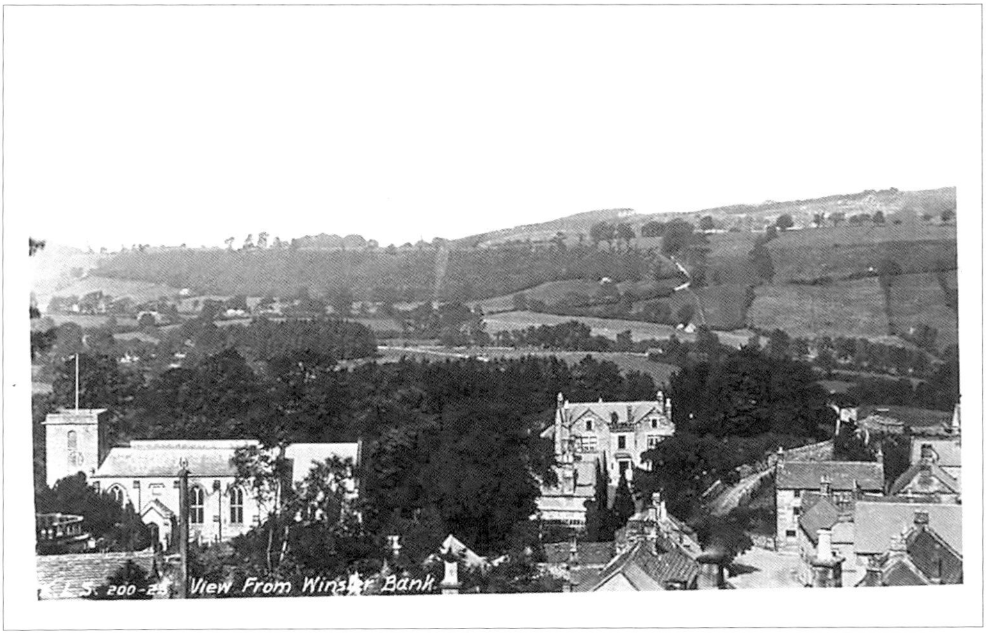

From Winster Bank E.L.S. 200-23

CHAPTER 10

J. CROWTHER COX

J. Crowther Cox, was another Edwardian itinerant postcard publisher based at 12 The Crofts, Rotherham. His real photographic postcards are also of high quality and there is a small collection of four of his "Ivanhoe Series" Winster cards here. The numbering sequence he used (at bottom left of each card) is suggestive of him publishing at least ten Winster cards. The earliest number in this collection is 38722 and the latest is 38732. Only one of these cards (of the Methodist Chapel) was postally used (on 27 October 1914). It was posted by JAB (whom we met earlier) and his colleague, B. Boam, both Methodist lay preachers, about their next preaching assignment at Ashley Hay, Wirksworth. The message reads:

"Dear Sir, God willing we shall be with you on Nov 22nd instead of last Sunday. J.A. Brassington, B. Boam."

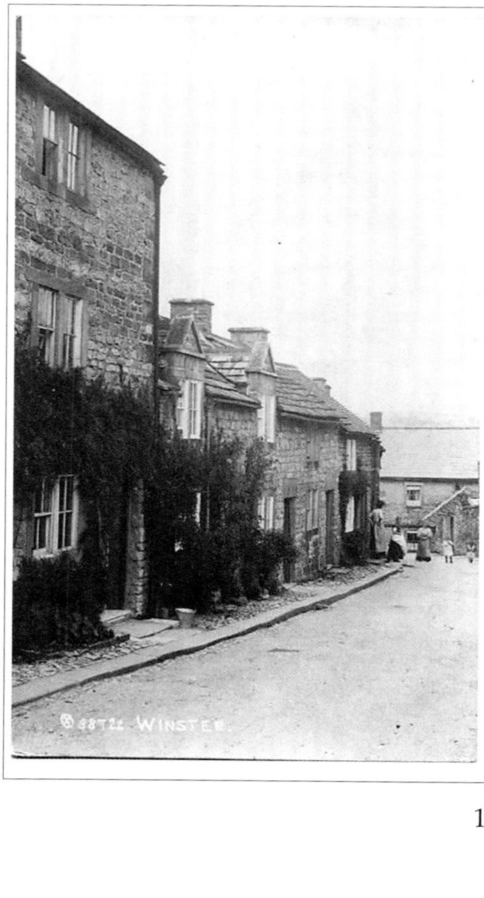

Woolley's Yard. Nod. 38722

The message on the back of the Woolley's Yard card reads:

"This is a great "*town*" of these parts where everyone goes to do their shopping.
We are in the middle of nowhere. Some of the nicest country I have seen & whether you believe it or not we are having a very good time & enjoying ourselves hugely.
Just off to meet Ada,
In haste W.N"

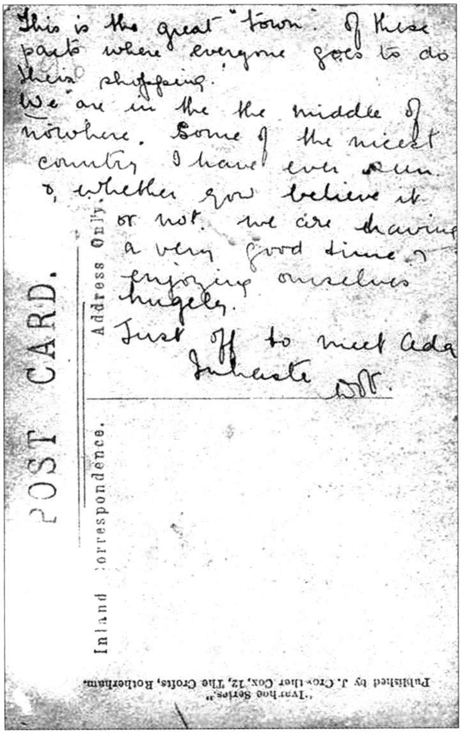
This is the great "town" of these
parts where everyone goes to do
their shopping.
We are in the the middle of
nowhere. Some of the nicest
country I have ever seen
& whether you believe it
or not we are having
a very good time &
enjoying ourselves
hugely.
Just off to meet Ada
In haste W.N.

POST CARD.
Address Only.
Inland Correspondence.
Published by J. Crowther Cox, 12, The Crofts, Rotherham.
"Ivanhoe Series."

Back Of Woolley's Yard Card
Nod. 38722

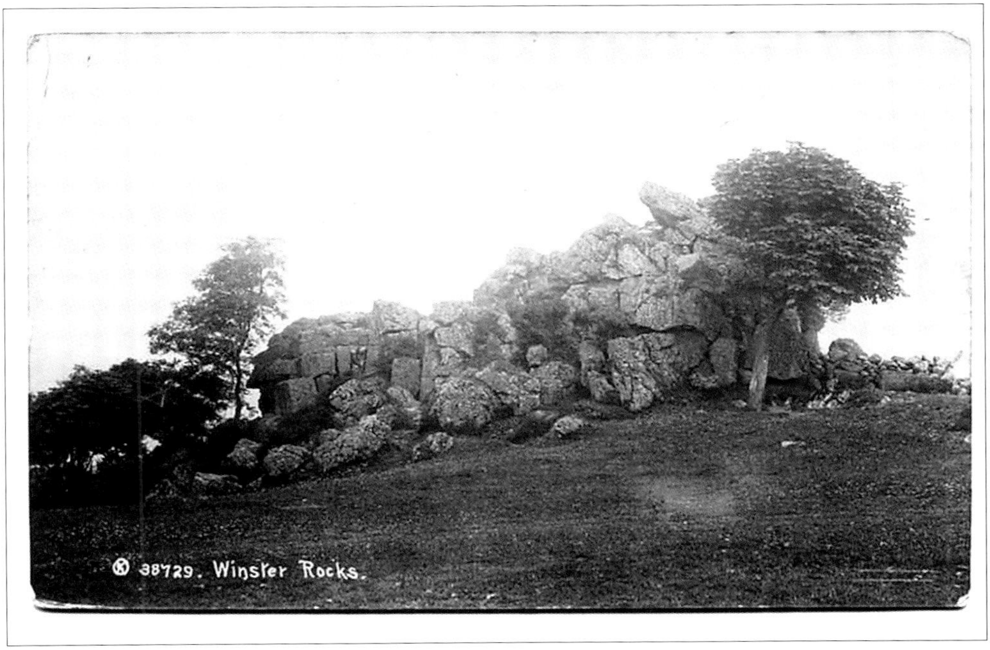

Winster Rocks Nod. 38729

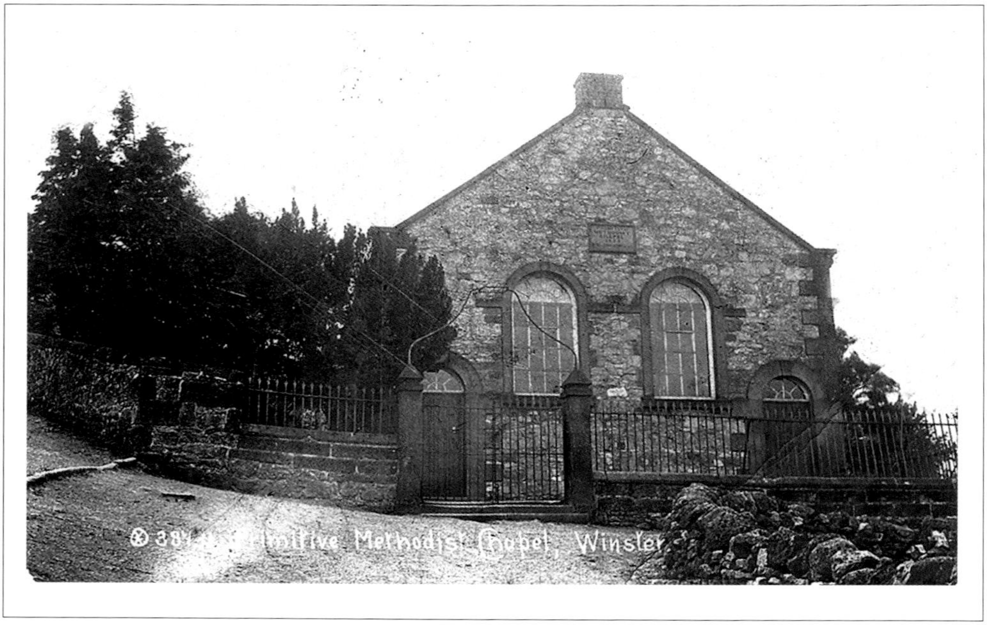

Methodist Church Nod. 38731 Reproduced by courtesy of Steven White

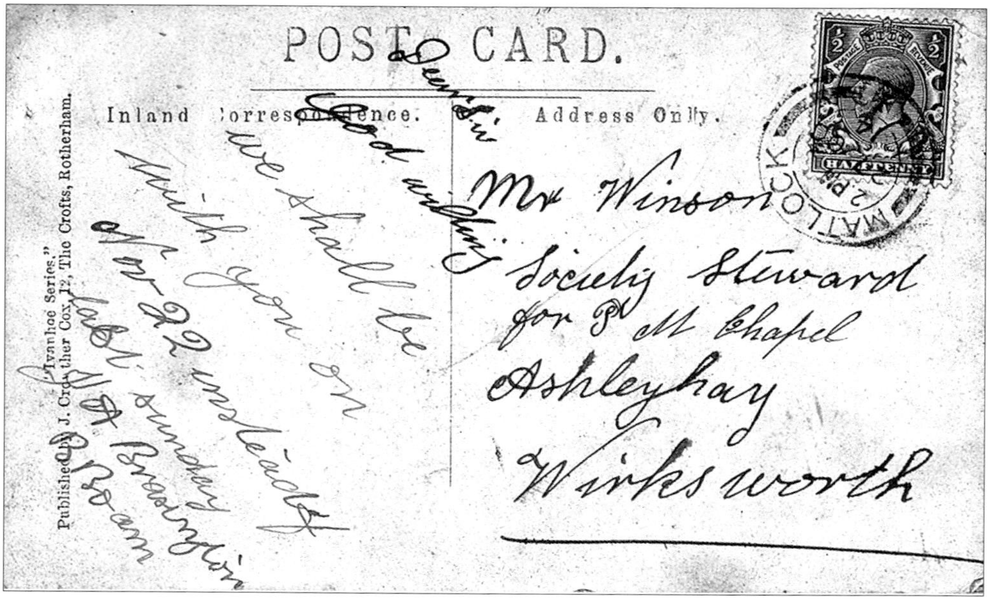

Back of Methodist Church Card Nod. 38731

The last card is a view of West Bank and of the blacksmith's wares spread out almost into the middle of the road. The man pictured may have been the blacksmith. In *"Winster – A Peak District Village Remembers"* (page 24) Betty Dexter recalled:

"Where your garage is (West Bank House), Mr. Vincent used to be there. He had that as a smith. This was when I was a little girl (Betty was born c1918). And sometimes the horses would be queuing down West Bank waiting to be shod."

In the 1911 Census, William Vincent, aged 30, was living in Winster (the address is not given). His birthplace was given as Norfolk and his occupation as blacksmith – he was an employer working *"at home."* He had been married for one year and his wife was Florence Mabel Vincent (nee Allen), aged 20, who was born in Manchester. Their marriage (on 1 August 1910) was reported in the *Parish Magazine* in 1910.

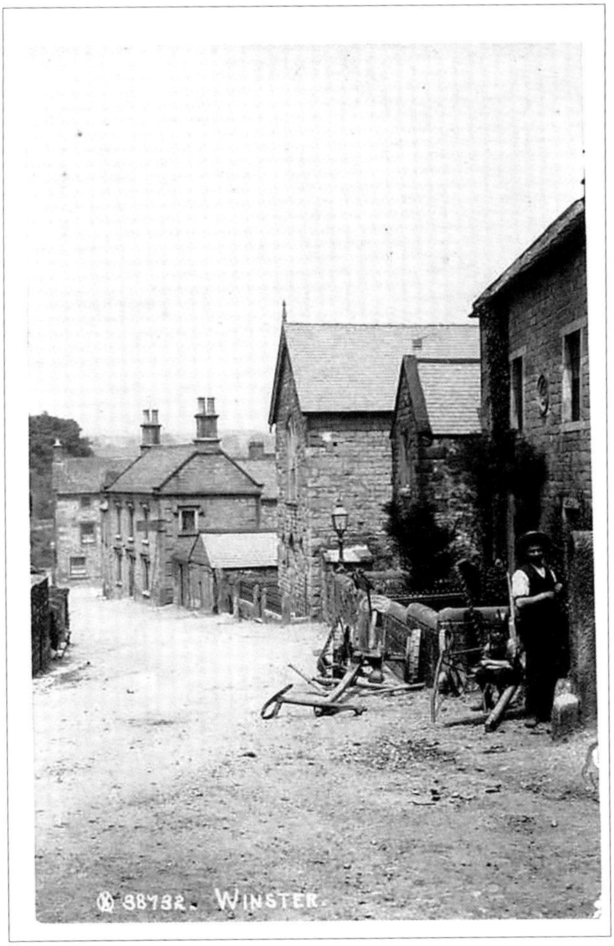

West Bank – Blacksmith Nod. 38732

CHAPTER 11

ERNEST HEATHCOTE (1873 – 1953)

Ernest Heathcote was born into a prominent Winster family on 17 February 1873. His father, Henry Charles Heathcote, (1843 – 1921), also born in Winster, trained as a druggist in Liverpool. At various times he was a justice of the peace and a member of the parish council. By 1901 he was a chemist, druggist and dentist working on his own account from his premises in Main Street next to Bank House. The same premises were continuously used as a Post Office until the business was transferred in 2010 to the Village Shop in Market Place. By 1901 Heathcote (Ernest) was the sub-postmaster. Henry's other son, Gilbert, was a medical student. The 1901 household was completed by Annie Gregory, aged 18, employed as a domestic servant. In 1904 Heathcote was postmaster and held this position until 1925. By 1911, aged 38, Heathcote was living with his parents and their servant Maud Mary Greatorex at Mooresfold, Elton Road. He died at Mooresfold on 25 June 1953. In 1937 The Heathcote Trust was created which still operates as a Charity (No. 215418) in Winster – one of its objects is to maintain the Heathcote Family graves in Winster Churchyard.

There is a memorial window to Heathcote's father in Winster Church. There is also a memorial to the pair in the bus shelter on Main Street. When I photographed this memorial in August 2009 it was then in need of some tender loving care. The inscription reads:

"The Heathcote Memorial Shelter
Erected To The Memory of the Late Henry Charles Heathcote
And
Ernest Heathcote

Ernest Heathcote (1873 – 1953)

Of "Mooresfold" Winster
In Appreciation Of Their Services To The Village."

Ernest Heathcote was the publisher of Edwardian Winster postcards. He was publishing postcards at the same time as Marshall but does not seem to have been as prolific. I have found no evidence that Heathcote was a photographer as Marshall was – he may have published photographs that were taken by Marshall. If he did, then it's strange that he did not give Marshall (or the photographer) a mention on the cards themselves. My guess is that Heathcote was not the photographer of the postcards he published – but I may be wrong! There are just eight examples of Heathcote's work illustrated here – he may have produced many more. Six of these cards are colour tinted (Marshall produced no coloured cards as far as I know although his wife published some later) and all are printed whereas the bulk of Marshall's postcard output was real photographic. Presumably Heathcote was interested in supplementing his income as a postmaster by selling postcards some of which he published in collaboration with Geo. Marsdsen & Son of Wirksworth. Many of the postcards in the examples illustrated here are printed on the back with the imprint of Marsden's *"Derbyshire Artistic Series"* and are numbered on the back at top right and also at bottom right. Confusingly, each individual card bears different numbers on the back of each card – one at top left and one at bottom right. All these cards have identical backs.

None of the backs of the postally used cards have messages of interest to Winster local historians and the backs have not been illustrated here save for one (Main St. Nod. 3010 and 7729) which is of interest as it has a Winster cancellation strike. Unfortunately, part of the strike with the year is illegible. However, Wilson (*"Postal History of Matlock And District* by Harold S. Wilson published by Derbyshire Postal History Society") usefully includes examples of strikes in use at Winster for different periods and thus it appears that the strike on this card was used between 1884 and 1911. It is clearly the latter part of this period as the strike is on a green Edwardian (1901 – 1910) half penny postage stamp as are all the other used cards.

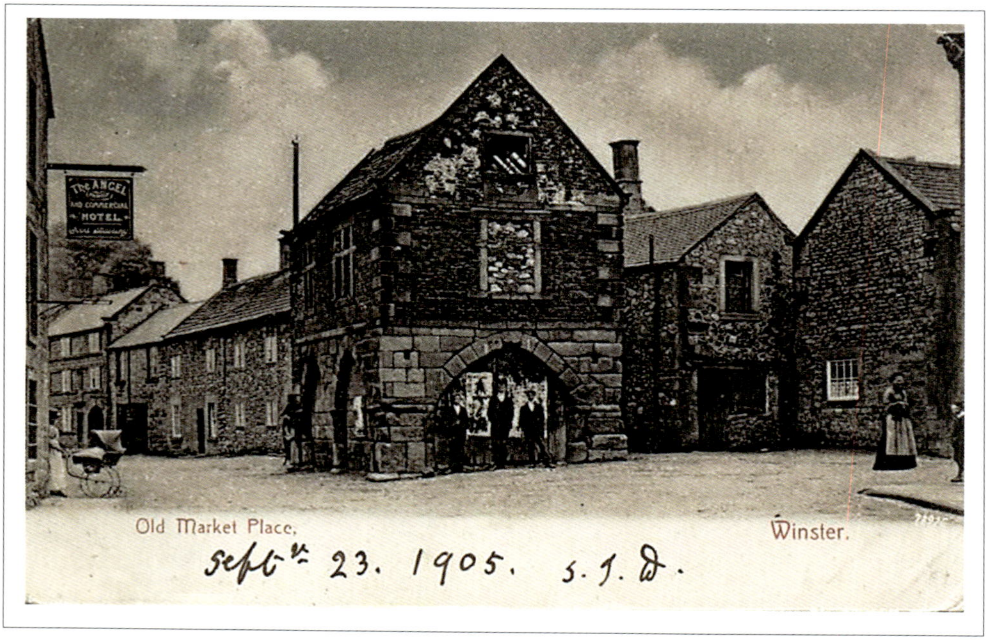

Posted from Matlock Bath on 23 September 1905 to Mrs. Daltry, 14 Broad St., Warwick. Strangely, there is no message

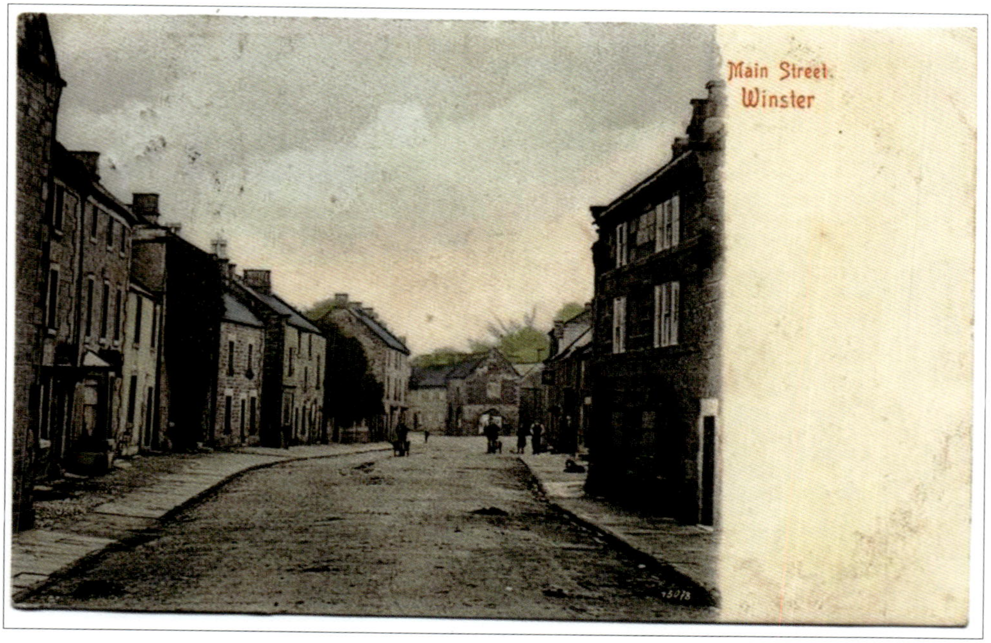

Posted on 19 October 1906 to Miss Brownson, 38 Arboretum Avenue, Monks Rd., Lincoln

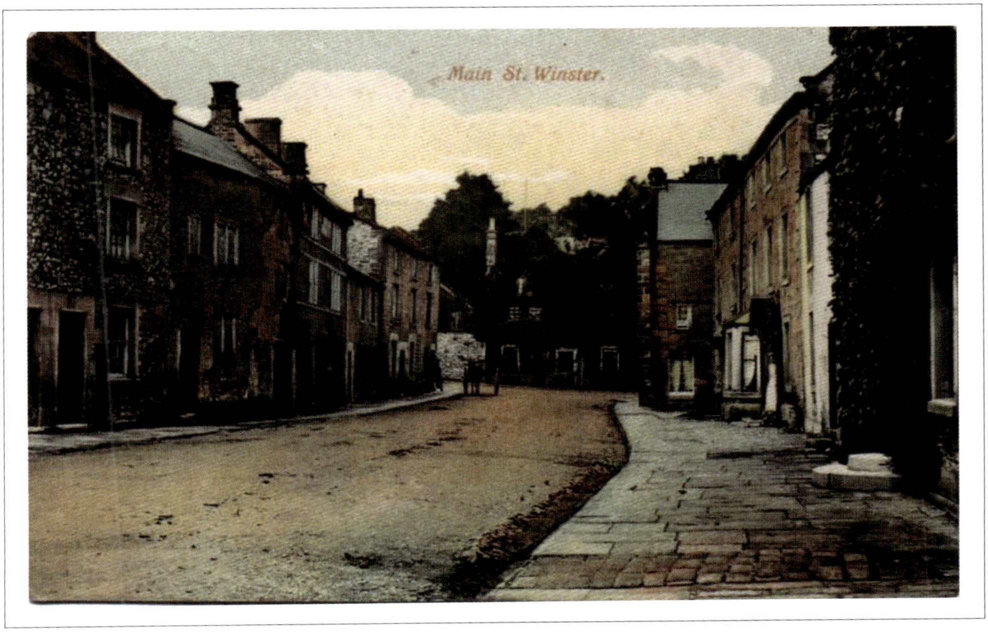

Posted from Winster on 9 May but the year is illegible to Miss Speed, c/o Mrs. Pinder, Elm Bank, Redcliffe Road, Nottingham

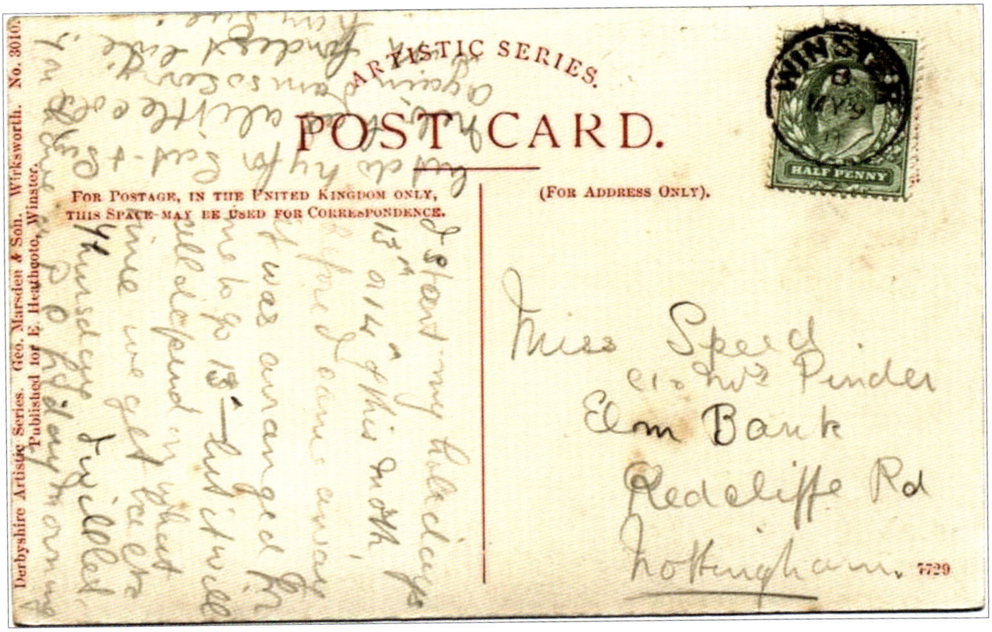

The Misses Thompson

I illustrated earlier in Chapter 9 a Scrivens card of the Market House which had a dated message (19 April 1920) and was sent to a Miss M.E. Thompson, 83 Sheffield Moor, Sheffield. There are 5 other postcards (3 of them Heathcote cards) sent to Miss Gladys Thompson (and one sent by Gladys to Miss Marian Thompson) which it is convenient to discuss here. Only one of these cards also has a dated message (14 April 1904) and none of them have survived with their postage stamps. The postcard collectors and family historians amongst you will know that cards of a particular location (such as Winster) are just as interesting if the collector is able to identify either the sender or the people to whom the cards were sent. In this case, I have enough information to be able to answer the question:

"Who Were the Misses Thompson And What Was Their Connection With Winster Vicarage?"

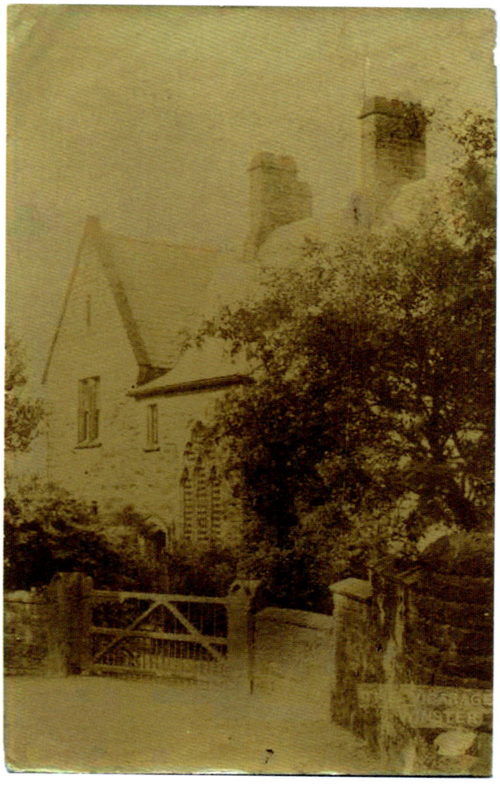

Winster Vicarage c1904. Real photo by unknown publisher

Throughout the Edwardian period the Vicar of Winster was The Rev. W.H. Nixon who married Victoria Thompson: they were Gladys and Marian's uncle and aunt. Members of the Thompson family, including the sisters, must have been regular visitors to Winster Vicarage. The girls' parents were John Thomas Thompson and Laura Agnes née Hardcastle. In 1901 the family were living at 83 South St Moor, Sheffield. J.T. Thompson, aged 44, was a Cycle Agent and manufacturer and was an employer. Marian and Gladys were living with their parents at this address, aged 11 and 8 respectively. The family also had a servant living with them. Next door, at 85 South St Moor, was the girls' uncle and aunt, William Henry Thompson, aged 41, and his then wife, Lilian, aged 32. William Henry was a Jeweller and Cycle Agent and manufacturer and also an employer. Were the girls' father and their Uncle Bill in business together? It seems highly probable. William and Lilian had a family too: Lilian, aged 13, Margaret, 12, and Albert, 10.

By 1911, Gladys and Marian and their parents were in occupation of both 83 and 85 South St Moor, Sheffield. Both parents were by this time Jewellers and Cycle Dealers. Marian Elsie and Gladys were then aged 21 and 18 respectively. Marian was a student and Gladys was at "*School Painting*." The family still employed a servant. Also by 1911 the girls' Uncle Bill was living with his two daughters, Lilian, aged 23, and Margaret, aged 22, both single and Margaret described as a Student, at 44 Bingham Road, Woodseats, Sheffield. Uncle Bill was still a Jeweller and Cycle Dealer and may still have been in business with his brother, John Thomas Thompson. There is no mention in the 1911 Census of Lilian, the girls' Aunt, so she may have died by this date.

Gladys may have married in later life: Marian Elsie probably did not. A Marian Elsie Thompson died in 1975 in the Bakewell Registration

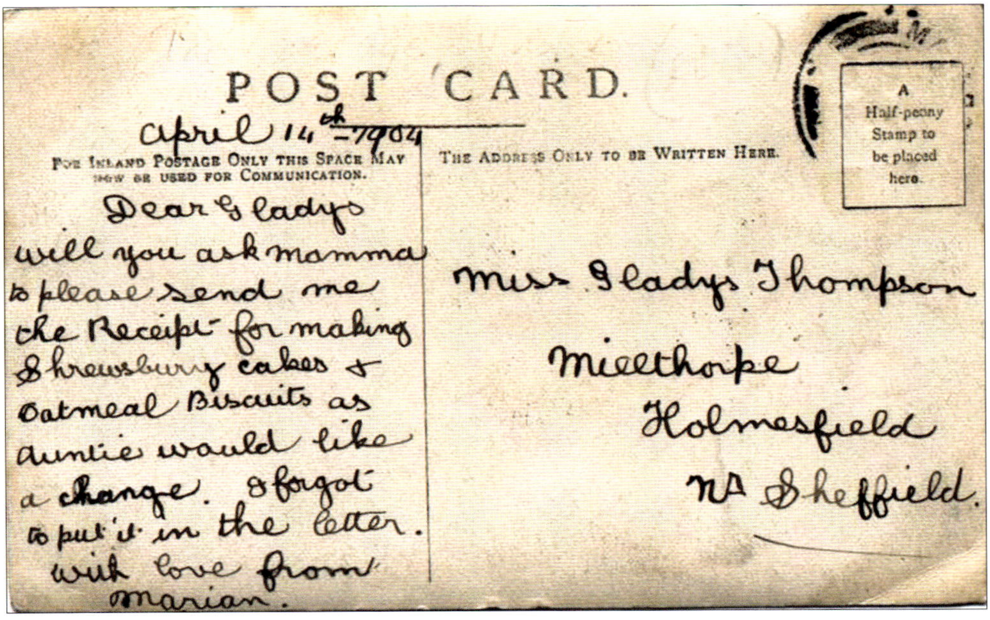

POST CARD.

April 14th 1904

FOR INLAND POSTAGE ONLY THIS SPACE MAY NOW BE USED FOR COMMUNICATION.

Dear Gladys
will you ask mamma
to please send me
the Receipt for making
Shrewsbury cakes &
Oatmeal Biscuits as
auntie would like
a change. I forgot
to put it in the letter.
with love from
Marian.

THE ADDRESS ONLY TO BE WRITTEN HERE.

A Half-penny Stamp to be placed here.

Miss Gladys Thompson
Millthorpe
Holmesfield
Nr Sheffield.

The back of Winster Vicarage c1904 and usefully dated 14 April 1904

District: the public record gives her date of birth as 23 March 1890. This person may have been our Marian Elsie – a reader who has done more extensive research into the Thompson family(ies) may already have the answer!

Now, let's enjoy these Thompson cards:
This next card is a recent addition to my collection – in November 2009 I saw it for sale on E-Bay. The picture side is a printed view of Thorpe Cloud, Dovedale, just the sort of picture which is unlikely to be collected. What attracted my attention was the Winster address and the Thompson name. I made a bid for the card – there was no competition – and was surprised when it arrived to see that someone (presumably Gladys) had written *"83 Sheffield Moor"* on the picture side. Again, the postage stamp was missing but it was clearly posted in Sheffield.

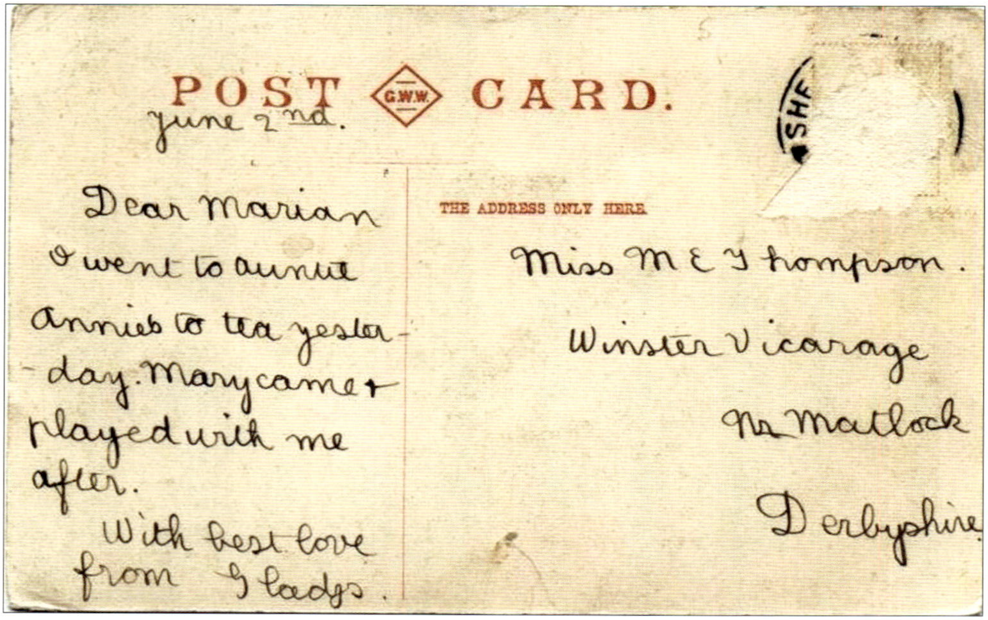

Back of card sent from 83 Sheffield Moor

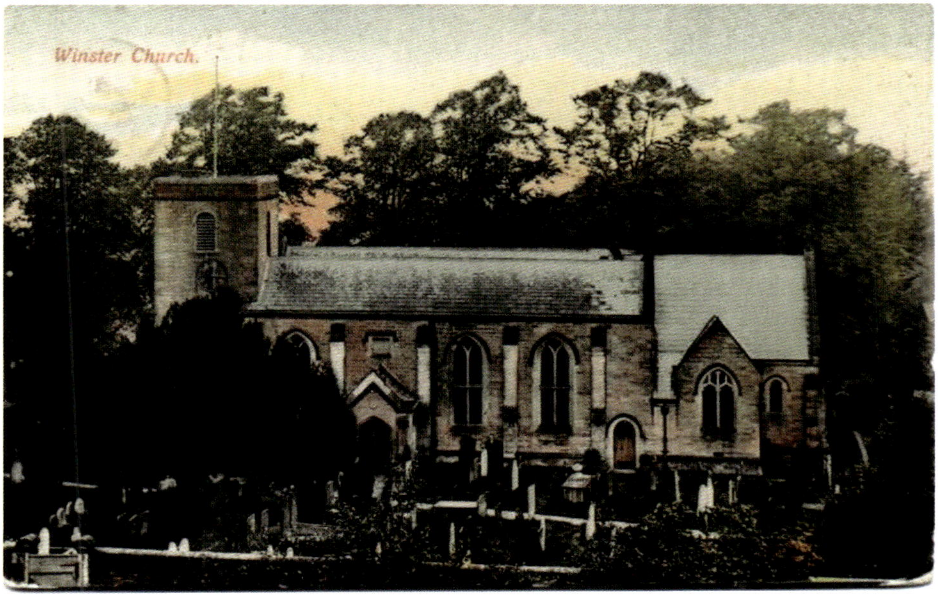

Nod. 3013 & 7732

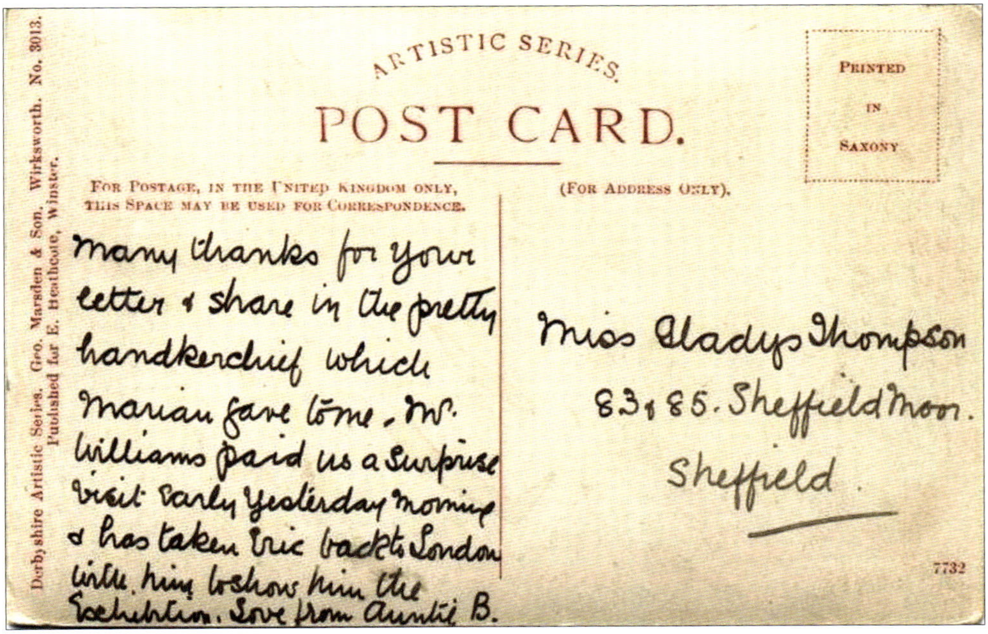

"Auntie B," the sender of this card, was Beatrice M. Thompson born 1870

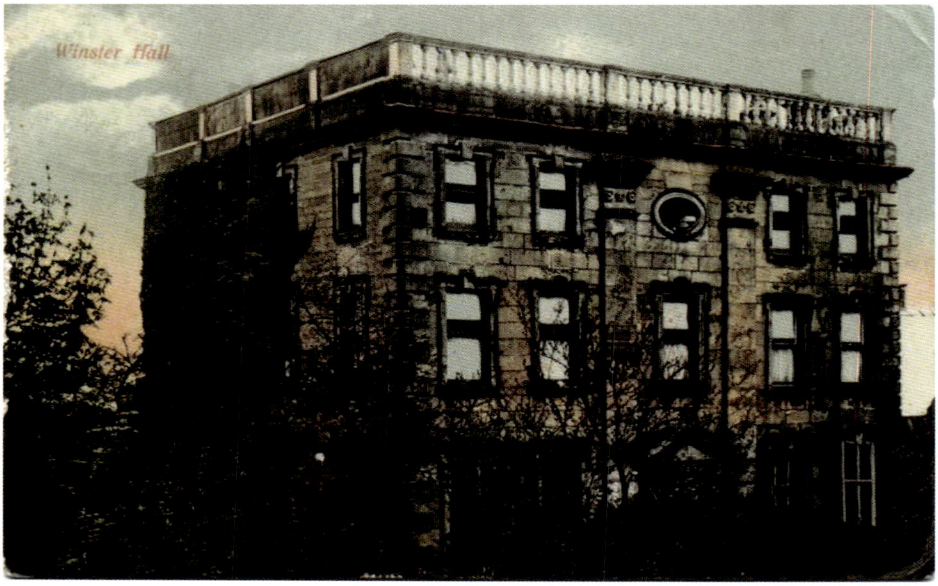

Winster Hall Nod. 3009 – other number illegible

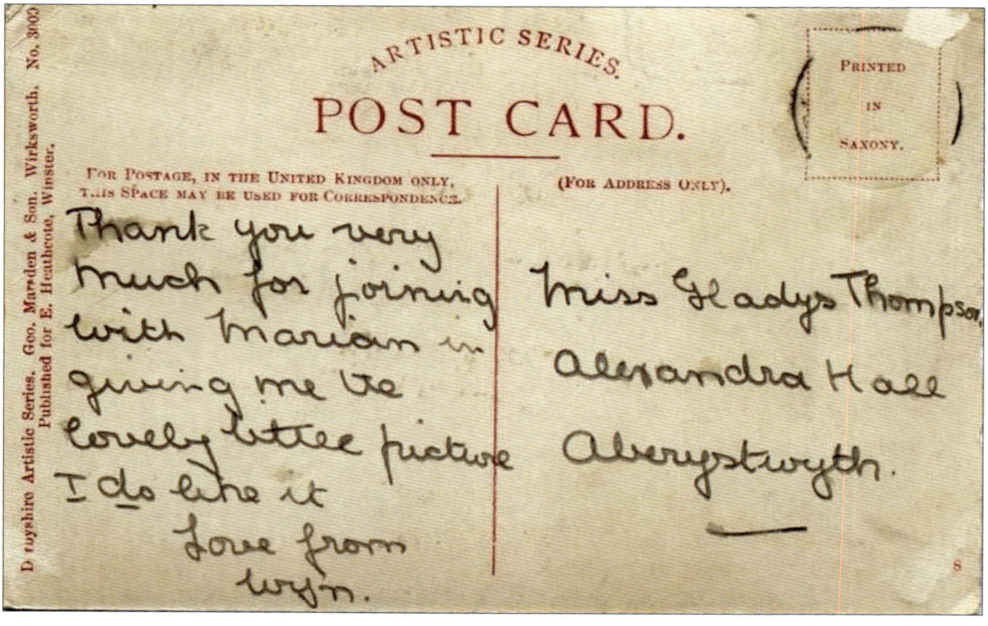

Back of Winster Hall card

You will note that the card (bottom of p.148) was sent to Gladys at Alexandra Hall, Aberystwyth. In 2010 this building, on the Sea Front, was still in use as a hall of residence for the University of Aberystwyth, and provided accommodation for 254 students. The building was built in 1895 as an all-girls hall and was opened on 26 June 1896 by the Princess of Wales after whom it was named. The University was one of the first institutions to admit women. By March 2010 the University had no record of either Gladys or Marion being full-time students between 1905 – 1915. The University then offered short courses in subjects ranging from dairying to horticulture and it might be that Gladys went to Aberystwyth to enrol on one of these courses but, unfortunately, the University does not have any records of attendance for them so there is no evidence to support this theory. What a pity – it would have been interesting to have this probable theory supported with some evidence.

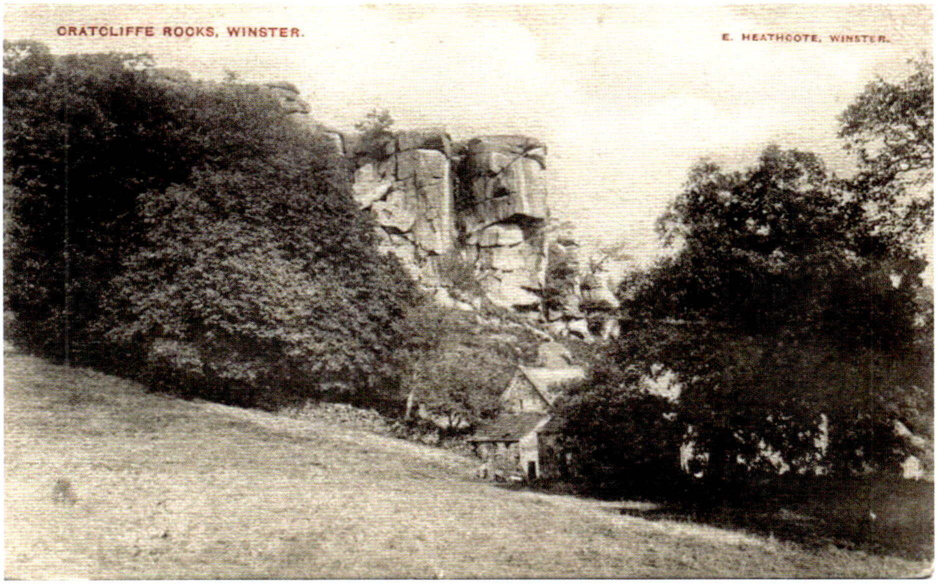

Cratcliffe Rocks

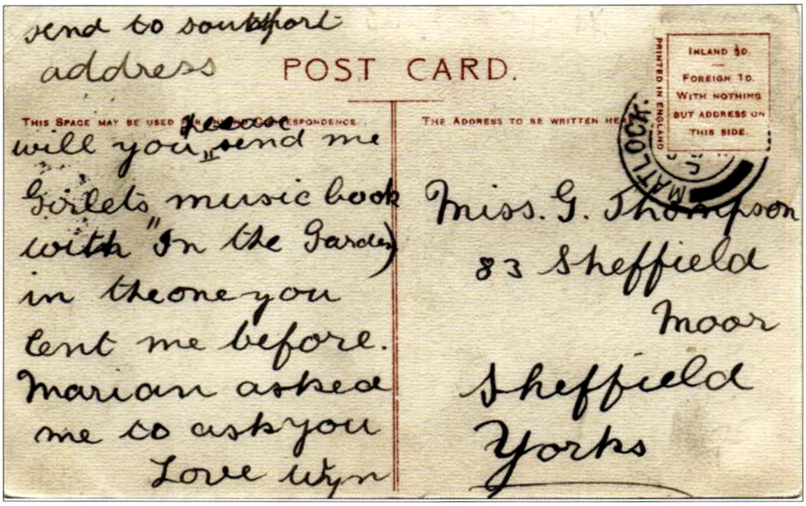
send to southport address

POST CARD.

THIS SPACE MAY BE USED FOR INLAND CORRESPONDENCE.

THE ADDRESS TO BE WRITTEN HERE.

PRINTED IN ENGLAND

INLAND ½D. FOREIGN 1D. WITH NOTHING BUT ADDRESS ON THIS SIDE.

MATLOCK.

please will you send me Goilets music book with "In the Garden" in the one you lent me before. Marian asked me to ask you Love Wyn

Miss G. Thompson
83 Sheffield
Moor
Sheffield
Yorks

Back of previous card

This last card has no association with the Misses Thompson.

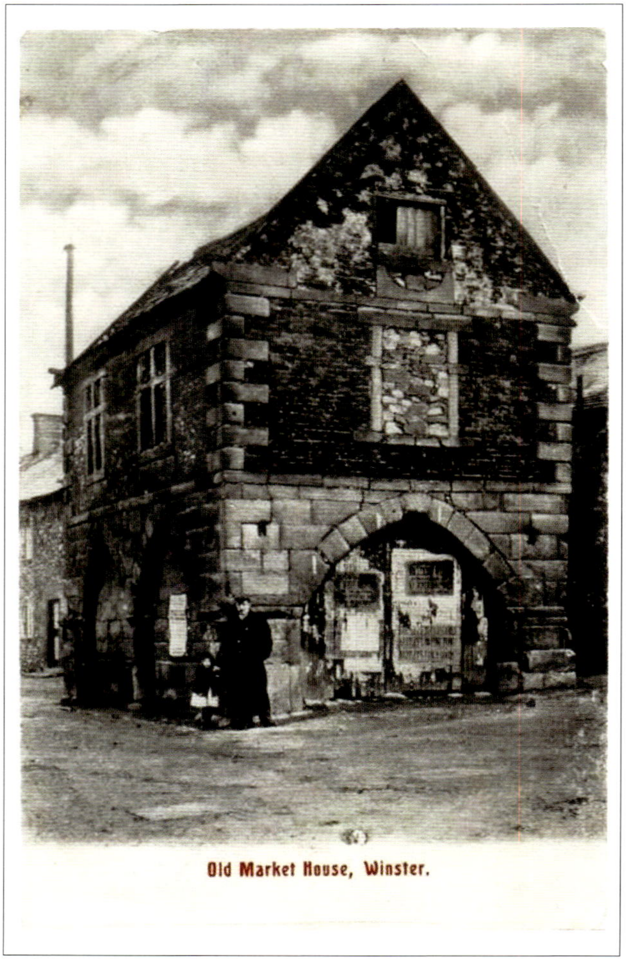

Nod. 3012 & 7732 – not postally used

CHAPTER 12

A.W. BOURNE

With the topographical postcards of A.W. Bourne we leap forward from the Edwardian period to the 1950s/60s. It was fitting that the first card illustrated in the introduction to this book should be by Bourne, the "*Approach To Winster*" card sent to me in 1961. Since then I have only managed to collect five Bourne cards of Winster including the 1961 card. There are two cards of West Bank and The Church which I have not yet added to my collection – there may be others of Winster too. I fell in love with Bourne's beautifully crisp black and white images almost as soon as I started to collect them. Bourne of 32 Babingly Drive, Leicester, was a real photographic postcard publisher who published postcards widely throughout the midland counties in the 1950s and 60s. He was a direct descendant of the early real photographic publishers and has left many images which record the topography of midland counties in the mid 20th century. Unfortunately, Bourne did not number his cards so we do not know how many cards he produced of Winster. All the backs of the cards included here are identical (see the "*Approach to Winster*" card in the Introduction) save for his multi-view card which, strangely, is not printed on the back with his usual identification details – it is, however, obviously his work as it includes views which are identified as by him.

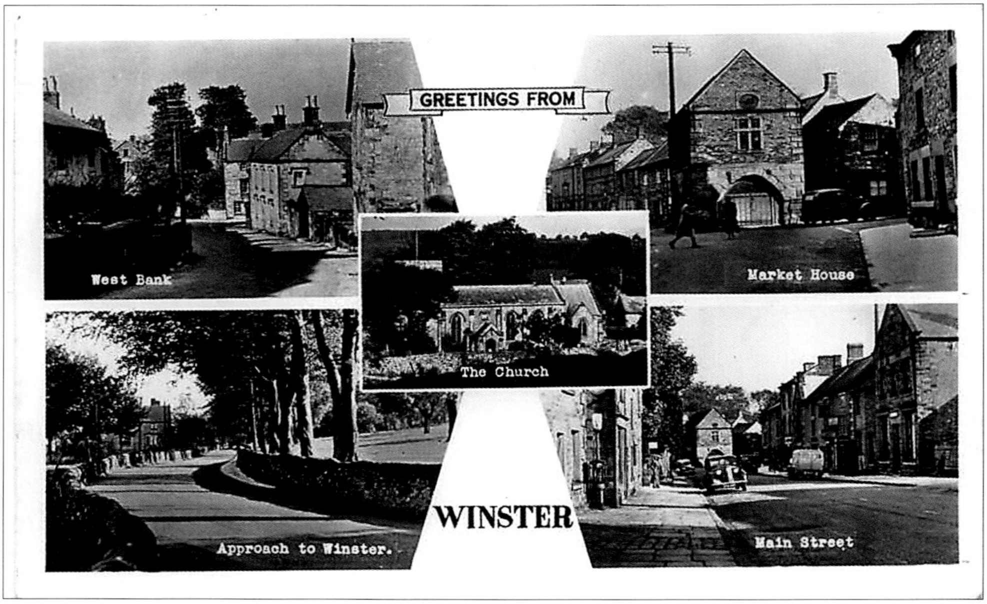

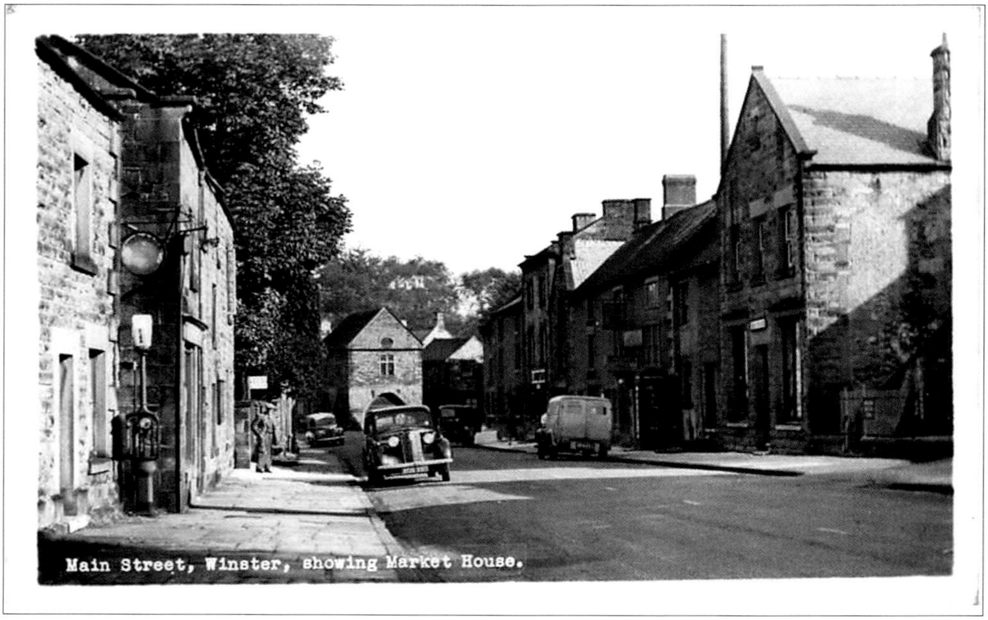

The petrol pump at left was operated in the 1950s by Tom Edward Gregory (known to me as a 1950s Winster boy as *"Putty"* Gregory). The pump was outside his house, *"Stonehaven."* *"Putty,"* during my childhood, was a strange, quiet (hardly said a word to me), almost brooding man. I treated him with childish caution. My recollection is that he lived alone, dispensed petrol and oil as required and also repaired bicycles. It was as a result of this latter aspect of his work that I came into contact with him. When my Dad could not repair my bike (which seemed to be often) he would tell me to *"take it to "Putty" Gregory."* *"Putty"* had a small shed at the bottom of his path which ran alongside *"Stonehaven."* When I called to collect the bike after repairs *"Putty"* would lead me silently down this path to the shed where he kept my bike. I have no recollection of paying him for his services but my Dad probably sent me to collect the bike with some money or else he settled direct with him. In trawling my memory about *"Putty"* I glanced too at the 1955 Register of Electors. I was surprised to see that registered with him at *"Stonehaven"* were also Annie Gregory, Thomas W. Gregory and Thomas Bernard Gregory. Were these people *"Putty's"* siblings? I have no memory of them at all.

Look again at this postcard: you will see a man at left looking towards the camera. There are many examples of people recognising themselves or their relatives on published postcards. In this case a relative of this man informed me that it was Ernest Boam (1880 – 1958) outside his home, Glendare. The shop sign at right middle is *"Burton's"*, The Crown Inn (advertising Offilers Ales) is at right middle and the railings at right are outside William & Glyn's Bank.

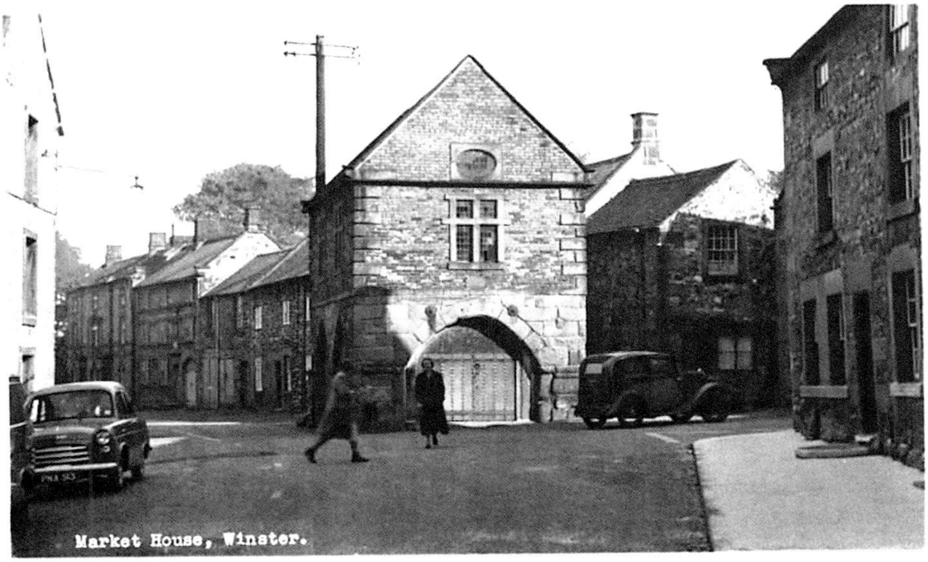
Market House, Winster.

No-one has yet come forward to identify the two people in the Market House card but who knows – it is still a possibility. It has, however, been possible to identify the vehicles! The Ford Anglia at left (parked outside Mosley's shop) has a registration number PNA. The registration number of the vehicle at right (at the bottom of East Bank) appears to be JJ 5353 – it is a Series One or Pre-Series Morris Eight of 1933 to 1936.

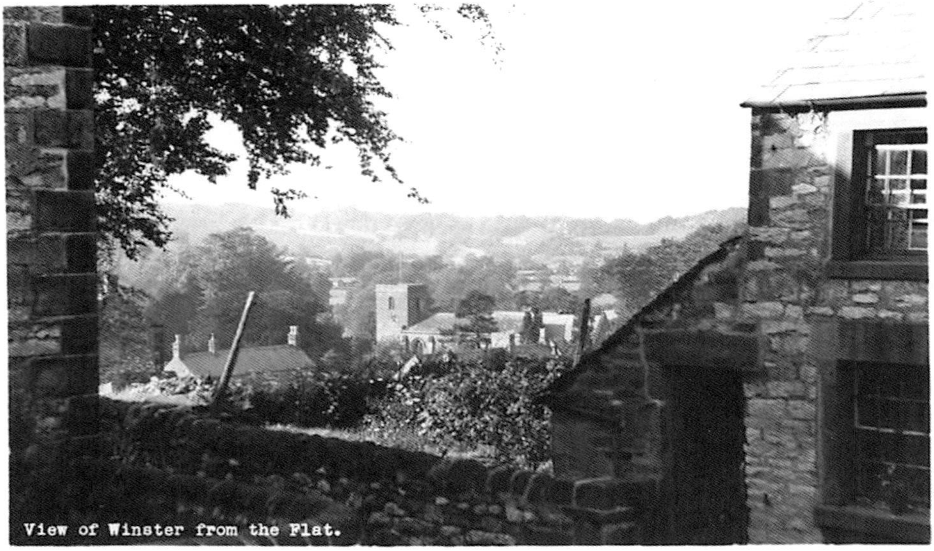
View of Winster from the Flat.

The house at right (now called Orchard Cottage) shown on the "*View of Winster from The Flat*", was occupied in the mid-1950s by Benjamin White and his wife, Sarah E. White and their son, Malcolm. Ben White was the village's part-time blacksmith at this time and had his "*black-smith's shop*" towards the top of East Bank. Again, as a child, I watched him shoe cart-horses in the small yard outside the shop and occasionally had the opportunity to peep inside to wonder at the blazing coals and to watch him hammering away. Malcolm White played local football for a number of teams and was also a part-time professional player with Matlock Town FC. The last card in this collection (General View From The Rocks) was postally used from Vernon House (on Main Street) on 5 August 1962 to an address in Berkshire. The message reads:

"Dear Toffee
Went to see the Shadows on Friday night, fabulous. It is not a bad life down here a bit dull at times. The photo shows where I am staying now and is marked

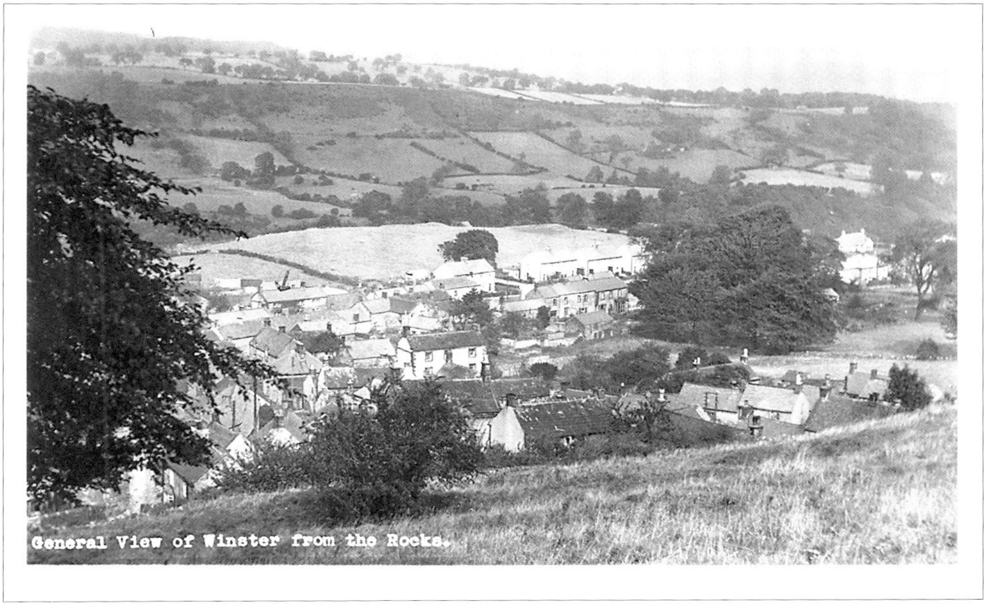

with an arrow (look hard)."

Those readers younger than 50 or so may not realise that "*the Shadows*" were a popular 1960s pop group who at one time supported the solo artist, Cliff Richard. This card also shows in the middle distance the Leacroft Road Estate as it was initially built in the late 1940s.

CHAPTER 13

MISCELLANEOUS

This Chapter includes some images not naturally finding a place in the earlier Chapters.

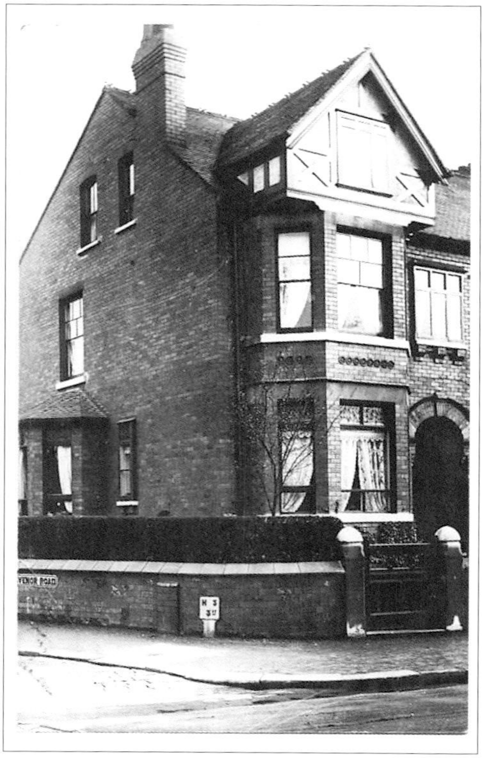

"Winster House" is cut into the stone at the top of the gateposts. The back of this card is marked "From Lizzie"

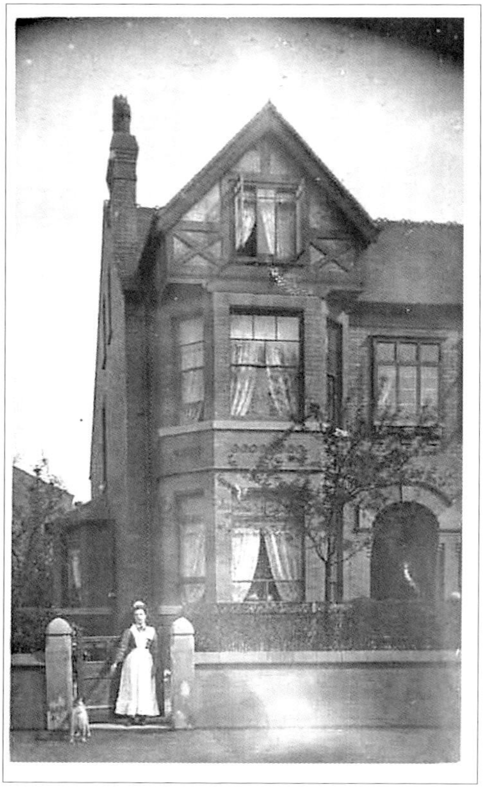

Another view of "Winster House"

A Winster House Mystery

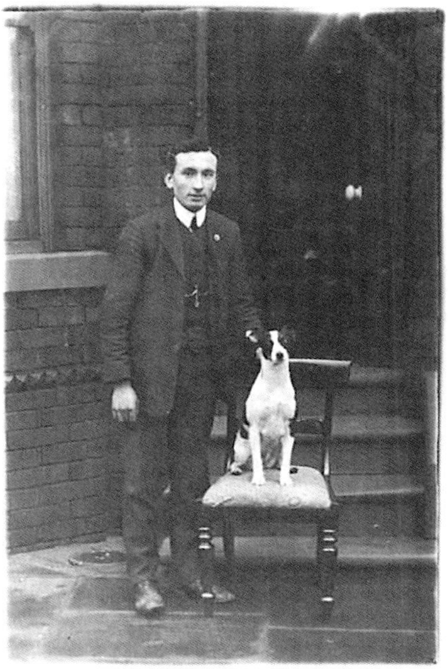

An unidentified man (and dog) outside "Winster House"

This provides you with the opportunity to continue some Winster research using the three cards illustrated – a start has been made on this work and you might be able to add to it.

The cards and the circumstances in which they have survived and the clues which they offer, illustrate the fun (and the frustration) to be had from trying to link postcards with the era and the people when they were produced. Here goes.

First, the circumstances in which the cards have survived. They were in the Eric Brassington Collection. To remind you, Eric inherited a collection of postcards, photographs and memorabilia associated with his Winster Brassington family and the Winster families of Barnsley, Newton and Gregory all of whom were at some time inter-related.

When Eric reviewed the cards the only clue which he had was that the comment *"From Lizzie"* was written on the back of one as all three cards were postally unused. Then he looked at computer scans of the cards and noticed that *"Winster House"* was carved on the gateposts. Lizzie must have been someone in the various Winster families or a friend or otherwise connected with them. Was *"Winster House"* and the building behind the gateposts and the people and the dog somehow connected with Winster itself? They must have been. But where was the house? Who were the people and what was the dog's name? So many questions.

As you will note if you take time to study the cards all three appear to show the same building but were probably taken at different times as the tops of the gateposts are coloured white in one card but not on another as was the bay window sill in one card but not on another. Two of the cards have the same postcard back (take my word for this) but not the third.

Eric did some research and tentatively concluded that Lizzie was Elizabeth Sellars (nee Hodgkinson) (b 1865). In the 1901 Census she was living with a family called Toplis at 59 Booth Street East, Urmston, South Manchester. Many of these people were born in Winster and Joseph Toplis was a Stone Mason. *"Who better to carve "Winster House" on a sandstone gatepost than a Stone Mason there must be more in this…"* as Eric commented.

I subsequently picked up the research mantle on this topic but have not been able to make progress towards identifying the address of the building shown in the cards least of all the identity of the man and woman. O.K, I always suspected that I might not be able to find the name of the dog!

And so I offer some notes as clues which you might want to follow yourself. If you have some success, then do please contact me. The value of the cards will increase dramatically if the location and the people can be identified. Sorry, the cards are not for sale – they are destined to be donated to a Winster area museum which undertakes to preserve them so you approach this task for fun and not for financial reward. Here are the clues in no particular chronological order:

Also in the Toplis household in the 1901 Census was Zilpah Hodgkinson, Joseph Toplis' brother in law. Also there was Zilpah's daughter, Eliza L Hodgkinson, aged 5 and a servant Eliza Howard also born in Winster.

In the 1911 Census Joseph Toplis was at 64 Mornington Street, Manchester. He was still a Stone Mason and also a Stone Merchant. His wife, Mary Ann nee Hodgkinson was with him as were four of their sons (born Bonsall, Winster and Manchester), and adopted daughter, born in Starkholmes, Matlock, Joseph's brother, William, born in Winster, and two borders, one born in Cornwall and the other (John Rouse) born in Winster.

In 1911 Eliza Lomas Hodgkinson, aged 15, was living with her father, Zilpah, at 20 Booth Street West, Chorlton-on-Medlock, Manchester. Zilpah was an employer with a book shop.

On one of the cards you'll see part of a road nameplate. Could this be Grosvenor Road? I found five Grosvenor Roads in Manchester. My guess is that the building is at the junction of Grosvenor Road with Flixton Road, Urmston, although the building at this junction in 2010 cannot be identified as the building in the postcards.

On the same card as the part road nameplate there is a sign for a fire hydrant? Are there records of these old signs?

Good luck!

Miss Lane And The Beeston Connection

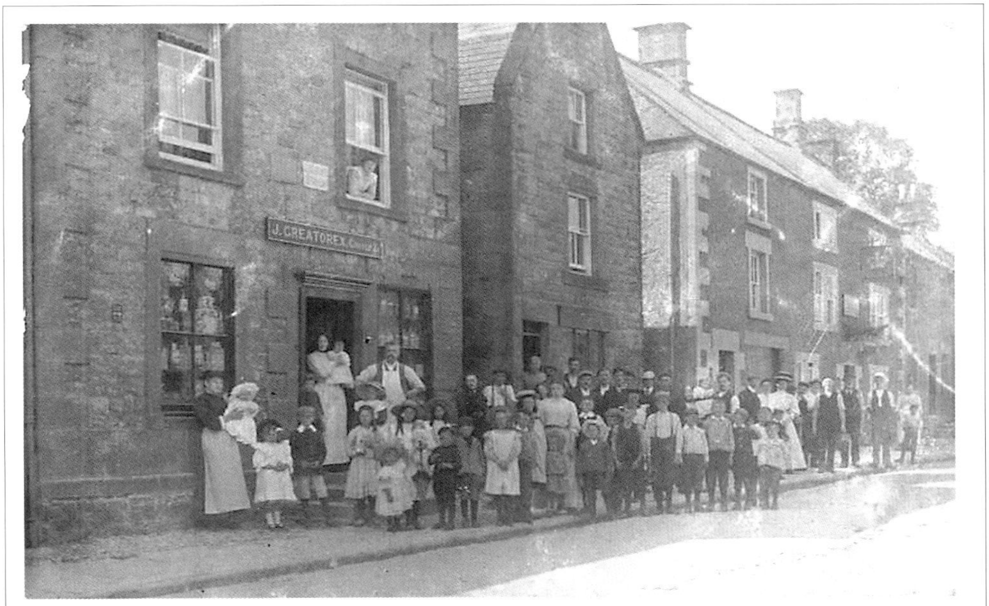

Outside J. Greatorex's Shop, Main Street

The first card in this section has a crowd of people outside J. Greatorex's shop, Main Street, and has been published elsewhere many times. It is a classic Edwardian real photograph, by an unidentified itinerant photographer, hence the crowd of locals whom he has managed to use to good effect. To the left of the right upstairs window of the shop is a sign advertising "*Colman's Starch*." The card is unused.

Joseph Greatorex (1846 – 1905) is listed in *Kelly's Directory*, 1891, as a grocer. In 1901 the shop was run by his wife Ellen Greatorex (nee Durden) (1853 – 1944) who was living at the shop along with her two step-daughters (Mary Ann Greatorex (1875 – 1934) and Sarah Jane Greatorex (1881 – 1923). On Census night Joseph was "*at home*" at the Bowling Green Inn which he ran on his own account. The card probably dates from after Joseph's death in 1905. One of Joseph's sons was Josiah Greatorex (1883 – c1941). In the 1911 Census he is in Winster but, unfortunately, the address is not given as seems to be the case with many of the 1911 Returns. He is described as "*Grocer (Provisional)*" and was an employer working at home. My guess is that the card dates from around this period and is of his shop. Josiah was living at the time of the 1911 Census with his wife Mabel (nee Williams) (1885 – 1973). Also captured on the same census with them was a male visitor and Sarah Jane Andrews (1895 – 1988) a general domestic servant who was born in Elton.

Many years ago a collection of cards (but not the one of the above shop), which might have been started by Sarah Andrews, came into my possession. The cards were posted during a period spanning 1911/12 and all have legible cancellation strikes; they provide lots of clues for Winster sleuths to follow. It is the message side of these cards which are of interest to Winster although the pictures (not illustrated here) may be sought by postcard collectors/local historians of other areas, particularly Beeston in Nottinghamshire, as we shall shortly see. Some of the puzzles posed by these cards (and which have not been solved by me) are:

Who Was Miss Lane?

Where was Beeston House, Winster?

What are the family stories behind the link with Winster and Beeston and the senders and recipients of these cards?

Unfortunately, I have no idea at all about who Miss Lane was; I haven't a clue about the whereabouts of Beeston House although I can make a good guess. These stark admissions may provoke a reader (it might be you) into trying to complete the jigsaw suggested by these messages.

You might like to have these unresolved questions at the back of your mind as you consider the cards in chronological sequence by the dates of the cancellation strikes:

9 August 1911

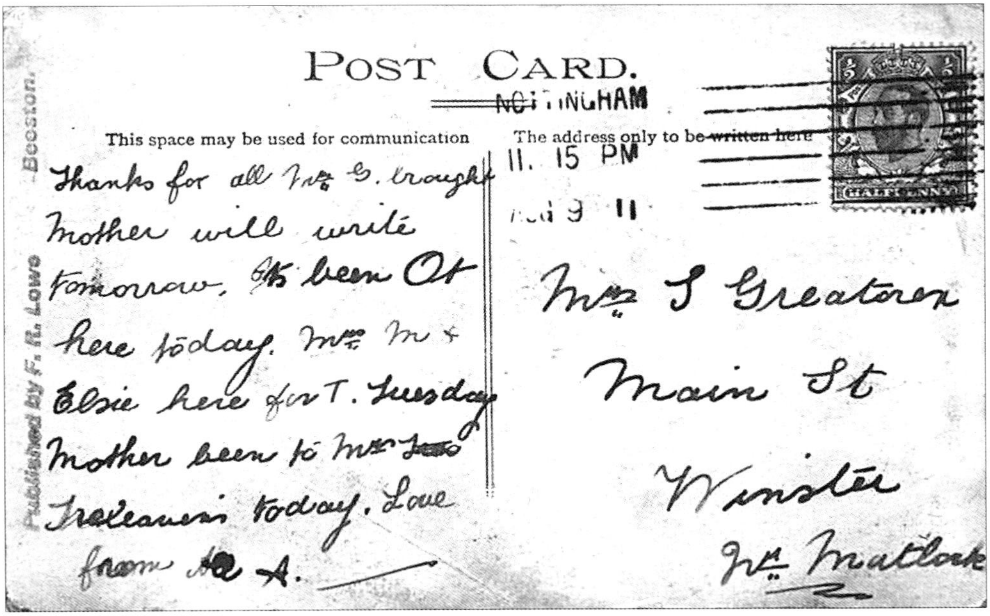
POST CARD.

NOTTINGHAM
11. 15 PM
AU 9 11

This space may be used for communication

Thanks for all Mr G. brought
Mother will write
tomorrow. Its been Ot
here today. Mrs M &
Elsie here for T. Tuesday
Mother been to Mrs
Treleaven's today. Love
from A & A.

The address only to be written here

Mrs S Greatorex
Main St
Winster
Nr Matlock

HALFPENNY

Published by F. R. Lowe, Beeston.

The picture side is a real photograph of a marching band led by a policeman marked *"Coronation 1911"* at bottom left. It was published by F. R. Lowe, Beeston, and the message reads:

"Thanks for all Mr. G. brought Mother will write tomorrow. Its been Ot here today. Mrs. M & Elsie here for T. Tuesday. Mother been to Mrs Treleaven's today. Love from A & A."

Who were these people? What was their relationship to Mrs. S. Greatorex, Main Street? What was the link with Beeston? Here are some clues which might assist you.

In 1911 Michael Vyne Treleaven, a 61 year old Architect and Surveyor, lived with his wife, son and a servant at 228 Station Road, Beeston. None of these people were born in Winster. *"Mr. G"* was probably Josiah Greatorex (1844 – 1941) who was born in Winster. In 1901 Josiah was living with his older brother William Henry Greatorex (1870 – 1903) at 1 Glebe Street, Beeston. At that time Josiah was an apprentice confectionary and William was a traveller for wholesale grocery. William was still in Winster in 1881 but by 1891 he was a boarder at 37 Mona Street, Beeston, employed as a grocer's assistant. William was in Beeston at 1 North Glebe Street in 1901 and died in 1903 in the Bridlington area. His widow, Minnie, (nee Burton) was in Beeston in 1911 at 1 Bramcote Road. She outlived her husband by 57 years dying in 1960. The couple are both buried in Winster churchyard and the headstone refers to William Henry as *"Late of Beeston."* So, in all probability the card to Mrs. S. Greatorex was sent by a Beeston relative.

But who was Mrs. S. Greatorex? In 1911 the Mrs. Greatorex at the shop on Main Street was Mrs J (Josiah) or she might have been addressed as Mrs M (Mabel) Greatorex (her maiden name was Mabel Williams). But we know this card was addressed to Mrs. S. Greatorex. Why? I recall from my childhood a possible clue. My mother sometimes referred to a "Mrs Siah ..." Was this a corruption of *"Mrs Josiah?"* I think it was. This is perhaps confirmed on p.20 of *Winster A Peak District Village Remembers* where Bert Boam in reference to *"The Old Brewhouse. Village Stores."* (likely Beeston House in Edwardian times – it is the same shop as shown in the card which introduces this section) says:

"First belonged to 'Siah Greatorex...."

Here a listener to Bert might have thought that he was referring to a "Mrs S. Greatorex" and would probably address a card to her as heard. I believe that both my mother and Bert when referring to *"Mrs 'Siah ..."* were in fact referring to the shortened version of *"Mrs Josiah."*

This card is signed with initials which look to be A D A. The next card is clearly signed with these same initials but the cards are by different hands so may have been sent by different people. This card might have been sent by a child – the handwriting is not as neat as the next card. Finally, this card refers to "Elsie" but I cannot trace anyone of this name.

28 September 1911

The picture side of this card is a Glossy Real Photo (Glossy Photo Series by The Photochrom Co. Ltd. London) of Carnarvon Castle From Queens Gate Nod. P.C. 36223 but you will see from the back that it was posted from Beeston.

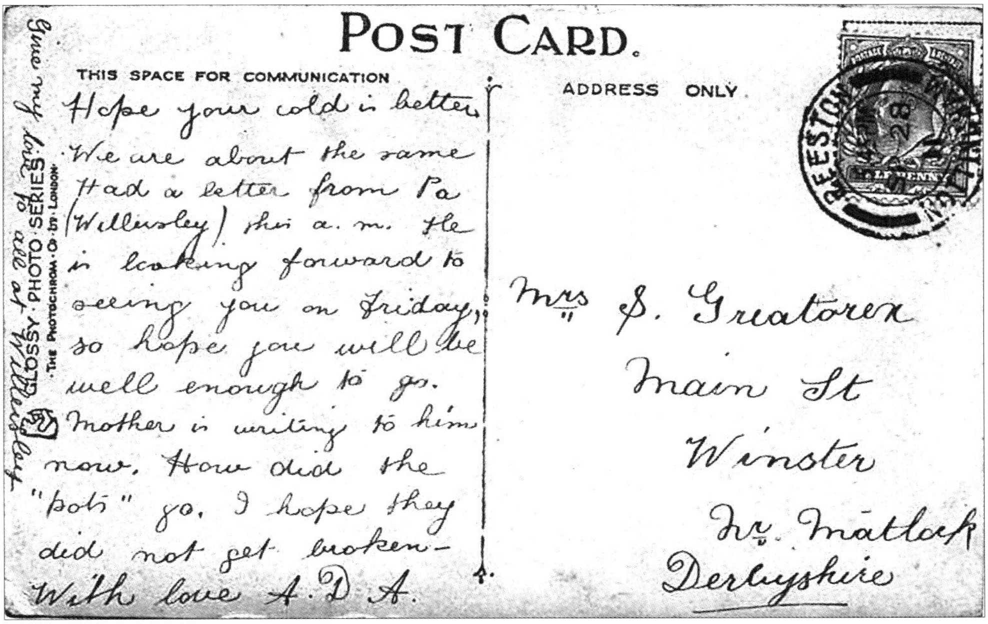

POST CARD.

THIS SPACE FOR COMMUNICATION

ADDRESS ONLY

GLOSSY PHOTO SERIES. THE PHOTOCHROM CO. LTD. LONDON

Hope your cold is better
We are about the same
Had a letter from Pa
(Willersley) this a. m. He
is looking forward to
seeing you on Friday,
so hope you will be
well enough to go.
Mother is writing to him
now. How did the
"pots" go. I hope they
did not get broken -
With love A. D. A.

Give my love to all at Willersley

BEESTON

Mrs S. Greatorex
Main St
Winster
Nr. Matlock
Derbyshire

The message reads:

"Hope your cold is better. We are about the same Had a letter from Pa (Willersley) this a.m. He is looking forward to seeing you on Friday, so hope you will be well enough to go.Mother is writing to him now. How did the "pots" go. I hope they did not get broken. With love A.D.A. Give my love to all at Willersley."

Willersley could well have been the Willersley near Cromford.

7 March 1912

The picture is a printed coloured view of Boscombe Chine by Boots Cash Chemists *"Pelham Series"* and was posted from Boscombe.

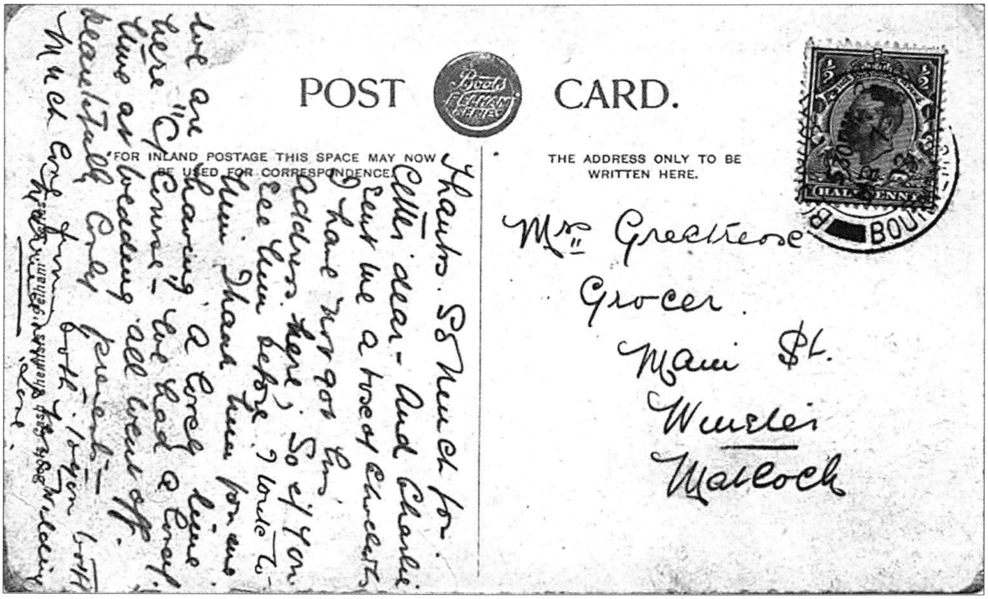

The message reads:
"Thanks so much for letter dear – And Charlie sent me a box of chocolates. I have not got his address here; so if you see him before I write to him thank him for me. We are having a lovely time here "of course" – we had a lovely time at wedding. All went off beautifully lovely presents – much love from both to you both."

Presumably a wedding in Dorset area – the name Harriet possibly Wilding. Surely progress can be made here. I have looked long and hard at the signature on this card and draw different conclusions each time!

5 June 1912

A real photograph of The River Trent And House Boats, Beeston, No. 3161 in the Kingsway Real Photo Series.
The message reads:

"We arrived home quite safe. We just got in home when down came the rain. With much love. Ma + Toby has being looking for you."

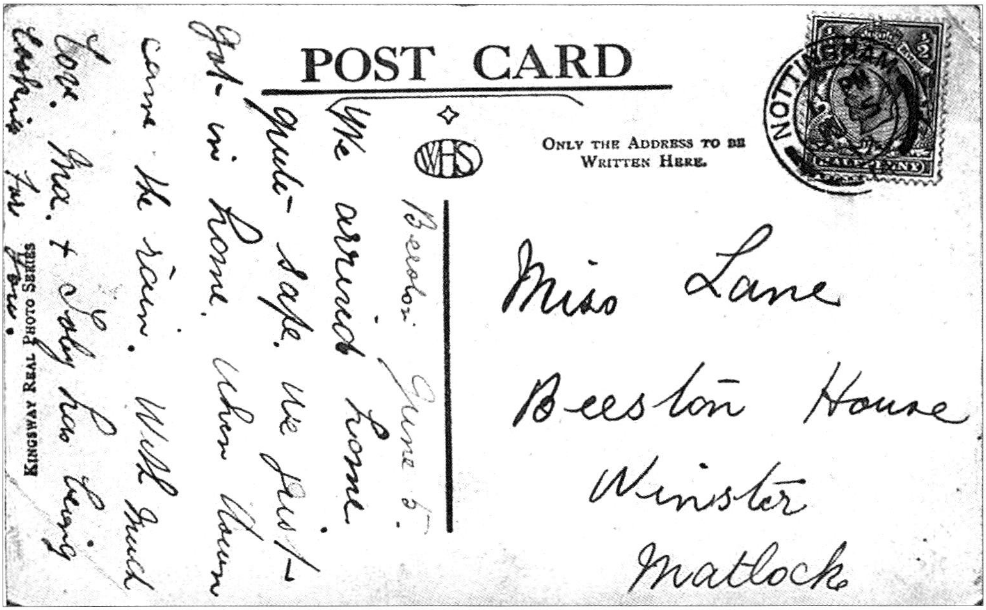

And yet another name to conjure with!

10 June 1912

A printed view of the Cunard R.M.S. *"Carmania"* And *"Caronia."*

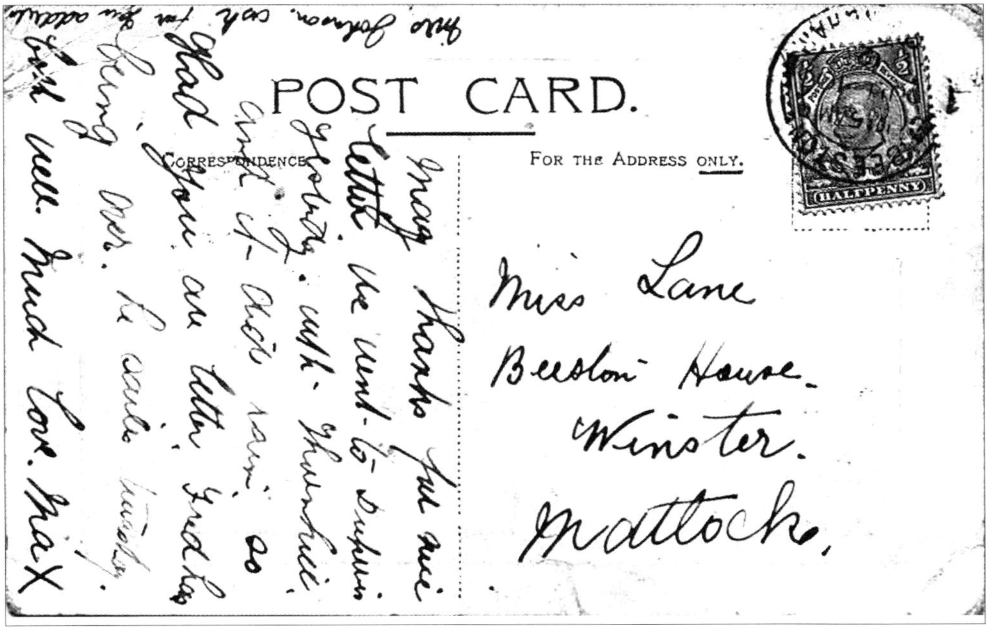

The message reads:

"Many thanks for nice letter. We went to Dukeries yesterday with Thornhill and it did rain so glad you are better. Fred has being over. He sails Tuesday. Mrs. Johnson ask for your address. Both well. Much love. Ma X"

More names, some boats and a trip on the briny. The picture of the ships may be of interest to shipping enthusiasts. In June 2010 I googled the name of the ships and found a site devoted to them and their history. The two ships were known as *"The Grand Dames of the Atlantic."* They entered service in 1905 on Cunard's Liverpool to New York service. Was Fred sailing from Liverpool to New York on one of these ships?

11 June 1912

A real photograph of The Cross, Beeston, No. 166 by W.H.S. & S.N. This shows a group of people posing behind The Cross.

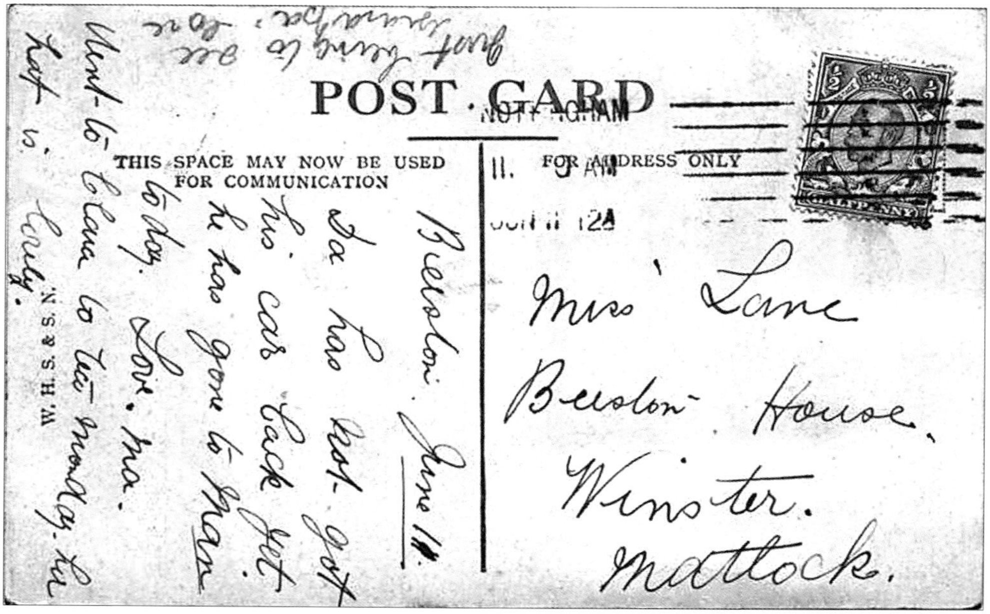

The message reads:

"Da has not got his car back yet. He has gone to Man today. Love Ma. Went to Clara to tea Monday. Her hat is lovely. Just being to see Grandpa. Love."

Good grief, someone with a car in 1912. That surely narrows the search down a little.

20 August 1912

A coloured printed multi-view of *"Peculiar Properties of the Isle of Wight"* by J. Welch & Sons, Photographic Publishers, Portsmouth.

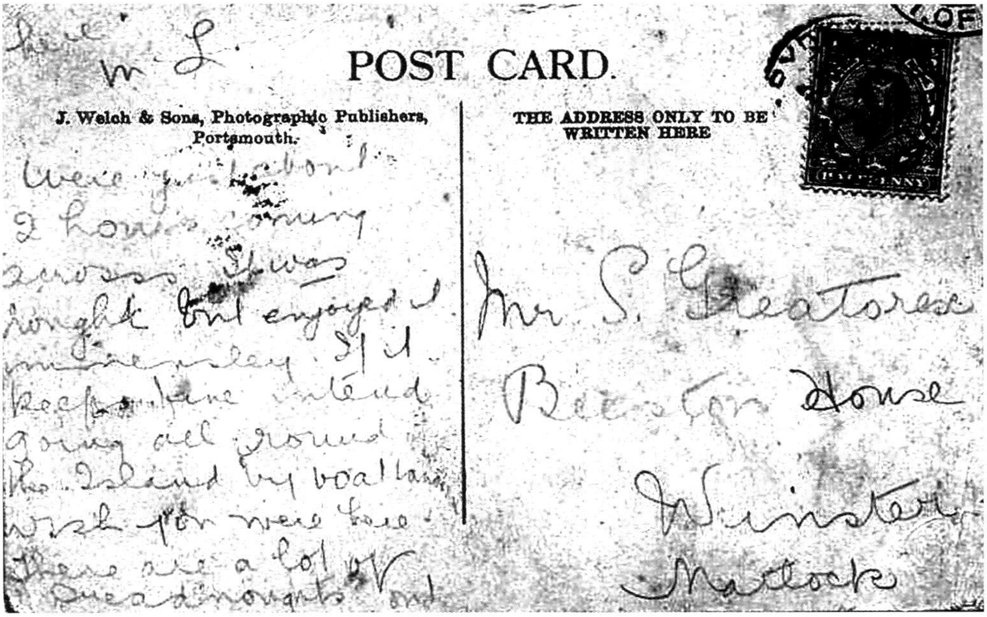

The message was written in pencil and is well-nigh illegible – it reads:

"Were you about 2 hours coming across. It was tonight but enjoyed it immensely. If it keeps fine intend going all around the island by boat. Wish you were here. There are a lot of dreadnoughts on here. M.L."

29 August 1912

A printed view of Eardisley by Raphael Tuck & Sons *"Collotype"* card.

The message reads:

"Ask Mr. G. to post the 2 "Womans Worlds" on please. I believe there is a large envelope amongst the books that will fit. Hope you are getting on all right. Shall soon be home again. M.G."

Mr. G. was probably Josiah Greatorex and the card to Miss Andrews was probably sent by Josiah's wife, Mabel.

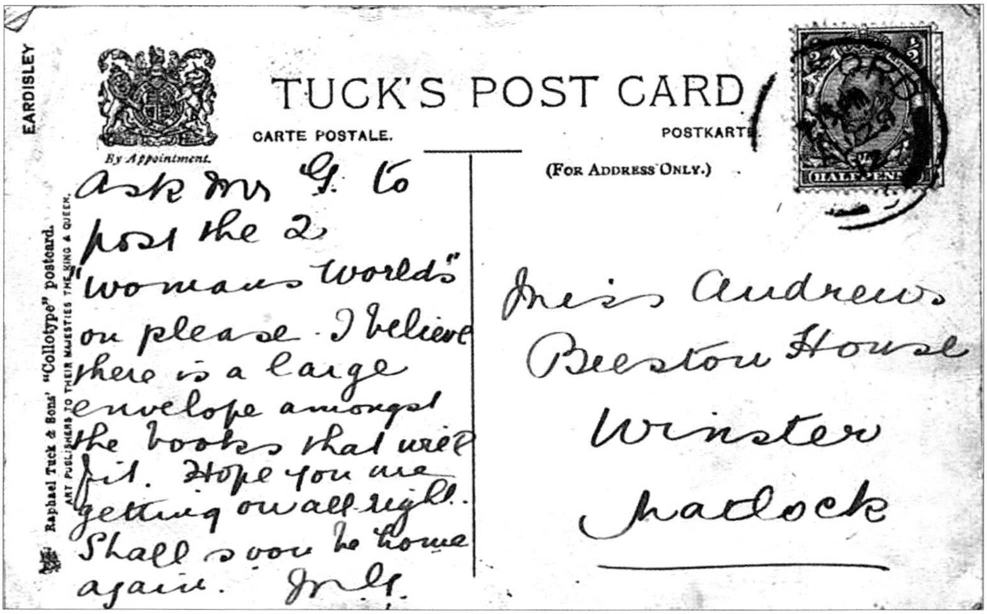

Good luck with all these clues.

Merry Xmas & A Bright New Year From Howden 1904

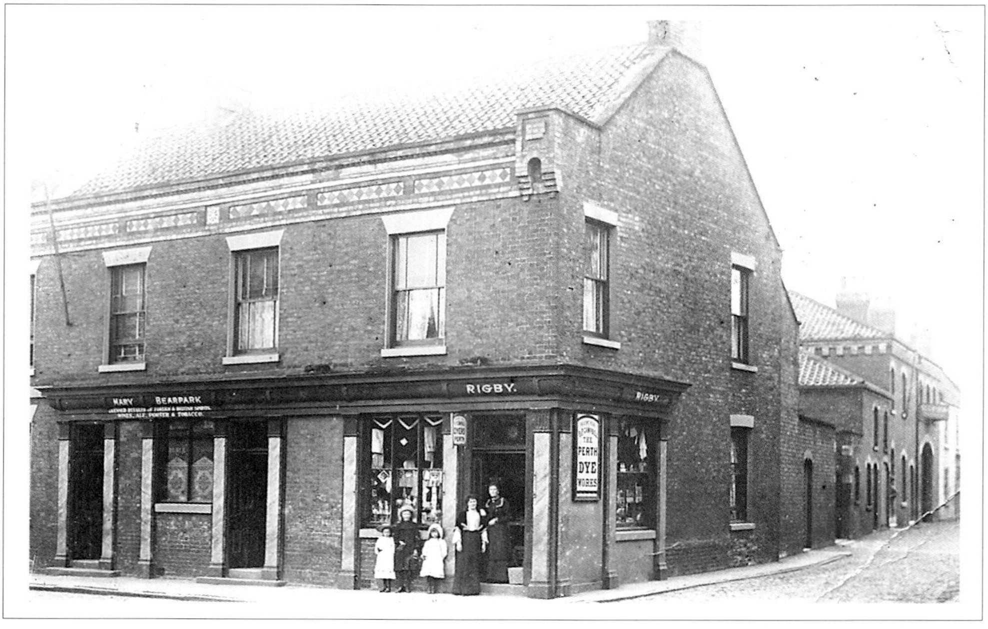

Harriet Ann Fearn outside Rigby's Shop, Howden, before 1904

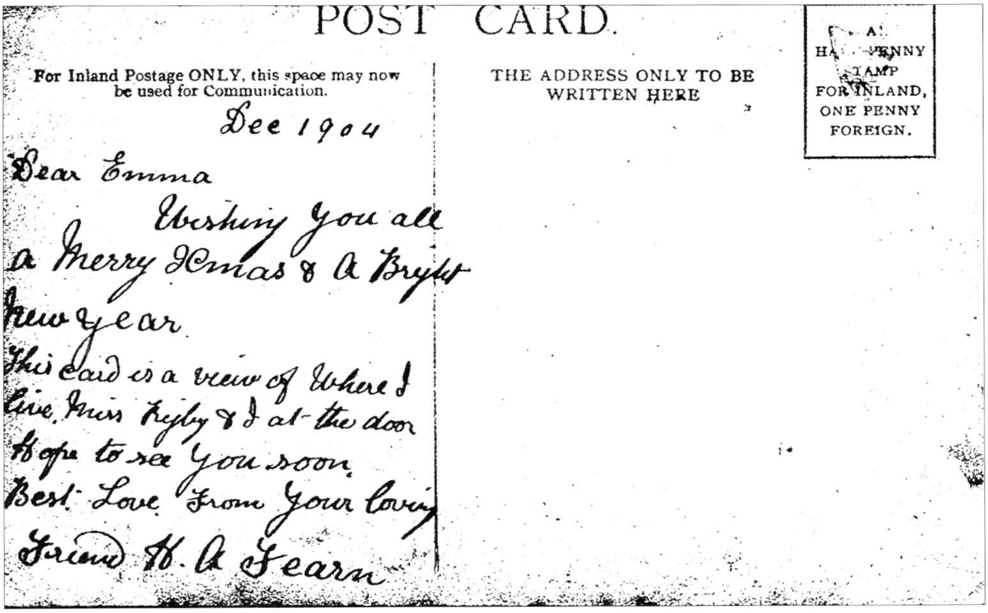
POST CARD.

For Inland Postage ONLY, this space may now be used for Communication.

THE ADDRESS ONLY TO BE WRITTEN HERE

A HALFPENNY STAMP FOR INLAND, ONE PENNY FOREIGN.

Dec 1904

Dear Emma

Wishing you all a Merry Xmas & A Bright New year.

This card is a view of where I live. Miss Rigby & I at the door

Hope to see you soon.

Best Love From your loving Friend H. A Fearn

The message side of the previous card sent by Harriet Ann Fearn in Dec. 1904 to her friend, Emma Brassington, in Winster.

This postcard has nearly everything that a postcard collector enjoys about a single card. In 2009 the card was among Eric Brassington's collection of Winster memorabilia – it had been sent to his grand-mother, Mary Emma Brassington (nee Barnsley) by her friend, H.A. Fearn.

The picture side of the card is obviously not a view of a Winster building. It is, however, a gem of a real photographic card and includes two elements which are popular amongst postcard collecting themes, a shop and a pub. It also has a group of people posing outside the shop and collectors know that there is half a chance that some of these people may be identified if only the message contains some clues. Here the clues in the message are generous. Although the card was not postally used it was dated by the sender *"Dec 1904."* That assists as it is obvious that the photograph was not taken later than this date. Secondly, the sender says "this card is a view of where I live" and goes on to say *"Miss Rigby and I at the door."* The link with Winster is through "Dear Emma" being confirmed as the Winster recipient of the card. That led to uncovering this further information.

H.A. Fearn was Harriet Ann Fearn who was born about 1877 in Winster. When she sent the card in 1904 she was about 27 and single. Her friend, Emma, also born in Winster in 1877 (on 1 April), had married in 1902. Emma and her husband made their home on East Bank. In 1901 Harriet was living at home on Main Street with her parents and family – her father was an insurance agent. By 1904 Harriet was living at the shop. But where was this shop?

The picture shows the name "*Rigby*" above the shop door and the name "*Mary Bearpark*" is above the next door pub. Research revealed that the shop was at Howden, Yorkshire. In 2008 the building (the pub and the shop) was still in use and known as the Minster Hotel. It was quite a surprise to find a modern image of the Hotel on the internet and for it to be unmistakeably the same building as in the 1904 postcard. Check this out for yourself by having this book open at the page displaying the picture side of the card – then google "*Minster Hotel Howden*" and see what turns up. If you are doing this within a reasonable time of 2008 then you may see for yourself the confirmation that the two images are of the same building.

In Bulmer's 1891 *Trade Directory* the landlord of the Black Swan, Howden, is given as John Bearpark. In 1901 Mary Bearpark (born about 1843) was the Publican (and a widow) at the same pub, the Black Swan. The pub was on Penfold Street, Howden. Mary's daughter, Elizabeth Whittaker, aged 25, lived with her and was a schoolteacher. The previous entry on the Census Return but described as St. John Street shows Rigby's shop was run by Hannah H. Rigby, aged 55, on her own account. Her live-in shop assistant was Lellu White, aged 31. Hannah probably died in 1909.

By 1911 Mary Bearpark was still living with her daughter but by this time Elizabeth was married to West Anderson and he and Elizabeth had two children and they were all living on Bridgegate, Howden. West was a fruiterer working on his own account and Elizabeth assisted him in the business. To add to this confusion, by 1911 Harriet Ann Fearn was married to John Charles Jenkinson. The couple had married in 1906 in the Bakewell District and in 1911 were living along with their son, John Edward, in Howden. Unfortunately, the 1911 Census does not give us the addresses in Howden where the Anderson and the Jenkinson families were living. Harriet's husband was a General Draper and employer with a shop assistant and a servant. Harriet was said to be assisting in the business. Is it possible that by this time one of these families was in business in the former Rigby's shop?

Turning back to the card we can deduce with some confidence that Miss Hannah Rigby is the older woman standing on the door step. Harriet Ann Fearn of Winster is the younger woman standing alongside her.

A View Down Woolley's Yard Before 1906

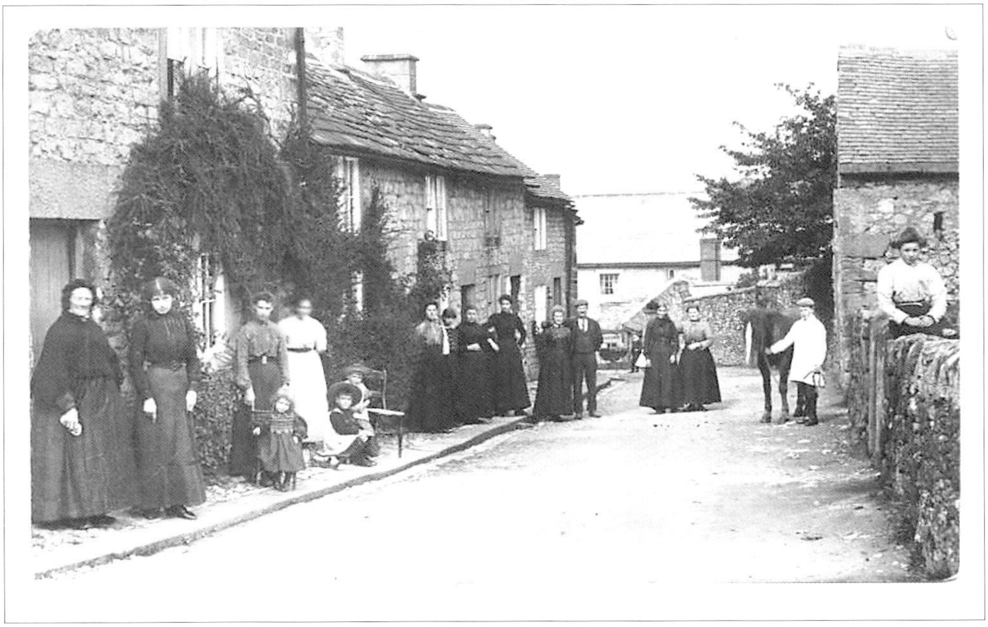

Woolley's Yard before 1906

This superb card was posted on 9 April 1906. It is by an unnamed professional who has taken care to group the locals including the boy holding the pony. It was sent to James Rowland, 24 Chaucer Road, Bedford. The message reads:

"Dear Jim I am very sorry I have not written before as I have not had time. I have left school now. We have flitted in Marshalls house against the Market House now. Be sure you come down for Friday. I shall be in work by the next time you come if all being well. We like our new house very much. Geo Thomas works for Dick Coates at the top of the town. I think this is all this time. Yours truly Dick"

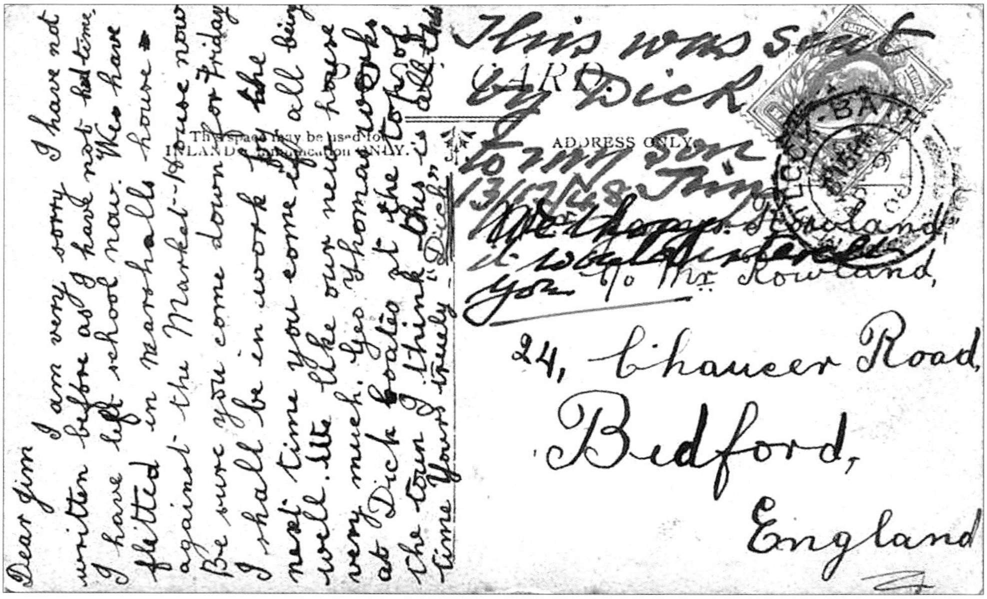

Back of previous card

And also on the back the address has been overwritten *"This was sent by Dick to my son Jim. 13/12/48. We thought it would interest you."*

James Walter Rowland (1890 – 1944) (the possible addressee) was born in Bedford. His father James Rowland (1861 – 1951) (also the possible addressee) was born in Winster where his ancestors had lived since 1776. The Geo. Thomas mentioned in the message may have been George Durden Thomas born in 1895 and aged about 11 at the time the card was sent.

Three More Soldiers

We met some soldiers earlier when discussing cards associated with the Gregory and Newton families. Here are three more:

Bernard Boam

Bernard was born on 7 December 1896 in Winster. In the 1901 and 1911 Census, he was living with his parents and family at Holly Bank (probably on East Bank). He was Private 241691 in the Notts & Derby Regiment (Sherwood Foresters). The card is printed at left back on the

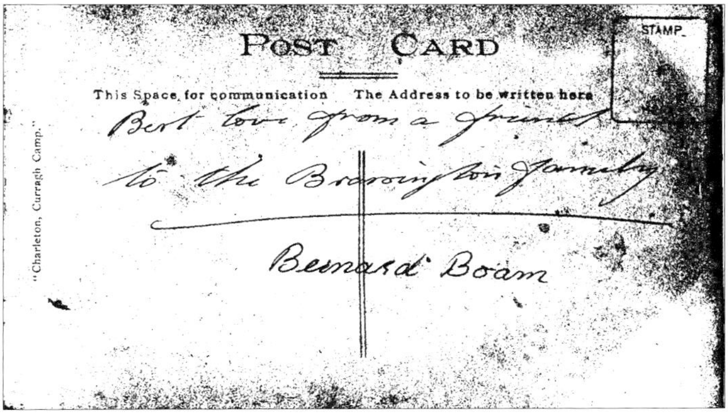

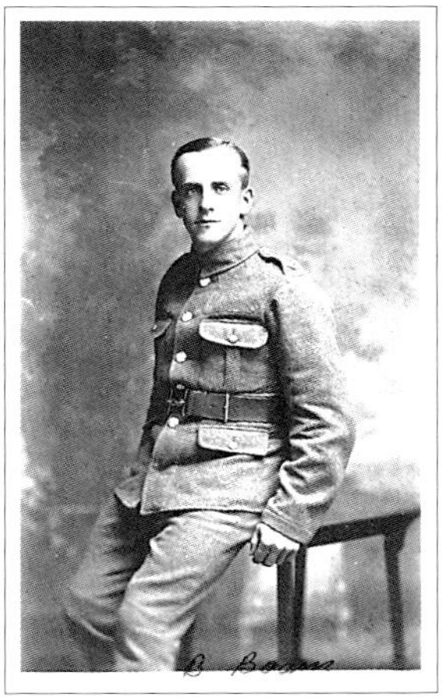

Bernard Boam and message from him on back.

message side *"Charleton, Curragh Camp."*

In 1919/20 Bernard married Emma C. Burton and the couple set up home at Waingroves, Nr. Ripley, where Bernard lived for the remainder of his life. He died on 11 February 1972.
Bernard served for over 30 years as a member of Ripley Town Council and was also Chairman of the Council. He was awarded the British Empire Medal in the Queen's Birthday Honours 1955.

Lewis Edwin Boam

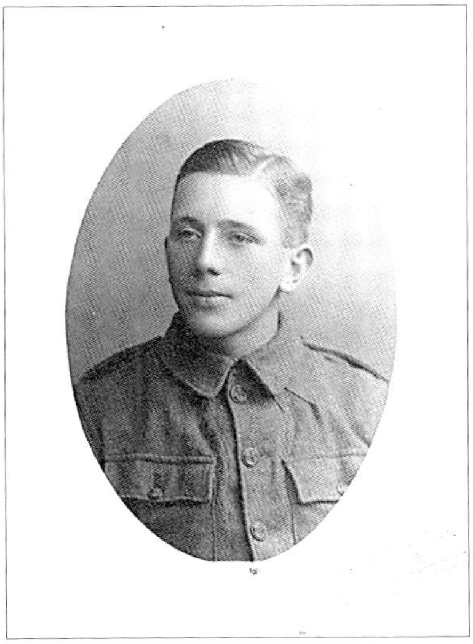

Lewis Edwin Boam
by W.E. Wright, Forest Gate

Lewis was born on 26 July 1892 and died on 10 October 1918.

In 1901 he was living at Wensley Road with his father (George) and his mother (Jane) and his six other siblings. By 1911 the family were on Main Street. He was buried at the Poznan Old Garrison Cemetery, Poland.

At some unknown time Lewis married Annie who lived at 31 Appletree Road, Stanfree, Clowne, Chesterfield. Lewis is commemorated on Bolsover War Memorial. At the time of his death he was in the 16th Battalion of the Sherwood

Foresters (Notts & Derbys Regiment) and had attained the rank of Lance Corporal. The card is embossed at bottom right with the name W. E. Wright & Sons, Forest Gate & Branches.

Daniel Corless

The 1901 Census records that, aged 1, Daniel was at home on East Bank with his parents, John and Annie Corless. His dad was a lead miner who was born in Ireland. By the 1911 Census the family lived on Main Street. Daniel had six brothers: three of whom also served in the Great War, namely Bernard, Frank and Thomas.

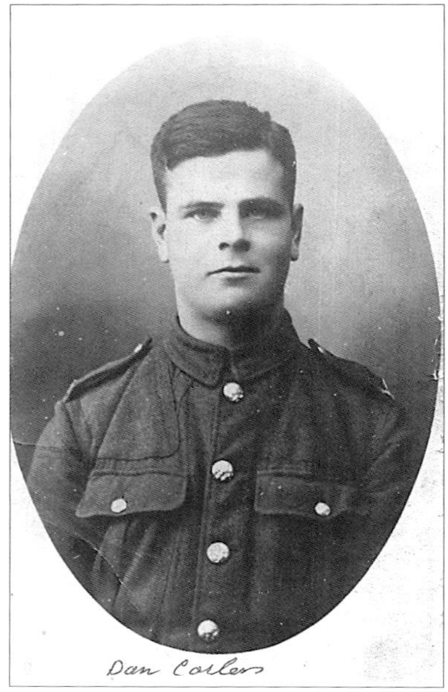

Daniel Corless by W.N. Statham probably copied from a photograph by an unknown photographer

In the Great War Daniel was Private No. 88334 in the 22nd Bat., Manchester Regiment attd Royal Munster Fusilers. He died on 7th January 1920, aged 20. He is buried in the Arquata Scrivia Communal Cemetery Extension, Italy. (Grave Reference/Panel Number: II.B.1).

The card is by W.N. Statham, The Studio, Matlock. There is another card in the Eric Brassington Collection (not illustrated) which is clearly the same photograph as that illustrated here but this card has a different back to the Statham Card – this one has a divided back but without the words *"Post Card"* and without the usual division of the back into *"For Correspondence"* and *"Address Only"* and also lacks the attribution of Statham. There is a small inked stamp on the back with the numbers *"7614."* The interest of this card is that the back probably has a message in pencil from Daniel himself – it reads:

"Hope you don't laugh too much it is not a very good one the(y) cant take photos our here like Blighty."

So, was this photo of Daniel taken on the continent and did the Corless family have it copied by Statham?

Winster School

The following three photos of groups of schoolchildren were probably taken in 1908 on the same day and by the same unknown photographer. You can see that the photos were taken in the same part of the school-yard although the window at right is in a different position in each photo. The sign held by the child at front centre appears to be dated Nov. 1908 and the first image has *"C78 No. 1,"* on the sign too, then No. 2 and so on. The last card illustrated is No. 4 and No. 3 is not illustrated here. Hopefully it has survived in another collection or has been published elsewhere. The numbering is presumably to assist the photographer in taking orders for copies of the four photographs.

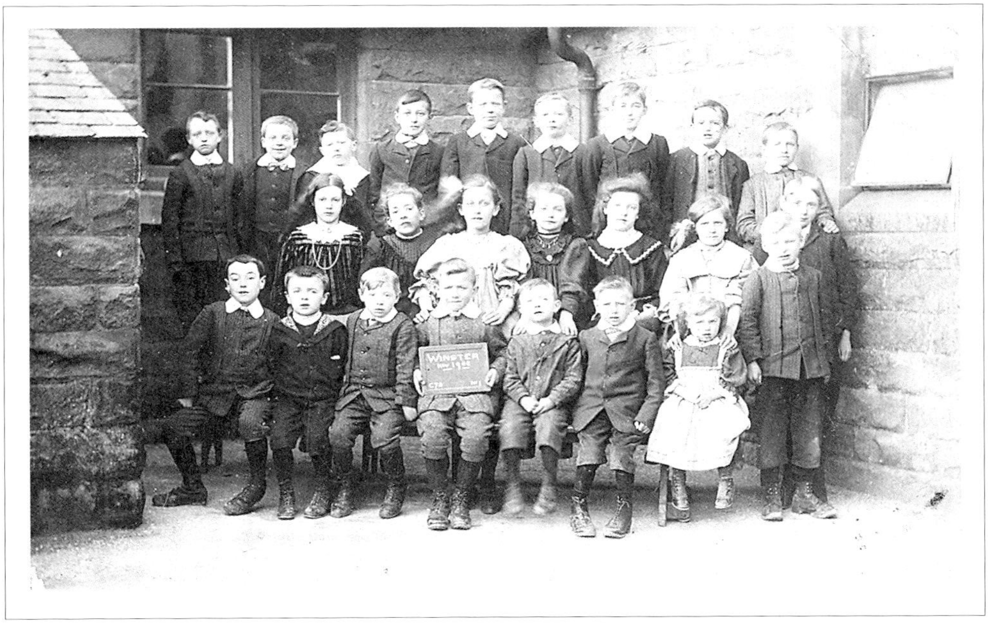

School Group C78 No. 1 Nov 1908. The boy 2nd from left back row is Joe Rains and the boy 2nd from right front row is Ben Brassington

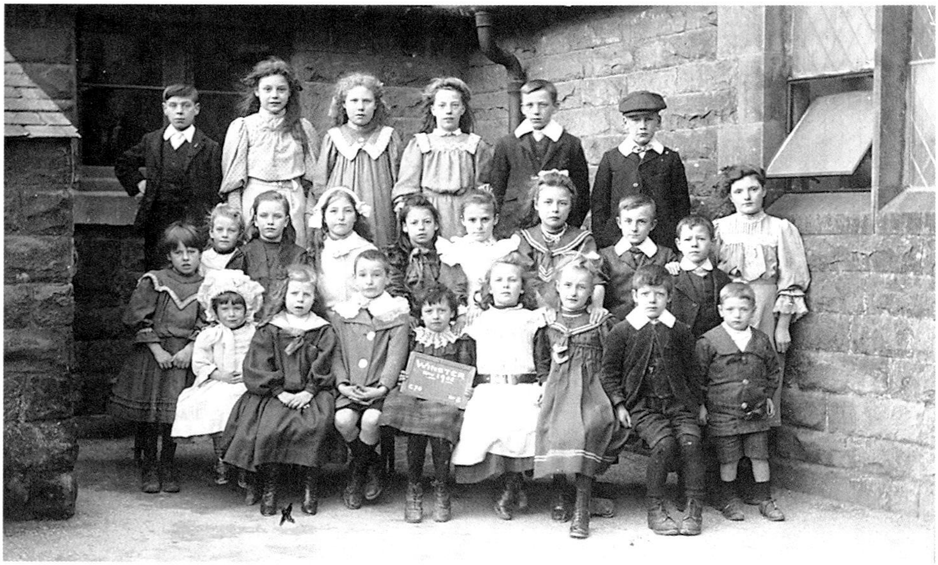

School Group C78 No. 2 Nov 1908. The girl 2nd from left on the front row (there is a cross between her shoes) is Ada Newton

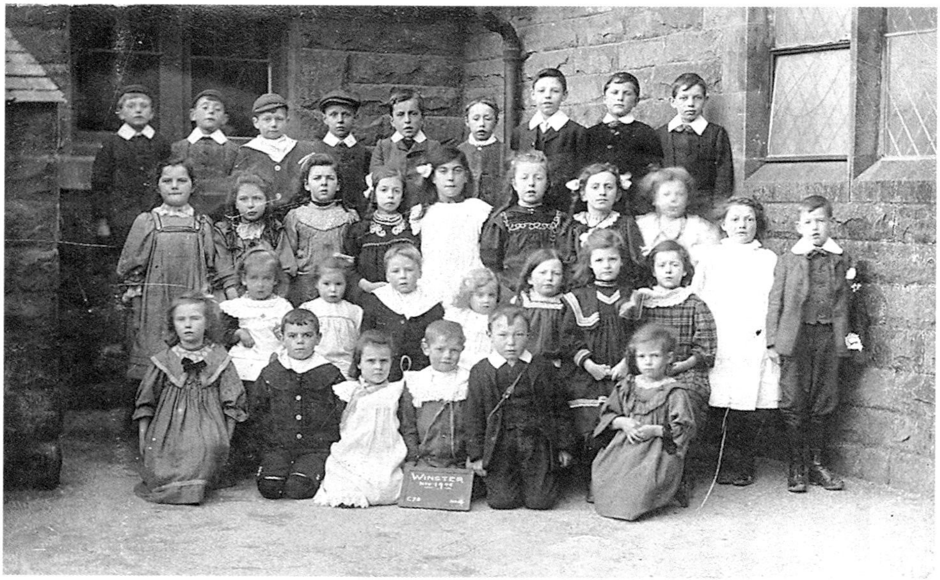

School Group C78 No. 4 Nov 1908.
Image reproduced by kind permission of Roland Corfield

POSTCARD PUBLISHERS/PHOTOGRAPHERS

Artistic Publishing Co, The - 9 Bury Court, St. Mary Axe, London
Bamforth & Co., Holmfirth
BB London Series
Boots Pure Drug Co. Ltd (Pelham Series)
Bourne, A.W., 38 Babingly Drive, Leicester
Bricklebank, Sheffield
Cooper, Will & Son, 125 Wellington Terrace, Blackpool
Cornall, Thos. A., Station Studios, Harrogate
Cox, J. Crowther, 12 The Crofts, Rotherham
Cumbe, V.B., Gibralter
Denny's Innovation Series, Matlock
Drake, J.V, Matlock
Evans, E.T. & T.C. , Youlgrave
Fennells (Chemist) Ltd., Skegness
Gale's Studios Ltd
Gill, Harry, Matlock
Hawke, A.H, Helston
Heathcote, Ernest, Winster
Howell, Charles, Official Photographer, Pleasure Beach, Blackpool
Jerome (Branches Everywhere)
Kingsway Real Photo Series
Lewis, C. & A.G., Sherwood Street, Nottingham
Lowe, F.R., Beeston
Maclean, D.A., Promenade, Blackpool
Marsden, Geo. & Son, Wirksworth
Marsden, Geo. & Son, Wirksworth (Derbyshire Artistic Series)

Marshall & Son, Winster
Marshall, Albert, Winster
Marshall, Mrs. E. A. & Son, Winster
Nield, Allen, Leeds
Parisian Studio, 118 Liverpool Road, Patricroft
Photochrom Co, The Ltd LondonRadium Co, Pleasure Beach,
Blackpool
Raphael Tuck & Sons Ltd
Revell's Series, AlrewasScott, W.S., 208 Derby Road, Chesterfield
Scriven, E.L., Doncaster
Statham, W.N., Matlock
Valentine's
W.H.S. & S.N.Welch, J. & Sons, Portsmouth
While U Wait Studios, Blackpool
Wolstenholme, Ellis, Blackpool
Wright, W.E. & Sons, Forest Gate & Branches

INDEX – PEOPLE

INDEX OF PLACES

There are two Indices: the first of Winster and the second of other places. Places such as The Market House appear often both in the pictures and the text and such references have not been included here. Where other places have a specific mention either in a picture or in the text, then they have been indexed but not single or general references.

Winster Index

Well-known Winster places such as East & West Banks, Main Street, St. John the Baptist Church, Market Hall/House (I prefer Market House) and Market Place, are mentioned frequently throughout the book and have not been indexed. This is a selected index – it does not attempt to be exhaustive.

Other Places

Again, this index is not exhaustive

Bibliography

Bulmer's Trade Directory 1891
Derby Mercury, The - 8th July , 1863
Derbyshire Times, The - 1st June. 1918
Fordham, D. & Thomas, G., E.L. Scrivens of Doncaster - Picture Postcard Monthly Magazine, October 2002
Greatorex, Michael – Winster, Derbyshire, Images – http://www.flickr.com/photos/winsterderbyshire/
High Peak News, The - 12 July 1873 and 1 June 1918
Kelly's Directory
Loyal Triumphant Hope Lodge No. 1546, The - Register of Members 1836 - 1911 (on deposit at Derbyshire Record Office, Matlock)
Rodger, Margery: A Winster Scrapbook No. 4 Winster Parish Records. August 1985.
Scotting, Dawn – Winster Ancestry - http://winster-ancestry.blogspot.com/2009/05/oddfellows-members.html
Wilson, Harold S., Postal History of Matlock And District (published by Derbyshire Postal History Society)
Winster Festival of Britain Celebrations, July 1951, Official Souvenir
Winster Local History Group, Winster - A Peak District Village Remembers published 2000
Winster Parish Magazine (various dates) (Deposited at Derbyshire Record Office, Matlock).